Attitudes, Aspirations and Welfare

Peter Taylor-Gooby • Benjamin Leruth
Editors

Attitudes, Aspirations and Welfare

Social Policy Directions in Uncertain Times

palgrave
macmillan

Editors
Peter Taylor-Gooby
School of Social Policy, Sociology
and Social Research
University of Kent
Canterbury, UK

Benjamin Leruth
Institute for Governance and Policy Analysis
University of Canberra
Canberra, ACT, Australia

ISBN 978-3-319-75782-7   ISBN 978-3-319-75783-4 (eBook)
https://doi.org/10.1007/978-3-319-75783-4

Library of Congress Control Number: 2018935690

© The Editor(s) (if applicable) and The Author(s) 2018
This work is subject to copyright. All rights are solely and exclusively licensed by the Publisher, whether the whole or part of the material is concerned, specifically the rights of translation, reprinting, reuse of illustrations, recitation, broadcasting, reproduction on microfilms or in any other physical way, and transmission or information storage and retrieval, electronic adaptation, computer software, or by similar or dissimilar methodology now known or hereafter developed.
The use of general descriptive names, registered names, trademarks, service marks, etc. in this publication does not imply, even in the absence of a specific statement, that such names are exempt from the relevant protective laws and regulations and therefore free for general use.
The publisher, the authors, and the editors are safe to assume that the advice and information in this book are believed to be true and accurate at the date of publication. Neither the publisher nor the authors or the editors give a warranty, express or implied, with respect to the material contained herein or for any errors or omissions that may have been made. The publisher remains neutral with regard to jurisdictional claims in published maps and institutional affiliations.

Cover image © Malte Mueller
Cover designed by Thomas Howey

Printed on acid-free paper

This Palgrave Macmillan imprint is published by the registered company Springer International Publishing AG part of Springer Nature.
The registered company address is: Gewerbestrasse 11, 6330 Cham, Switzerland

The research discussed in this book was supported by NORFACE under grant 462-14-050 for the project 'Our Children's Europe' as part of the *Welfare Futures* programme.

Acknowledgements

We are grateful for the support of Wim van Oorschot, Femke Roosma and Tijs Laenen, University of Leuven; Stephen Elstub, University of Newcastle; Adrienn Győry, University of Kent; Vegard S. Svågard and Kjetil Klette Bøhler, NOVA Institute and many others for this project.

Contents

1 **New Challenges for the Welfare State and New Ways to Study Them**   1
   Peter Taylor-Gooby and Benjamin Leruth

2 **Individualism and Neo-Liberalism**   29
   Peter Taylor-Gooby and Benjamin Leruth

3 **European Welfare Nationalism: A Democratic Forum Study in Five Countries**   63
   Christian Albrekt Larsen, Morten Frederiksen, and Mathias Herup Nielsen

4 **Attitudes to Inequalities: Citizen Deliberation About the (Re-)Distribution of Income and Wealth in Four Welfare State Regimes**   93
   Jan-Ocko Heuer, Steffen Mau, and Katharina Zimmermann

5 **Intergenerational Solidarity and the Sustainability of State Welfare**   137
   Mi Ah Schøyen and Bjørn Hvinden

Contents

6   The Provision of Care: Whose Responsibility and Why?   183
    Heejung Chung, Maša Filipovič Hrast, and Tatjana Rakar

7   Healthcare Futures: Visions of Solidarity
    and the Sustainability of European Healthcare Systems   215
    *Maša Filipovič Hrast, Ellen M. Immergut, Tatjana Rakar,
    Urban Boljka, Diana Burlacu, and Andra Roescu*

8   Labour Market Challenges and the Role of Social
    Investment   243
    Katharina Zimmermann, Heejung Chung, and Jan-Ocko Heuer

9   Democratic Forums and Welfare State Attitudes   273
    Peter Taylor-Gooby and Benjamin Leruth

**Appendix: Details of the Participants in the Democratic
Forums**   297

Author Index   309

Subject Index   311

Notes on Contributors

Urban Boljka is Senior Researcher at the Social Protection Institute of the Republic of Slovenia and University of Ljubljana, Faculty of Social Sciences. His research interests include: social and family policies, child well-being indicators and universal basic income.

Diana Burlacu is Postdoctoral Researcher at Humboldt University of Berlin. Her research focuses on the interaction between public opinion and political institutions, in particular the feedback effects policies have on social policy preferences.

Heejung Chung is Reader in Sociology and Social Policy at the University of Kent. Her research deals with cross-national comparison of labour markets, working conditions and work-life balance issues focusing on the role institutions and socio-economic factors play therein.

Morten Frederiksen is Associate Professor at Aalborg University. His research interests are values and the process of evaluation—in particular trust, solidarity and the symbolic boundaries between state, market and civil society.

Jan-Ocko Heuer is Postdoctoral Researcher at the Humboldt University of Berlin. His current research focuses on welfare state change, financialisation and social inequality.

Maša Filipovič Hrast is Associate Professor at the University of Ljubljana, Faculty of Social Sciences, and a member of the Centre for Welfare Studies. Her research interests focus on social policy, housing policy and social exclusion.

Bjørn Hvinden is Professor in Sociology and Senior Researcher at NOVA, Oslo and Akershus University College of Applied Sciences, Norway. His main research interests are comparative European welfare, social citizenship, climate change, sustainability, disability and solidarity.

Ellen M. Immergut holds chairs in Comparative Politics and Political Sciences at the EUI and at Humboldt University. Her research interests are in political theory, state theory, neo-institutionalism, comparative political science and theories of policy analysis.

Christian Albrekt Larsen is Professor at the Centre for Comparative Welfare Studies (ccws.dk) at Aalborg University, Denmark. His research focuses on welfare attitudes, social trust and migration.

Benjamin Leruth is Assistant Professor in Politics and Public Administration at the University of Canberra. His research focuses on comparative European politics, Euroscepticism, differentiated integration in the European Union and public attitudes towards immigration and the European welfare state.

Steffen Mau is Professor of Sociology at the Humboldt University of Berlin. His research focuses on social policy, social inequality, migration and Europeanisation.

Mathias Herup Nielsen is Postdoctoral Researcher and lecturer at the Centre for Comparative Welfare Studies at Aalborg University. His research focuses broadly on discourses of welfare policies, including processes of justification and critique of policy programs.

Tatjana Rakar is Researcher and Assistant Professor at the University of Ljubljana, Faculty of Social Sciences, Centre for Welfare Studies. Her fields of research involve studies in social policy, family policy and civil society organisations.

Andra Roescu is Postdoctoral Research Fellow at the University of Southampton. Her research interests focus on comparative welfare state research, health policy, welfare attitudes, voting behaviour and policy responsiveness.

Mi Ah Schøyen is Senior Researcher at the NOVA research institute at Oslo and Akershus University College of Applied Sciences. She researches comparative welfare state studies, the welfare mix, intergenerational relations, public pension systems and the impact of climate change on welfare states.

Peter Taylor-Gooby is Research Professor of Social Policy at the University of Kent. He researches comparative social policy and social policy theory and writes novels with social policy themes.

Katharina Zimmermann is Postdoctoral Researcher at Humboldt University of Berlin. Her research interests lie in comparative welfare state research from a European and cross-national perspective, and her recent work covers welfare attitudes, social and employment policies in Europe and Europeanisation.

Acronyms

AfD	Alternative for Germany
AFDC	Aid to Families with Dependent Children
ALMP	Active Labour Market Policy
AROPE	At Risk of Poverty and Social Exclusion
BSA	British Social Attitudes Survey
CEE	Central and Eastern European countries
EC	European Commission
ECB	European Central Bank
EOPYY	Greek National Health Service Organisation
ESS	European Social Survey
EU	European Union
EU-15	First 15 members of the European Union
FN	Front National
GDP	Gross Domestic Product
GDR	German Democratic Republic
GMI	Minimum Income Guarantee
ILO	International Labour Office
IMF	International Monetary Fund
ISSP	International Social Survey Programme
ND	New Democracy
NPM	New Public Management
OECD	Organisation for Economic Co-operation and Development
OMC	Open Method of Co-ordination

SAP	Social Action Programme
SYRIZA	Coalition of the Radical Left (Greece)
UBI	Universal Basic Income
UK	United Kingdom
UMP	Union pour un Mouvement Populaire (France)
UNHCR	United Nations High Commissioner for Refugees
VAT	Value Added Tax

List of Figures

Fig. 3.1 The welfare state encourages immigration and immigrants' net gain/contribution to the welfare state (2008 ESS and 2015 Democratic Forums pre-survey) 71

Fig. 3.2 Attitudes to granting immigrants equal social rights across 28 countries 73

Fig. 4.1 Percentage of people who agree/strongly agree with the statement 'large differences in income are acceptable to reward talents and efforts' 99

Fig. 4.2 Percentage agreeing/strongly agreeing with the statement 'for a fair society, income differences in standard of living should be small' 100

Fig. 5.1 Public social expenditure: elderly and the working-age population, in 2007 and 2013 141

Fig. 5.2 At risk of poverty and social exclusion (AROPE) by broad age group 142

Fig. 5.3 Level and expected pace of population ageing by country 143

Fig. 6.1 Formal childcare by age group and duration (2015); total public expenditure on early childhood education (% GDP, 2013) 186

Fig. 6.2 Long-term care recipients and expenditure on long-term care (% GDP, 2014) 187

List of Figures

Fig. 7.1	Healthcare financing	217
Fig. 7.2	Willingness to include immigrants in publicly-funded healthcare	221
Fig. 7.3	Access to treatment	222
Fig. 8.1	Expenditure on active labour market services in 2010 and 2015 (% GDP)	249
Fig. 8.2	Passive labour market expenditure in 2010 and 2015 (% GDP)	250

List of Tables

Table 1.1	Key issues in the Democratic Forums	17
Table 2.1	Core issues in neo-liberalism and the concepts used to identify them in the forums	37
Table 2.2	Individualism and neo-liberalism in attitudes to the welfare state	55
Table 4.1	Basic coding scheme for analysis of attitudes towards economic inequalities	102
Table 4.2	Comparison of attitudes towards economic inequalities in four welfare state regimes	114
Table 4.3	Quotations used in this chapter	119
Table 5.1	Attitudes to the welfare state and to intergenerational issues	159
Table 5.2	Quotations used in the text	163
Table 6.1	Division of responsibility in the provision of care	192
Table 7.1	Coding list	224
Table 7.2	Healthcare solidarity in the Democratic Forums	238
Table 8.1	Labour market topics raised by democratic forum participants in the UK, Denmark, Germany and Slovenia	253
Table 8.2	Problems, their causes and their solutions	269

1

New Challenges for the Welfare State and New Ways to Study Them

Peter Taylor-Gooby and Benjamin Leruth

We urgently need to understand what people want for the future of the welfare state for two reasons. Firstly, European welfare states face severe challenges and are changing rapidly. Change is driven by long-run factors that include population ageing, globalization, labour market change, rising inequality, unprecedented levels of immigration in most European countries, constrained resources and a decline in the forces that traditionally supported public provision. We need to know what people expect from the welfare state and what reforms they will support.

Secondly, these challenges are exacerbated by immediate economic factors—the Great Recession, stagnation and more intense budgetary pressure—and by a new, global wave of radical populist politics, which mistrusts elites and experts and demands greater control over government.

P. Taylor-Gooby (✉)
School of Social Policy, Sociology and Social Research,
University of Kent, Canterbury, UK
e-mail: p.f.taylor-gooby@kent.ac.uk

B. Leruth
Institute for Governance and Policy Analysis, University of Canberra,
Canberra, ACT, Australia

We need to know what the implications of these changes are for public attitudes and for welfare state futures.

This book analyses welfare state attitudes and priorities and the way people justify them. It uses a new method, Democratic Forums. This method does not pre-categorise public opinion in the way that conventional quantitative surveys do, but seeks to give 'ordinary' people as much control as possible over the way attitudes are studied—as it were, a populism in social science research.

This chapter falls into five sections that consider, respectively, the following dimensions: current challenges to European welfare states; responses to these challenges and the importance of attitude studies; review of the existing literature on welfare state attitudes (almost entirely from pre-coded surveys); explanation of our new method, Democratic Forums; discussion of the contribution that our research makes to understanding current challenges; and lastly, we draw conclusions about the key themes in popular understanding of welfare state futures in different European countries.

Challenges to the Welfare State in Europe: Population Ageing, Austerity and the New Populism

The challenges confronting European welfare states have been discussed in an extensive literature (Ervasti et al. 2012; Pierson 2001; Van Kersbergen and Vis 2014) and in our companion book *After Austerity* (Taylor-Gooby et al. 2017). They may be divided into two groups: *structural threats* caused by continuing changes in the context of state welfare, and *political challenges* that result from the policies pursued by national governments in response. Into the first group fall population ageing with its attendant pressures on pension, health - and social - care spending, and the labour force; economic globalization which challenges the capacity of governments to maintain national employment policies; the inequality resulting from changes in the world of work and labour market dualisation; the competitiveness imperative that more open markets impose on national industries; and the high levels of immigration resulting largely from war and disorder, mostly in the Middle East and North Africa. The second group includes public spending cutbacks and the exacerbation of inequality as governments prioritise balanced budgets over state interventions at the national and European Central Bank (ECB) level; and a new wave of populist politics, especially on the right, that often promotes isolationism and foregrounds a welfare chauvinism that ring-fences public provision for nationals.

A series of reforms have contained pressures to escalate health and pensions spending across Europe (see Taylor-Gooby et al. 2017, Chaps. 1 and 10). Most governments have addressed labour-force issues by cutting back benefits and introducing stricter entitlement rules to promote flexibility and enhance work incentives, by investing in education and training to improve skills and productivity and by seeking to mobilise older people and those with young children into paid work, for example raising the pension age and subsidising childcare (Hemerijk 2013, Chap. 1). These policies are intended to enhance national competitiveness in a more globalized world and help address inequality and poverty.

Flexibility, Work First,[1] financial stringency and social investment have had varying success in different parts of Europe. The EU's *Europe 2020* programme seeks to draw national initiatives together to address a range of issues including climate change and energy production as well as productivity and inequality. It reports positive developments in education since 2008, particularly among women who also have higher levels of employment and a slow growth in their proportion of the working population, but no progress in the proportion of men in paid work, or progress in reducing poverty or inequality (Eurostat 2017a). More detailed analysis shows that success tends to be concentrated in Northern and Western Europe, while the most serious problems are found in Southern Europe and the post-socialist countries (Eurostat 2017b). Liberal Europe (notably the UK) does relatively well in employment but has failed to address poverty.

The majority of European governments and the EU as a whole have pursued 'balanced budget' programmes, requiring very substantial cuts in public spending, especially in those countries receiving bailout loans from the European Central Bank (ECB), the International Monetary

Fund (IMF) and the EU—Greece, Portugal, Spain and Ireland (De la Porte and Heins 2015). Greece and France's attempts to pursue neo-Keynesian state-led investment and social spending programmes in 2012–2016 achieved very little (see for example Petmesidou 2017; Leruth 2017).

The sense of economic and social malaise and the failure of governments to address the very real problems many people experience have contributed to the populist shift notably on the right in national politics across Europe, typically combining suspicion of established elites and of institutions such as the EU with programmes to end or reduce immigration, welfare chauvinism and higher spending on services for nationals.

Eurosceptic parties across Europe have considerably increased their influence since the advent of the Great Recession. Such parties have joined the government in Finland, Hungary and Poland and gained substantial numbers of votes elsewhere, but the UK is the only country to trigger the EU exit process, following a referendum on 23 June 2016. This has stimulated a process of 'differentiated disintegration' in the European Union (Leruth 2017; Leruth et al. 2018). The debate surrounding Greece's possible exit from the Economic and Monetary Union, which started in 2013, still continues as the country encounters severe difficulties in repaying EU-led bailouts. Following the results of national elections held across Europe in the course of 2017 (including Austria, Czech Republic, France and Germany), it appears that Euroscepticism remains a major political force and exerts strong influence on mainstream politics especially among those who feel 'left behind' (Kuhn et al. 2016).

Europe has experienced substantial immigration with over ten per cent of the population in all large countries foreign born and particularly high levels in Germany, Scandinavian countries and the UK (OECD 2016). In countries such as Denmark, Hungary or the UK, anti-immigration and/or anti-refugee programmes are typically bound up with a welfare chauvinism that assumes rigid controls will free up a fixed pool of jobs, housing and other resources for established residents. Resentment at austerity and concerns about immigration into Europe and between EU countries have fuelled a general trend to more emphatic nationalism in European politics.

The shift to a more populist and nationalist politics has led international commentators such as the OECD (2017) and International Monetary Fund (IMF 2017) to argue that countries should pursue social reforms as well as balanced budget and labour market flexibility programmes. These agencies have for some time claimed that more support for active labour markets and a strengthening of the rights of women and other disadvantaged groups in access to work and opportunities will enhance productivity. The new reports argue for broader redistributive programmes to enhance social equality and improve health (for example OECD 2017) and claim that these will also help by reducing the dissatisfaction that is seen to lie behind the growth of populism. They also present evidence (for example Ostry and Berg 2014) to show that redistribution does not damage medium-term growth.

This brief review points out why good quality, up-to-date attitude data is valuable in European welfare policy debates. Most European countries had addressed (or were on the way to addressing) most of the structural external challenges by the middle of the 2000–2010 decade. The reforms implemented in both pensions and healthcare were expected to meet commitments, and considerable progress had been made in improving the quality and quantity of labour to meet the competitive challenge of globalization. The Great Recession then set in train an ideological shift towards neo-liberalism and a general move to prioritise eliminating deficits over sustaining services. The impact of such policies on living standards and opportunities heightens dissatisfaction with existing policy elites. High rates of immigration provide a focus for blame. Any assessment of the development of the welfare state in Europe must take into account people's confidence in their governments and their response to immigration when analysing hopes and expectations for the future.

Findings from Recent Attitude Research

Public opinion, from what the quantitative attitude survey literature tells us, is generally not supportive of most aspects of the neo-liberal austerity programme, although austerity has dominated responses to the 2007–2008 financial crisis and its aftermath in European countries. There is backing for welfare chauvinism and the new populism, but also strong evidence of support for traditional provision, for inclusive, redistributive welfare states and also for social investment.

All the evidence shows that welfare states are popular with their citizens (Roosma et al. 2016), and that popularity has not diminished over time, at least since the 1980s (Papadakis and Bean 1993; Svallfors 2012a). The survey data is much less supportive of private provision (Taylor-Gooby 2002). Similarly, support for redistribution and for greater equality appears strong, although as Svallfors (2012b) and Taylor-Gooby and Martin (2010) point out, the details of question phrasing make a substantial difference to the findings. Approval of state welfare is evident in all regime types, despite differences of level in relation to redistribution and income differences (Arts and Gelissen 2001; Brooks 2012; Svallfors 1997).

So far so good for the traditional, non-liberal, non-populist welfare state—and an emerging puzzle as to how democratic governments succeed in pursuing welfare state contraction, austerity and individual responsibility programmes so obviously at variance with majority opinion. However, as an influential study by Roosma et al. (2013) points out, attitudes to the welfare state and the part it should play in redistribution and meeting need are complex and multidimensional. These authors distinguish seven dimensions in attitudes to the welfare state, including the goals, the range of service areas covered, the degree of redistribution, who should benefit and who should pay, and the efficiency and effectiveness of implementation. Our Democratic Forum method is designed to explore this complexity as ordinary people themselves understand it.

In summarising the structured survey literature we may group these dimensions under three headings. Firstly, *goals, range and redistribution*: many studies point to a division in support between benefits for older people, disabled people and healthcare programmes which are generally popular, and the much lower level of enthusiasm for benefits for able-bodied people of working age, evident in survey findings from the 1996 International Social Survey Project onwards, and which if anything have strengthened over time (Bonoli 2000; Ferrera 1993; Likki and Staerklé 2015; Taylor-Gooby 1982). Public opinion is notably less likely to support spending on unemployed people and inclined to distinguish more and less deserving groups even among the unemployed (Larsen 2008). The extent of actual or potential reciprocity makes a difference, especially in more corporatist countries (Mau 2003). These points are reinforced by findings from the few qualitative studies available (Taylor-Gooby et al. 2018; Taylor-Gooby and Martin 2010; Ullrich 2002). Welfare state support is nuanced and centres on mass services. While people favour the general idea of redistribution, they do not endorse practical policies directed at low-income people, so they do not back programmes leading to redistributive and inclusive outcomes.

Secondly, *who should benefit and who should pay?* Both interests (typically proxied by socio-demographic variables) and political ideology (proxied by political party support and orientation) play a role in support for social spending. Interests tend to be the most influential factor (Blekesaune and Quadagno 2003; Taylor-Gooby 2002). Both self-interest and ideology also influence attitudes to pensions and unemployment benefits and explain a major part of the difference in levels of support (Pederson 2014). National patterns of provision impact on support. Social class differences play a stronger role in the more liberal countries, whereas insider/outsider differences matter more in the more corporatist countries (Fong 2001; Linos and West 2003; Meier Jæger 2006). Carriero (2016) shows that, surprisingly, lower class people are more accepting of inequality in the more unequal countries.

Normative assumptions also fit within a national regime framework. Linos and West (2003) show that, in Anglo-Saxon liberal countries, the greater the extent to which people value social mobility, the less they are likely to support redistribution. The one qualitative study in the field shows that attitudes to inequality and redistribution vary markedly between Germany and the UK, and that this extends to the language used to discuss the concepts of opportunity and outcome (Burkhardt et al. 2011). Again, support in practice is likely to be much stronger for particular aspects of the welfare state than for state welfare as a whole.

Thirdly, *efficiency, effectiveness and tax*: many people are critical of what they see as government bureaucracy and lack of transparency. They are strongly concerned about benefit abuse, particularly by people of working age, and they believe that the incidence of taxation is unfair, particularly for lower- and middle-income groups (Edlund 1999; Andersen 1999; Svallfors 1999). This reinforces the shift to populism.

The strength of support for welfare state provision as a whole and for the most expensive aspects of state welfare (pensions and healthcare) in particular tells against the general programme of balanced budgets, cuts in state provision and the expansion of the market. On the other hand, concerns about the operation and effectiveness of welfare state institutions fit well with a general neo-liberal suspicion of big government. The parallel concerns that centre on provision for people of working age imply approval of the principle of individual responsibility, in this area at least. This suggests a nuanced individualism in public attitudes, growing rather stronger over time and immediately focused on an ethic of responsibility in the world of paid work.

Two other areas are currently important: the central focus of the current wave of European populism—the conviction that immigration damages the interests of national populations—and the endorsement of social investment to promote productivity and enhance individual opportunities by the EU and many national governments. In the first area, the claim promoted by Alesina and Glaeser (2005), that European welfare states rest on an essentially nationalist solidarity which will be undermined by mass immigration, has attracted considerable attention. While this claim is not supported by the empirical evidence on policy responses to immigration (Taylor-Gooby 2005; Chap. 3 this volume), attitude studies do at least show that immigrants come low in rankings of deservingness for benefits and services (Jaime-Castillo et al. 2016; Kootstra 2014; Mau and Burkhardt 2009; Reeskens and Van der Meer 2014; van Oorschot 2008). The welfare chauvinist thesis that couples support for generous welfare states to the exclusion of immigrants from provision is widely endorsed (Mewes and Mau 2012; Van der Waal et al. 2010). Conversely immigrants themselves are rather more in favour of mass state welfare than are the host populations (Luttmer and Singhal 2011).

When we come to examine individual rights and social investment, there is evidence that many people are in favour of state services that help mobilise groups like women with childcare responsibilities into paid work. Support for the provision of childcare by the state is high across Europe, rather higher in southern European countries than elsewhere

(Meuleman and Chung 2012). Women are more likely to support these policies than men (Bolzendahl and Olafsdottir 2008; Knijn and van Oorschot 2008). Support for childcare has increased somewhat since 1996 (Crompton and Lyonette 2005). Other aspects of social investment policies are not well covered by the surveys, but a recent eight-country study in Western Europe shows that social investment programmes are generally more popular than passive welfare or workfare programmes and are particularly supported by a broad coalition of the better-educated and left-libertarian leaning middle class (Busemeyer et al. 2017). In addition, a one-country study using a quasi-experimental design shows that the inclusion of training and employability enhanced support for active labour market programmes (Gallego and Marx 2016).

The data from the pre-coded surveys and other work shows a clear hierarchy of areas of provision and of the deservingness of different groups of recipients, with older and disabled people at the top and those closest to the labour market and recent immigrants at the bottom. This fits with the established theory which links deservingness to 'control over need, or to taking responsibility for it, level of need, reciprocity, closeness to us and gratefulness and compliance' (van Oorschot 2006, 29; Cook 1979; Coughlin 1979). Groups seen as needy, not responsible for their need, having contributed or being likely to contribute to society, similar to us and grateful for help are thought deserving. Support for state welfare in general and for redistribution seems reasonably high, highest in Nordic and corporatist countries, but also high in relatively weakly redistributive liberal and southern countries. The private sector is endorsed most strongly in liberal and also in post-socialist Europe.

Support for the welfare state is heavily nuanced and at odds with the traditional model of the inclusive and redistributive welfare state. There are clear differences in the level of support for different needs and the pattern of support is likely to undermine serious redistribution since the needs of able-bodied poor people of working age are generally viewed with suspicion. This approach does not support a simple austerity neoliberalism but might go some way towards approving more liberal labour market policies. The widespread anti-immigrant sentiments and concerns about big government fit well with populism and with welfare chauvinism. At the same time, the social investment stance receives considerable support in the few surveys that cover this area. Social investment is typically seen as a new approach to state welfare and one that could contribute to the traditional goals of greater equality and a better quality of life for most people (European Commission 2013; Morel et al. 2012).

These points suggest that the basis for a real shift in the politics of welfare may exist, but that we need to explore attitudes and their various dimensions in much more detail to understand how people fit the various ideas together and what the forward programme that most people expect or would support would be like.

In the next section we discuss a radically new approach to understanding people's attitudes in context based on the idea of 'democratic forums'. We then outline some of the findings from our research to demonstrate its merits and limitations.

Democratic Forums

Democratic Forums are relatively large (typically 30–40 participant) group discussions that take place over an extended period of time with limited moderation. The objective is to allow participants as much control over proceedings as possible and to limit opportunities for the conceptual frameworks of researchers and policymakers to influence the ideas they express. The opportunities for discussion in the forums and the time involved, typically extending over more than one day, allow people to develop ideas and to respond to arguments. Researchers can examine the way different positions are justified and the conceptual frameworks that are used by ordinary members of the public to link ideas together. In practice, plenary sessions are combined with breakout groups in most forums to facilitate participation from those who are less confident in large gatherings. One aspect of the authority of the group over the situation is that the participants are typically given the opportunity to request information to assist their discussion and this is then sought from independent experts by the researchers.

The background theory for the forums comes from two social science traditions. First, one of the major developments in recent democratic theory has been a shift away from an approach to democracy as a system for ensuring that governments respond to the wishes of a largely passive electorate (Almond and Verba 1963) and for managing disagreements about the overall direction of policy within that electorate (Dahl 1961; Lijphart 1999), to one of democracy as an active institutional framework for promoting more widespread deliberation and citizen engagement (Chambers 2003; Dryzek 2010; Goodin 2009; Mouffe 2000; see Floridia 2017 for a historical review). Secondly, and at the same time, attitude theorists have moved away from a positivist concept of attitudes as original within the individual—the 'file-drawer model' in which, as it were, one looks up one's attitudes inside one's head (Wilson and Hodges 1992)—to a more social account of attitudes as developing through interaction and expression in debate (Tajfel 1981).

These changes are bound up with a number of developments: economic approaches that shift away from a simple rational actor model to one which sees preferences as constructed within economic formations (for example, the New Institutionalism); the emergence of a whole range of groups and interests demanding engagement within the political process (Snow and Soule 2010); shifts in international aid and development towards programmes that require donor countries to consult with and actively engage with the populations as well as the governments of countries which receive aid (for example, the World Bank Civil Society programme: see World Bank 2014); developments such as the Porto Alegre participatory budget-holding initiative (de Sousa Santos 2005), now copied elsewhere; concern about citizen alienation in Western democracies; and a whole range of approaches associated with an increased emphasis on individual dignity and human rights. These have led to shifts in the way power-holders treat others in areas ranging from legal systems to medicine, from science to mental health and from risk policy to local government. A foundational argument underlying both democratic theory and theories about attitudes and values is Habermas' concept of legitimacy as based on the exemplar of an 'ideal speech situation' in which all those concerned can communicate with good will and outside the influence of interests and in which differences in political values can be negotiated justly (Habermas 1996). This basis makes the forum method particularly valuable in studying the ideas of ordinary members of the public, very often in rejection of the approach of an established policy elite.

The main use of Democratic Forums has been in extending participative democracy and consulting the mass public, for example by policymakers who will themselves make the final decision. This is particularly valuable in the case of areas of controversy and conflict. Renn (2008) describes an exercise in using forums to arrive at a community decision on the siting of an unpopular waste incinerator. No one wanted it but it had to go somewhere. The forums concluded that the possibly poisonous plant should be located upwind of the main regional administrative building. Their advice was considered and the plant not built. Another use is to legitimate a decision that is already preferred by policymakers, by allowing others to discuss it, or in testing out public reaction to a decision that has already been made: for example the UK consultation on Universal Credit and other reforms that was interpreted as endorsing the proposals despite widespread dissent (DWP 2010). Here we use the forums in a relatively unusual way and for the first time in studying welfare attitudes, as a research tool to examine how people justify their ideas and link them together.

We explore these linkages, which play an important role in determining priorities, through the idea of 'framing'. The framing approach emphasizes the point that social attitudes do not exist independently from ideas and values about other aspects of society. The entire pattern of ideas provides a supportive context which reinforces or legitimates attitudes (Druckman 2001). For example, a conceptual framework that includes the belief that the proportion of older people in the population is increasing and sees older people as net consumers of services will support the idea that pension spending will be a major problem in the future; the belief that unemployed people are lazy and that the cost of benefits for them is an important factor in public spending may justify benefit cuts and workfare programmes. This may be reinforced by a value-commitment to the work ethic. The view that immigrants are a net economic burden as consumers rather than an asset as workers fits with the view that immigration should be limited. Ideas about the relative costs of services for different needs and the social impact of the behaviours that particular welfare programmes are thought to encourage will influence spending choices. Framings link together understandings of the world of welfare with ideas about priorities and serve to justify the positions that people take up. They may be provided through mass media, the statements of politicians, celebrities, public intellectuals, media figures, neighbours or other communications (van der Pas 2014), or be understood as part of people's mental mapping of the issues (Chong and Druckman 2007).

The extended group discussions with which we are concerned are variously referred to as Democratic Forums, Deliberative Forums or Citizen's Assemblies (see e.g. Warren and Pearse 2008; Flinders et al. 2016) and more generally participatory government, depending on whether the central concern is the locus of authority in a research investigation, the deliberative process, or the interest in arriving at a consensus outcome on a public policy issue. The title 'Deliberative Poll' is particularly associated with the work of the Center for Deliberative Democracy at Stanford University. In this case we refer to our method by the general title of Democratic Forum. Our research method differs from other deliberative approaches in three ways. Firstly, we are concerned to give participants as much control as possible. Secondly, our interest is broader than that of a typical Citizens' Assembly, as we asked participants to reflect on the future of the welfare state, which encompasses a broad and loosely defined family of issues. Thirdly, one of the key objectives of our Democratic Forums is to compare attitudes between citizens of countries with different welfare traditions.

The forum approach has strengths and limitations compared with the main alternative, pre-coded surveys. The group participating in a forum is too small to provide statistical representation of the population. It is perhaps best thought of as a 'mini-public' that includes the main socio-demographic groups in which most researchers are interested. The material generated by a forum is not typically amenable to statistical examination but instead requires careful and detailed post-coding and protracted iterative content analysis.

The point of the forum is that, unlike a pre-coded questionnaire survey, it does not impose its own framing on the questions to be asked about an issue or the response categories into which answers will be fitted. The raw priorities of ordinary people, the justifications they think important and the conceptual framing they use to link ideas together can be captured. Goerres and Prinzen (2011) point to the failure of pre-coded surveys to capture ambivalence (a respondent may really wish to tick two of the exclusive boxes), non-attitudes (the respondent may have no strong views but offer one to be polite), inconsistency (people may hold logically contradictory attitudes, for which there is no place on the questionnaire) and uncertainty (the individual simply does not know what to think). The material from a Democratic Forum, since it includes the arguments used by participants expressed in an informal and unstructured way, is much more likely to allow the researcher access to such aspects of the way people understand an issue.

The justifications that people give in discussion may also bring out their background understanding; in the case of beliefs in the effectiveness of the current welfare state, for example, it may reveal their assumptions about the relative cost and numbers of claimers for different benefits. They may also indicate the significance of current framings of issues, for example, by mass media, and indicate which sources of information people trust and which they do not (see Larsen 2013; Slothuus 2007).

As part of the NORFACE-funded 'Welfare States Futures: Our Children's Europe' (WelfSOC) project, we used Democratic Forums to give new insight into how people think about the future of European welfare states. We were particularly interested in people's priorities and in how they justified them, the evidence they used to support their views and the way their ideas and beliefs fitted together into conceptual frameworks which legitimated particular policy directions.

We conducted two-day forums with between 34 and 36 participants in five countries (Denmark, Germany, Norway, Slovenia and the UK) in September and October 2015. The forums included a broadly representative sample of the population, consisting of older and younger, middle and working class, women and men and those with and without dependent children, and also some unemployed, self-employed, retired, ethnic minority and immigrant members. Participants were selected by research agencies commissioned by the WelfSOC team. The countries were chosen to represent Scandinavian, corporatist, liberal and post-socialist welfare state regimes, and co-ordinated market and liberal market varieties of capitalism. We offered the forums a deliberately broad and forward-looking question, encompassing several themes: '*What should the priorities of the government of [your country] be for benefits and services in 2040?*, but did not seek to direct the discussion through further questions.

The forums included a mix of breakout groups (consisting of 10–12 participants) and plenary sessions. On the first day of discussion participants were asked to select five themes based on what they saw as the key challenges in the future of the welfare state. This reversed the standard procedure whereby researchers will frame the discussion by presenting particular themes or issues and response categories in a structured survey questionnaire. The themes selected by our participants were (in order of priority) immigration; work; education; old age; and welfare state resources and inequality. Participants also were given the opportunity to request information at the end of the first day and this was provided at the beginning of Day Two. The second day of discussion was more structured, and participants were asked to reflect on five themes put forward by the research team: immigration, the labour market, population ageing, gender and inequality. These themes overlapped with those chosen by the participants on day one, the only real difference being the inclusion of gender and the omission of education. This structuring is the only aspect in which we departed from the standard Democratic Forum assumption that the participants should have greater control over proceedings than researchers. The object was to generate material that dealt with similar topics and could be compared directly across the five national studies. The value of the discussion was given added emphasis by requesting participants to provide bullet points for a report to government on the main issues at the end of the second day.

We carried out a brief pre-coded survey of attitudes before and after the forums, using questions from the European Social Survey, to establish attitude change, but were mainly interested in the details and process of the discussions, which were audio and video recorded. Further details of the conduct of the forums are available in the papers on our website (WelfSOC 2017) and in Appendix 1, which also gives a key to the participants' characteristics.

The use of Democratic Forums enables us to approach people's attitudes to welfare state futures with the minimum of preconceptions as to how the issues should be framed. The findings extend our understanding of how people think and argue about the state welfare in various European countries.

Our Findings: The Future of Welfare

In this section we present the various areas in which we analyse Democratic Forum findings in detail in Chaps. 2, 3, 4, 5, 6, 7, 8, and 9 of this book. The two main immediate challenges to traditional welfare states are the neo-liberal individualist agenda, given impetus since the 2007 crisis by stringent austerity programmes, and the welfare chauvinist/nationalist politics that has swept across Europe. These are analysed in Chaps. 2 and 3. We then go on to address attitudes to the problems that welfare states are designed to manage and which are becoming more pressing as a result of the longer-run challenges discussed earlier: inequality and poverty, intergenerational transfers and exchanges, child and elder care and gender issues, healthcare, education, and labour market regulation. We focus particularly on issues that are emerging or are expected to develop in the near future and include discussion of sustainability, population ageing and new policy directions such as social investment, the growth of the private sector, changing welfare citizenship and the tendency to shift responsibility for outcomes to individuals.

The way people think about welfare provision is influenced by a number of factors, including their interests (what they think will advantage them and their group), their ideology and value-assumptions, their ideas and beliefs about the current system and how it works and fits into the rest of society, and the institutions that form the existing welfare state regime. These various elements combine in a 'framing' which shapes the positions at which they arrive and the arguments with which they support them.

A detailed comparative analysis is presented in the final chapter together with the implications of our findings for the study of attitudes to the future of the European welfare state. Here we highlight the main points (see Table 1.1). Some parallel the main findings of quantitative work. These can be summed up by saying that the onward march of neo-liberalism across European welfare states is much exaggerated. Welfare states are popular. Most people want the greater part of the existing pattern of provision to be sustained with a shift of emphasis to younger people, to expand opportunities in work and improve support for families. In most countries they believe this is possible.

Table 1.1 Key issues in the Democratic Forums

	Denmark	Norway	Germany	Slovenia	United Kingdom
Starting point	Main services remain popular but spending is under rising pressure	Main services remain popular but pressure is anticipated	Main services remain popular but spending under some pressure	Main services popular but require increased spending and eradication of corruption	Main services remain popular but face major pressures and governmental capacity is weak
Case for the welfare state	Individual, social and economic benefit	Social, individual and economic benefit	Social, economic and individual benefit	Individual and social then economic benefit	Economic and then individual benefit
Threats	Internal: population ageing; workshy; external: MNCs	Internal: population ageing; external: MNCs	Internal: population ageing; external: MNCs	Internal: low spending, corruption; emigration	Internal: work-shy; cost of NHS, pensions; external: immigrants and MNCs
Ways forward	Reforms including less redistribution and greater flexibility; continued social investment	Reforms inc. some privatisation; intergenerational shifts in spending; continued social investment	Reforms inc. greater equality in education and health access; some privatisation; continued social investment	Control corruption; raise minimum wages and benefits for working age and for older people; progressive taxes	Decline of main services; expansion of private sector; cut immigrants' welfare rights; expansion of social investment
Confidence in state effectiveness	High	High	High	Adequate	Low
Overall	More flexible integrative universalism	Moderated integrative universalism	Meritocratic egalitarianism	Post-soviet egalitarianism	'Reluctant individualism' because no alternative is available

The more detailed analysis of attitudes in context provided by the forums nuances these findings in four ways. Firstly, they show that populations, even in the Scandinavian countries with the strongest welfare states, accept aspects of the liberal individualist model. They acknowledge the difficulties in sustaining high standards across all services in the face of population ageing and other pressures, and stress the importance of personal responsibility, particularly in relation to pensions.

Secondly, the established deserving/undeserving distinction remains strong, especially in Germany, Denmark and the UK. It links up with demands for greater personal responsibility in a way that challenges some aspects of state provision.

Thirdly, analysis of the framing of healthcare, the polar case of welfare state solidarity, points to national variations. Discussion in the Scandinavian countries is framed in terms of a universal solidarity, providing for all who need help. In Germany the debate is more status-oriented and includes consideration of how access for those who have contributed to the service through social insurance is damaged by queue-jumpers who pay privately for better treatment. Slovenian members of the forums value an egalitarian solidarity, want higher spending and resent the current role of private practice in promoting the corruption of gatekeepers. In the liberal UK, while participants value the service in terms of national solidarity, in keeping with their anti-immigrant ethos, they also see it as under threat from outsiders, and express anxiety about its sustainability. These notions of solidarity apply loosely to other service areas. Benefits for those of working age tend towards a universalist need-meeting in Scandinavia, are more focused on status or work history in Germany, are underpinned by support for greater equality in Slovenia, and are hedged by a determination to prevent outsiders (in this case those who infringe the work ethic) from claiming benefits in the UK. Solidarity is packaged in different ways in different countries.

Fourthly, the forum analysis brings out more strongly than does the quantitative literature popular support for social investment as a way of serving national economic and social objectives while containing future demands and compensating for constraints on services and pressures on solidarity. Again the balance varies from country to country. The services most commonly referred to are education and training (or apprenticeships) and childcare. The strongest individualism is found in the UK forums, both in relation to responsibility for maintaining oneself and in the demand for improved individual opportunities that will also benefit the economy. Here few participants see the object of social investment in terms of social cohesion or equality. In Denmark and Norway (where the high quality of training is generally accepted) and in Germany, where there is real concern about education inequalities, such investment is valued also for its contribution to social integration, and in Slovenia for reducing inequalities as well as reducing poverty.

In short, the main elements in existing welfare states remain popular, but with reservations, with national variations and with concurrent support for new directions addressing new social risks. Three further findings build on existing quantitative work and show new ways forward. These deal with the way current issues are understood, often counter-factually, how background assumptions and beliefs about one's society underpin what might be loosely understood as regime differences, and trust in government and confidence in its capacity to meet the demands placed upon it.

The most striking issue in the first area, the understanding of current issues, concerns immigration. While the UK has nowhere near the highest number of immigrants, its residents have far and away the strongest concern that immigrants are displacing existing residents in a fixed pool of available jobs or pre-empting welfare services, and demand the harshest restrictions on access to last-resort welfare for both immigrants and for residents (see Chap. 3). This fits with both the dominant overall liberal commitment to self-responsibility and the idea that greater conditionality generates stronger concerns about sharing. Elsewhere integrationist policies predominate over defensiveness in attitudes to immigration.

The second issue is the relationship between attitude patterns and regime structures: national patterns and concerns related to regime type emerge in the areas of inequality, responsibility, intergenerational transfers and labour market issues, again moderated by contextual factors (see Chap. 9). Thus the participants in the Danish forums stress their commitment to the values of inclusion and solidarity but are relatively relaxed about the regulation and taxation required to sustain redistribution and highlight the importance of individual labour market responsibility; Slovenian participants (at similar levels of inequality but with much lower general living standards) are determined that government should pursue strong progressive taxation, tighten labour market regulation and improve benefits and minimum wages. In the liberal UK there is a striking concern about wage levels and working conditions, particularly at the bottom, and demands for a higher minimum wage and an end to zero-hour contracts. But measures to strengthen unions or introduce other regulations are hardly mentioned, and higher taxes or benefits for non-workers are rejected. What is seen to require redistributive policies in one context fits into a more individualist ideology in another. In Germany many people feel that the dilution of rights for those in low-paid jobs damages the strongly held principle of valuing work but seem unwilling to call for changes.

Similarly most participants regard state support for childcare as important, but differ in their emphasis on the interests of society, the child, the parents or the economy, with the Scandinavian countries and the UK at opposite extremes. Interestingly, the degree of individual responsibility for financing childcare that is seen as appropriate tends to increase the more that the chief concern is to release women for paid work.

The third area, trust in government, has received little attention in quantitative work on welfare state attitudes but has a clear influence on national patterns and may well play a stronger role in the future. There are real concerns about the capability and effectiveness of national government in relation to multinational companies and other agencies advantaged by globalization and government's capacity to serve the interests of its own citizens. Across all the forums there is a strong sense that governments should regulate business more strictly in relation to taxation, employment practices, wages for lower-paid groups and security in work, and that this is increasingly difficult in a world where footloose capital can move at will. Interestingly it is the UK participants with the most market-centred and liberal approach to individual responsibility that see government as least effective in regulation of business.

Trust in government feeds into confidence in the sustainability of welfare state services, a real issue in all the countries studied. As pointed out earlier, participants in Scandinavian countries and Germany stressed the cost of population ageing and discussed strategies to maintain state services, including a degree of privatisation. In Slovenia the pressures of ageing are felt less intensely against the more immediate issue of improving services, and participants are in favour of higher and more progressive tax. Implicit in all these arguments is the belief that government is capable of implementing policies to achieve these ends. In the UK the forums reveal considerable misgivings as to the competence of government and an acceptance that standards in state healthcare and pensions will fall to the level where private services provide for most people. Similarly the effectiveness of government in protecting the benefits of the deserving poor from the fraudulent and workshy, or the health service, social housing and the whole welfare system from the demands of immigrants is called into question just as much as its capacity to regulate business. Thus far, quantitative work has not made the link between confidence in government and concerns about welfare state sustainability.

Perhaps the most useful feature of the Democratic Forum approach is its capacity to bring together issues that are often not directly linked in pre-coded questionnaires and to follow through the arguments of ordinary people to show how the points made about individual services and issues link together in an overall 'framing' of the welfare state and how it is likely to develop (see Table 1.1). The analysis shows differences between Denmark and Norway within the Nordic model, the continued emphasis upon equality in the German corporatist-conservative regime, how Slovenian post-socialism links strong commitments to fairness and greater equality to concerns about corruption, and how in the UK liberal individualism fits with anti-immigration strategies and disquiet about state capacity. These issues are developed further in the concluding chapter.

Conclusions: Welfare Going Forward

In this chapter we argue that the Democratic Forum approach offers a new and valuable method of investigating attitudes to the welfare state in Europe alongside our existing quantitative and qualitative techniques. We discuss and illustrate the advantages and disadvantages of the method and commend its use to explore the everyday life framing of social issues.

The following chapters provide a detailed account of attitudes to social provision and how they are likely to develop during the next quarter century in five representative European countries. They show that, despite facing broadly similar pressures of globalization, population ageing, austerity and, to some extent, immigration, people base their attitudes and expectations for the future on different background assumptions and framings of how society works and of the place of the welfare state within it. These lead to different expectations and aspirations for future development. The strongest overall themes are two. First there is continuing support for the main welfare state programmes, though with different degrees of confidence in their future sustainability. Secondly most people endorse social investment programmes to secure better training, childcare and education for the mass of the population as a way forward, though for different reasons in different countries. The UK stands out in the way its citizens mistrust the capacity of their government to sustain the main welfare state services.

Note

1. Work First programmes prioritize employment over benefit receipt for unemployed and disabled people.

References

Alesina, A., & Glaeser, G. (2005). *Fighting poverty in Europe and America*. Oxford: Oxford University Press.

Almond, G., & Verba, S. (1963). *The civic culture*. London: Sage.

Andersen, J. G. (1999). Changing labour markets, new social divisions and welfare state support: Denmark in the 1990s. In S. Svallfors & P. Taylor-Gooby (Eds.), *The end of the welfare state? Responses to state retrenchment*. London: Routledge.

Arts, W., & Gelissen, J. (2001). Welfare states, solidarity and justice principles: Does the type really matter? *Acta Sociologica, 44*(4), 283–299.

Blekesaune, M., & Quadagno, J. (2003). Public attitudes toward welfare state policies a comparative analysis of 24 nations. *European Sociological Review, 19*(5), 415–427.

Bolzendahl, C., & Olafsdottir, S. (2008). Gender group interest or gender ideology? Understanding U.S. support for family policy within the liberal welfare regime. *Sociological Perspectives, 51*(2), 281–304.

Bonoli, G. (2000). Public attitudes to social protection and political economy traditions in Western Europe. *European Societies, 2*(4), 431–452.

Brooks, C. (2012). Framing theory, welfare attitudes, and the United States case. In S. Svallfors (Ed.), *Contested welfare states: Welfare attitudes in Europe and beyond*. Stanford, CA: Stanford University Press.

Burkhardt, C., Martin, R., Mau, S., & Taylor-Gooby, P. (2011). Differing notions of social welfare? In J. Clasen (Ed.), *Converging worlds of welfare?* Oxford: Oxford University Press.

Busemeyer, M., Garritzmann, J., & Neimans, E. (2017, 15 September). *Public demand for social investment*. Paper presented at the ESPAnet annual conference, University of Lisbon.

Carriero, R. (2016). More inequality, fewer class differences: The paradox of attitudes to redistribution across European countries. *Comparative Sociology, 15*(1), 112–139.

Chambers, S. (2003). Deliberative democracy theory. *Annual Review of Political Science, 6*, 307–326.

Chong, D., & Druckman, J. N. (2007). Framing theory. *Annual Review of Political Science, 101*, 637–655.

Cook, F. L. (1979). *Who should be helped? Public support for social services*. Beverly Hills, CA: Sage Publications.

Coughlin, R. (1979). Social policy and ideology: Public opinion in eight rich nations. *Comparative Social Research, 2*, 3–40.

Crompton, R., & Lyonette, C. (2005). The new gender essentialism—Domestic and family 'choices' and their relation to attitudes. *British Journal of Sociology, 56*(4), 601–620.

Dahl, A. (1961). *Who governs?* New Haven, CT: Yale University Press.

De la Porte, C., & Heins, E. (2015). A new era of European integration? Governance of labour market and social policy since the sovereign debt crisis. *Comparative European Politics, 13*(1), 8–28.

de Sousa Santos, B. (2005). Participatory budgeting in porto alegre: Toward a redistributive democracy. In B. De Sousa Santos (Ed.), *Democratizing democracy: Beyond the liberal democratic canon*. London: Verso.

Department for Work and Pensions. (2010). *Better welfare for the 21st century*, Cm. 7971. London: Department for Work and Pensions.

Druckman, J. (2001). The implications of framing effects for citizen competence. *Political Behavior, 23*(3), 225–256.

Dryzek, J. (2010). *Foundations and frontiers of deliberative governance.* Oxford: Oxford University Press.

Edlund, J. (1999). Progressive taxation farewell? Attitudes to income redistribution and taxation in Sweden, Great Britain and the United States. In S. Svallfors & P. Taylor-Gooby (Eds.), *The end of the welfare state? Responses to retrenchment.* London: Routledge.

Ervasti, H., Andersen, J. G., Fridberg, T., & Ringdal, K. (2012). *The future of the welfare state: Social policy attitudes and social capital in Europe.* Cheltenham: Edward Elgar Publishing.

European Commission. (2013). 'Communication from the Commission to the European Parliament, the Council, the European Economic and Social Committee and that Committee of the Regions', towards social investment for growth and cohesion-including implementing the European Social Fund 2014–2020. COM (2013) 83 final. Brussels: European Commission.

Eurostat. (2017a). Europe 2020 headline indicators: Scoreboard. Retrieved August 11, 2017, from http://ec.europa.eu/eurostat/web/europe-2020-indicators/europe-2020-strategy/headline-indicators-scoreboard.

Eurostat. (2017b). Labour productivity per hour worked. Retrieved July 10, 2017, from http://ec.europa.eu/eurostat/web/products-datasets/-/nama_10_lp_ulc.

Ferrera, M. (1993). *EC citizens and social protection.* Brussels: European Commission.

Flinders, M., Ghose, K., Jennings, W., Molloy, E., Prosser, B., Renwick, A., Smith, G., & Spada, P. (2016). Democracy matters: Lessons from the 2015 citizens' assemblies on English devolution [online]. Retrieved August 11, 2017, from https://eprints.soton.ac.uk/391972/1/Democracy%2520Matters%2520final%2520report.pdf.

Floridia, A. (2017). *From participation to deliberation.* Colchester: ECPR Press.

Fong, C. (2001). Social preferences, self-interest, and the demand for redistribution. *Journal of Public Economics, 82*(2), 225–246.

Gallego, A., & Marx, P. (2016). Multi-dimensional preferences for labour market reforms: A conjoint experiment. *Journal of European Public Policy, 24*(7), 1027–1047.

Goerres, A., & Prinzen, K. (2011). Can we improve the measurement of attitudes towards the welfare state? *Social Indicators Research, 109*(3), 515–534.

Goodin, R. E. (2009). *The Oxford handbook of political science.* Oxford: Oxford University Press.

Habermas, J. (1996). Three normative models of democracy. In S. Benhabib (Ed.), *Democracy and difference: Contesting the boundaries of the political* (pp. 21–30). Princeton, NJ: Princeton University Press.

Hemerijk, A. (2013). *Changing welfare states*. Oxford: Oxford University Press.
IMF. (2017). Growth that reaches everyone: Facts, factors, tools. Retrieved October 27, 2017, from https://blogs.imf.org/2017/09/20/growth-that-reaches-everyone-facts-factors-tools/.
Jaime-Castillo, A. M., Marques-Perales, I., & Alvarez-Galvez, J. (2016). The impact of social expenditure on attitudes towards immigration in Europe. *Social Indicators Research, 126*(3), 1089–1108.
Knijn, T., & van Oorschot, W. (2008). The need for and the societal legitimacy of social investments in children and their families: Critical reflections on the Dutch case. *Journal of Family Issues, 29*(11), 1520–1542.
Kootstra, A. (2014). *The deservingness of immigrants: Evidence from survey experiments in the UK and the Netherlands*. Paper presented at the ESPAnet Conference Oslo.
Kuhn, T., van Elsas, E., Hakhverdian, A., & van den Burg, W. (2016). An ever wider gap in an ever closer union: Rising inequalities and Euroscepticism in 12 West European democracies, 1975–2009. *Socio-Economic Review, 14*(1), 27–45.
Larsen, C. A. (2008). The institutional logic of welfare attitudes: How welfare regimes influence public support. *Comparative Political Studies, 41*(2), 145–168.
Larsen, C. A. (2013). *The rise and fall of social cohesion*. Oxford: Oxford University Press.
Leruth, B. (2017). The Europeanization of the welfare state: The case for a differentiated European social model. In P. Taylor-Gooby, B. Leruth, & H. Chung (Eds.), *After austerity: Welfare state transformation in Europe after the great recession*. Oxford: Oxford University Press.
Leruth, B., Startin, N., & Usherwood, S. (Eds.). (2018). *The Routledge handbook of euroscepticism*. London: Routledge.
Lijphart, A. (1999). *Patterns of democracy*. New Haven, CT: Yale University Press.
Likki, T., & Staerklé, C. (2015). Welfare support in Europe: Interplay of dependency culture beliefs and meritocratic contexts. *International Journal of Public Opinion Research, 27*(1), 138–153.
Linos, K., & West, M. (2003). Self-interest, social beliefs, and attitudes to redistribution. Re-addressing the issue of cross-national variation. *European Sociological Review, 19*(4), 393–409.
Luttmer, E., & Singhal, M. (2011). Culture, context, and the taste for redistribution. *American Economic Journal, 3*(1), 157–179.

Mau, S. (2003). *The moral economy of welfare states: Britain and Germany compared*. London: Routledge.
Mau, S., & Burkhardt, C. (2009). Migration and welfare state solidarity in Western Europe. *Journal of European Social Policy, 19*(3), 213–229.
Meier Jæger, M. (2006). What makes people support public responsibility for welfare provision: Self-interest or political ideology? A longitudinal approach. *Acta Sociologica, 49*(3), 321–338.
Meuleman, B., & Chung, H. (2012). Who should care for the children? Support for government intervention in childcare. In H. Ervasti, J. G. Andersen, T. Fridberg, & K. Ringdal (Eds.), *The future of the welfare state: Social policy attitudes and social capital in Europe*. Cheltenham: Edward Elgar.
Mewes, J., & Mau, S. (2012). Unravelling working-class welfare chauvinism. In S. Svallfors (Ed.), *Contested welfare states: Welfare attitudes in Europe and beyond*. Stanford, CA: Stanford University Press.
Morel, N., Palier, B., & Palme, J. (2012). *Towards a social investment welfare state?* Bristol: Policy Press.
Mouffe, C. (2000). *The democratic paradox*. London: Verso.
OECD. (2016). Key statistics on migration in OECD countries. Retrieved March 21, 2017, from http://www.oecd.org/els/mig/keystat.htm.
OECD. (2017). Going for growth. Retrieved March 21, 2017, from http://www.oecd.org/economy/goingforgrowth.htm.
van Oorschot, W. (2006). Making the difference in social Europe: Deservingness perceptions among citizens of European welfare states. *Journal of European Social Policy, 16*(1), 23–42.
van Oorschot, W. (2008). Solidarity towards immigrants in European welfare states. *International Journal of Social Welfare, 17*(1), 3–14.
Ostry, J., & Berg, A. (2014). Treating inequality with redistribution: Is the cure worse than the disease? Retrieved March 21, 2017, from https://blog-imfdirect.imf.org/2014/02/26/treating-inequality-with-redistribution-is-the-cure-worse-than-the-disease/.
Papadakis, E., & Bean, C. (1993). Popular support for the welfare state: A comparison between institutional regimes. *Journal of Public Policy, 13*(3), 227–254.
van der Pas, D. (2014). Making hay while the sun shines: Do parties only respond to media attention when the framing is right? *Journal of Press/Politics, 19*(1), 42–65.
Pederson, J. (2014). Where should the money go? A six-country comparison of attitudes toward spending on public pensions and unemployment programs. *International Journal of Social Science Studies, 2*(1), 38–50.

Petmesidou, M. (2017). Welfare reform in Greece: A major crisis, crippling debt conditions, and stark challenges ahead. In P. Taylor-Gooby, B. Leruth, & H. Chung (Eds.), *After austerity: Welfare state transformation in Europe after the great recession* (pp. 155–179). Oxford: Oxford University Press.

Pierson, P. (Ed.). (2001). *The new politics of the welfare state*. Oxford: Oxford University Press.

Reeskens, T., & Van der Meer, T. (2014). *Conditions for social solidarity with immigrants. A survey experiment into deservingness criteria.* Paper presented at the 72e Annual Conference of the Midwest Political Science Association, Chicago.

Renn, O. (2008). *Risk governance*. London: Earthscan.

Roosma, F. (2016). *A multidimensional perspective on the social legitimacy of welfare states in Europe*. Tilburg: Tilburg University.

Roosma, F., Gelissen, J., & van Oorschot, W. (2013). The multidimensionality of welfare state attitudes: A European cross-national study. *Social Indicators Research, 113*(1), 235–255.

Roosma, F., van Oorschot, W., & Gelissen, J. (2016). A just distribution of burdens?: Attitudes toward the social distribution of taxes in 26 welfare states. *International Journal of Public Opinion Research, 28*(3), 376–400.

Slothuus, R. (2007). Framing deservingness to win support for welfare state retrenchment. *Scandinavian Political Studies, 30*(3), 323–344.

Snow, D., & Soule, S. (2010). *A primer on social movements*. New York, NY: W.W. Norton & Co.

Svallfors, S. (1997). Worlds of welfare and attitudes to redistribution: A comparison of eight western nations. *European Sociological Review, 13*(3), 283–304.

Svallfors, S. (1999). The middle class and welfare state retrenchment. In S. Svallfors & P. Taylor-Gooby (Eds.), *The end of the welfare state? Responses to state retrenchment*. London: Routledge.

Svallfors, S. (2012a). Welfare attitudes in Europe: Topline results from round 4. *European Social Survey*. Retrieved August 24, 2017, from http://www.europeansocialsurvey.org/docs/findings/ESS4_toplines_issue_2_welfare_attitudes_in_europe.pdf.

Svallfors, S. (2012b). *Contested welfare states: Welfare attitudes in Europe and beyond*. Stanford, CA: Stanford University Press.

Tajfel, H. (1981). *Human groups and social categories*. Cambridge: Cambridge University Press.

Taylor-Gooby, P. (1982). Two cheers for the welfare state: Public opinion and private welfare. *Journal of Public Policy, 2*(4), 319–346.

Taylor-Gooby, P. (2002). The silver age of the welfare state: Perspectives on resilience. *Journal of Social Policy, 31*(4), 597–622.
Taylor-Gooby, P. (2005). Is the future American? *Journal of Social Policy, 34*(5), 661–672.
Taylor-Gooby, P., & Martin, R. (2010). Fairness, equality and legitimacy: A qualitative comparative study of Germany and the UK. *Social Policy & Administration, 44*(1), 85–103.
Taylor-Gooby, P., Leruth, B., & Chung, H. (Eds.). (2017). *After austerity: Welfare state transformation in Europe after the great recession*. Oxford: Oxford University Press.
Taylor-Gooby, P., Leruth, B., & Chung, H. (2018). Political legitimacy and welfare state futures. *Social Policy and Administration*. Available at: https://kar.kent.ac.uk/id/eprint/65845, accessed on 3 April 2018.
Ullrich, C. G. (2002). Reciprocity, justice and statutory health insurance in Germany. *Journal of European Social Policy, 12*(2), 123–136.
Van der Waal, J., Achterberg, P., Houtman, D., De Koster, W., & Manevska, K. (2010). 'Some are more equal than others': Economic egalitarianism and welfare chauvinism in the Netherlands. *Journal of European Social Policy, 20*(4), 350–363.
Van Kersbergen, K., & Vis, B. (2014). *Comparative welfare state politics: Development, opportunities, and reform*. Cambridge: Cambridge University Press.
Warren, M. E., & Pearse, H. (Eds.). (2008). *Designing deliberative democracy: The British Columbia citizens' assembly*. Cambridge: Cambridge University Press.
WelfSOC. (2017). Welfare state futures: Our children's Europe. Retrieved July 10, 2017, from http://welfsoc.eu.
Wilson, T., & Hodges, S. (1992). Attitudes as temporary constructions. In L. L. Martin & A. Tesser (Eds.), *The construction of social judgments*. Hillsdale, MI: Erlbaum.
World Bank. (2014). *The World Bank and Civil Society Engagement* [online]. Retrieved January 31, 2018, from http://web.worldbank.org/WBSITE/EXTERNAL/TOPICS/CSO/0,,contentMDK:20092185~menuPK:220422~pagePK:220503~piPK:220476~theSitePK:228717,00.html.

2

Individualism and Neo-Liberalism

Peter Taylor-Gooby and Benjamin Leruth

Neo-liberal ideas exert increasing influence on welfare state policies in Europe. Neo-liberalism has a particular theoretical analysis of the state and stresses the importance of the individual in society. The policies that it helped develop take those ideas in particular directions, devaluing intervention and stressing individual responsibility as well as opportunity. This in turn highlights particular themes in public attitudes (deservingness, obligation and choice) and downplays others (solidarity and community).

This chapter falls into five sections: a review of individualism and neo-liberalism and their influence on European welfare states, an account of how these themes emerge in public attitudes, the findings from our Democratic Forums, a discussion of how people link these ideas together

---

P. Taylor-Gooby (✉)
School of Social Policy, Sociology and Social Research,
University of Kent, Canterbury, UK
e-mail: p.f.taylor-gooby@kent.ac.uk

B. Leruth
Institute for Governance and Policy Analysis, University of Canberra,
Canberra, ACT, Australia

© The Author(s) 2018
P. Taylor-Gooby, B. Leruth (eds.), *Attitudes, Aspirations and Welfare*,
https://doi.org/10.1007/978-3-319-75783-4_2

in framing the welfare state, and concluding comments on the implications for public policy and for inequality, solidarity and sustainability.

Individualism and Neo-Liberalism

The use of the term neo-liberalism developed in the 1930s to describe a political economy that placed the market at the centre, but differed from the laissez-faire liberal approach of the nineteenth century based on unregulated free markets (Springer et al. 2016, 2). 1930s neo-liberalism blamed this approach for the crises of the 1920s and 1930s and advocated a social market economy regulated by a strong state with limited direct interventions to transfer resources to needy groups and build infrastructure (op.cit. Chap. 1). Both share the neo-classical *homo oeconomicus* analysis of the individual as essentially independent and self-directed in a world consisting of other such individuals. This contrasted with the post-World War II Keynes-Beveridge approaches which promoted a greater degree of collectivism: government redistributed more than a third of GDP to ensure good standards in public services, promote greater social equality, pay benefits to those outside the labour market and provide infrastructure (Sen 1977). The welfare state as it has developed has been increasingly informed by a more social conception of human motivation and behaviour with greater roles for solidarity, trust and collective support.

As governments became more committed to interventionism, neo-liberal ideas moved back towards classical free market liberalism, drawing on the work of Hayek and Friedman and promoted by the Mont Pelerin society (Higgs 1997). Such modern neo-liberalism is informed by confidence in the self-regulating capacity of markets and suspicion of the state and of collectivism. It aspires to roll back government at national and international levels. In practice neo-liberalism has failed to attain these goals but has been increasingly influential. As realised in the policies promoted across the Anglo-Saxon world by Margaret Thatcher and Ronald Reagan in the 1980s, it has been associated with de-nationalisation, deregulation, free trade, enhanced labour market flexibility, reduced state spending and lower taxes. Comparable policies have been influential to different degrees in mainland Europe, where in many countries there is a stronger commitment to corporatist and social democratic systems and to co-ordinated rather than liberal market economies.

The analysis of the person associated with neo-liberal political economy centres on individual independence rather than societal membership. This leads to a greater emphasis on choice and responsibility for outcomes and to the reinforcement of the work ethic. So far as the welfare state goes, the outcomes have been spending constraint, a much greater role for the private sector, welfare-to-work benefit systems, the weakening of trade unions, greater tolerance of inequality and much more reliance on the use of internal markets within state-financed services (Piven 2015).

Recent Policy Developments

Much greater use of markets and competitive principles in the allocation of state services is evident across Europe. One outcome has been a general trend to greater inequalities, even at times of positive economic growth (Cantillon 2011). The constraints of the EU's Growth and Stability Pact in 1997 and more recently the stronger enforcement mechanisms contained in the so-called Six-Pack (European Commission 2011) and Two-Pack (European Commission 2013) impose stricter market discipline on Eurozone governments. The ECB's overriding commitment to contain inflation rather than promote employment signals a determination to prioritise the stability of the market over equality (Stiglitz 2016).

The move towards neo-liberalism has been associated with the shift towards stronger individual rights. The decline in collective workplace rights has been paralleled by anti-discrimination legislation and the development of rights and provisions that enable under-represented groups, most importantly women with children, to participate in paid work. In the case of disabled and unemployed people rights in work are accompanied by cutbacks in support outside the labour market.

The dominance of the market and individual-centred approach has also encouraged proponents of interventionism to advocate a 'social investment strategy' (see Chap. 8), intended to reposition state welfare as an investment in labour rather than a burden on the productive economy (Vandenbroucke et al. 2011; Morel et al. 2012). The primary areas where such investments can be expected to show a return (Nolan 2013) lie in enhancing the quality, quantity and allocation of labour through education and training, mobilisation, and greater mobility and meritocracy. This approach has influenced the national policies mentioned above. It explains why there is much greater investment in mobilising younger women (a better educated and more active group) through improved childcare than middle-aged women through better care for the very old. It is the middle-aged group who are burdened with informal elder care in many countries (Knijn and Komter 2004). It is also contained in the targets of the EU's *Europe 2020* programme which include increasing the employment rate to 75 per cent from the current (2013) 68 per cent, reducing the early leaving rate from education from about 12 to ten per cent, increasing the share of 30–34 year olds with degrees from 37 to 40 per cent and reducing poverty from 122 to 97 million (European Commission 2015, 3).

Neo-liberal and individualist ideas have received strong support from influential analyses of globalization and post-industrial shifts in work. These argue that the rapid expansion in international trade and consequent intensification of competition, the weakening of industrial bargaining power associated with the shift towards service sector economies in the West (Jessop 2002), the rapid expansion in the use of IT and robotics, which devalues an ever-wider range of skills and enormously enhances managerial capacity, and the concentration of power among a hyper-wealthy elite (Hacker and Pierson 2010) diminish the interventionist authority of governments and massively expand market opportunities.

Two more recent developments are relevant to how neo-liberal policies are pursued in practice: first, the response to the global economic crisis has been overwhelmingly neo-liberal. Recovery plans, intended to curb high levels of indebtedness, place much greater emphasis on spending cuts than on tax increases or higher borrowing (OECD 2011; Gough 2011). The UK, Germany and other countries are committed to reduce net borrowing to zero, and the Eurozone as a whole is on course for net borrowing of about half of one per cent of GDP by 2021 (IMF 2017).

Secondly, the recent political success of populist parties across many Western countries indicates a rejection of the outcomes of neo-liberalism by groups who see themselves as losers in a more globalized and competitive world (Kriesi et al. 2012). Analyses of the Front National in France, UKIP in the UK, AfD in Germany and other parties shows that the main body of supporters are working-class people with low or obsolescent skills who live in deindustrialised areas, see their jobs as threatened by newcomers and feel abandoned by an increasingly remote elite (Hobolt 2016; Hakhverdian et al. 2013).

Neo-liberal endorsement of a strong role for free markets, the self-responsible individual and a weaker role for government (other than promoting market freedom and individual self-direction) has exerted a considerable influence on public policy at all levels across Western countries. The repercussions for welfare states have been spending and taxation cutbacks, privatisation, greater inequality and limited redistributive capacity, curtailing of collective rights and weakened labour market regulation. There has also been an influence on anti-discrimination policies, better childcare, education and training policies and stronger concerns about opportunity and mobility, intended to support individuals in taking responsibility for their own life-chances.

We move on to consider how these shifts are reflected in public attitudes.

Public Attitudes

Neo-liberalism rejects an interventionist or redistributive role for the state. It also implies a general suspicion of government: state provision is seen as inefficient and managed according to bureaucratic rather than consumer interest. Governments stifle market enterprise. Taxes are onerous and unfair. Coupled with individualism it implies that attitudes will be anti-state and very much driven by self-interest. In practice it may also imply greater support for social investment, which enhances individual opportunities and promotes enterprise.

The pattern of attitudes discussed in Chap. 1 accords with some of these points but not others. The strength of support for welfare state provision as a whole and for the most expensive aspects of it (pensions and healthcare: Bonoli 2000; Ferrera 1993; Taylor-Gooby 1982, 2002; Roosma et al. 2013; Likki and Staerklé 2014) in particular tells against the general programme of substituting market for state. On the other hand, concerns about the operation and effectiveness of welfare state institutions (Andersen 1999; Edlund 1999; Svallfors 1997) fit with a general neo-liberal suspicion of the state. The parallel concerns that centre on provision for people of working age (Larsen 2008) imply endorsement of the principle of individual responsibility, in this area at least. This suggests a nuanced individualism in public attitudes, growing rather stronger over time and immediately focused on an ethic of responsibility in the world of paid work.

When we come to examine individual rights and social investment there is evidence that many people are in favour of state services that help mobilise groups like women with childcare responsibilities into paid work; support is especially strong where provision is weakest (Meuleman and Chung 2012; see also Chap. 8). The limited evidence available indicates that training and education programmes are also strongly endorsed (Busemeyer et al. 2017).

Immigration and related issues are not covered in most analyses of individualism and neo-liberalism: market principles apply equally across borders. Ideal typical neo-liberal approaches imply freedom of access to work and say nothing about restrictions by nationality or ethnicity. In practical politics many on the political right support restriction of immigration despite mistrust of government interventions (Mewes and Mau 2012; Van der Waal et al. 2010).

This brief review shows that the relationship between public opinion and neo-liberal individualism at the general level is complex. The high level of overall support for the welfare state and for redistribution conflicts with the foregrounding of the independent individual actor. Similarly there is strong approval of provision for groups who are of less economic value (pensioners, the sick and disabled), and this appears to rest on both self-interest and norms of need, contribution and deservingness. The concerns about workshy unemployed people fit more closely with the ideal of individual responsibility. However, the level of enthusiasm for childcare and the indications of support for training programmes suggest public endorsement of at least some aspects of the social investment strategy. This approach arguably harnesses individualism to promote state welfare.

Overall we may conclude that neo-liberalism has a substantial influence on recent development in European welfare states. The individualism associated with it, however, appears to be only one among several forces shaping current politics. Liberal individualism is most evident in relation to unemployed people. Support for many aspects of the welfare state and for a role for government in redistribution and the promotion of equality remains highly significant; equally there is considerable enthusiasm for childcare and social investment and for chauvinist restrictions on welfare for immigrants. There is good evidence that national differences in welfare state regime have a strong bearing on attitudes, as do people's recognised self-interest, socio-demographic position and political values.

The Democratic Forums

Our democratic forums took place in five countries with very different welfare state regimes (UK: liberal; Norway and Denmark: social democratic; Germany: corporatist; Slovenia: post-socialist: see Chap. 1). The trajectory of recent policy is analysed in our companion book (*After Austerity*, Taylor-Gooby et al. 2017). The UK has led Europe for a number of years in its commitment to market-centred ideology (forcefully promoted by Thatcher in the 1980s, moderated to a Third Way market-socialist approach in the early 2000s and then reasserted in the austerity programme after 2010), although it retains mass services in healthcare, pensions and education. Investment in education and training is relatively low and childcare fees are among the highest in Europe. Norway, followed by Denmark, has remained most vigorously committed to a substantial welfare state, although policies that foreground individual choice between suppliers financed by the state in health and social care have gained ground in both countries. In Denmark there has been a stricter move towards the imposition of a work ethic on unemployed people in the context of flexicurity policies and attempts to introduce tax cuts. These countries and particularly Norway have the strongest support both for individuals to enter and progress in the labour market and for the family.

Germany has probably gone furthest in reforms designed to maintain current standards in the main services but contain future spending on pensions and healthcare. A new regime imposes lower benefits and much greater compulsion on unemployed people to enter into paid work, and measures to expand the availability of low-paid jobs and free up the labour market have been introduced. The country has a strong international reputation for the quality of its apprenticeship and training programmes. It is only recently that Germany has made substantial investment in childcare and support for gender equality, but here it has moved fast. Slovenia did not pursue a straightforward market path after the break-up of former Yugoslavia but retained major state responsibilities. Much of the debate now is about the poor quality of state health and social care services and about the regulation of work. Training, education and childcare support, all the policies that make up social investment, are not well developed.

Our brief review of current directions in welfare state institutions indicates: that the UK is pursuing the most liberal/individualist approach in terms of curbing the state and requiring individuals to take greater responsibility; that liberal initiatives in some areas in Germany are paralleled by strong commitments to state services and in Slovenia by support for the expansion of the state; and that Denmark and Norway share a major commitment to state-led collectivism. However, the countries fall into a different order if social investment individualism, which is concerned to enhance opportunities, is highlighted: Norway and Denmark, followed by Germany, Slovenia and the UK, and this is the order in which we present them.

Table 2.1 provides the main questions and concepts used to trace the issues of individualism and neo-liberalism in our analysis. Since the discussion differs substantially between the countries, we consider the pattern of attitudes in each country and then bring the analysis together.

Norway

The Norwegian participants identified three issues similar to those in the UK: tax evasion, lack of accountability and sustainability.

Tax evasion:

> I think about globalization, that we might have great wage inequalities in the world too, and then the politicians have to take an active part interna-

Table 2.1 Core issues in neo-liberalism and the concepts used to identify them in the forums

Issues	Concepts
Roll back the state	Concern about inefficiency (waste; bureaucracy) and incapacity (lack of 'transparency' and 'accountability'; unfairness in state services); belief that the interventionist state is incapable of meeting future challenges. Contrasts with collectivism (concern for vulnerable people and support for state provision to meet their needs and also promote solidarity; support for redistribution and greater equality)
Promote the market	Privatisation; use of pricing, acceptance of inequality. Opposition to taxation. Support for private property rights
Individual responsibility	Belief that people should 'stand on their own two feet'; concerns about moral damage of welfare dependency, about benefit cheats and about work incentives
Active individualism	Support for better training, life-long learning, education, education grants and maintenance allowances, more/cheaper/better quality childcare (also elder care and for other dependents)
Relation of neo-liberalism to individualism	A successful market requires limitation of state power and greater individual responsibility; individuals should be independent and self-sufficient as far as possible vs. successful use of individual abilities requires support from the state and is justified both for economic success and for individual benefit

tionally to prevent an exodus of tax payers. ...Make an international framework to prevent people from hiding from tax. If Norwegians spend money, it should be taxed in Norway. (NO-24)

Accountability and transparency (but in the context of general support for the state and valuing of its achievements):

[i]t is important that we tax-payers have a closer understanding of where the money goes.... Sometimes it feels like the money disappears more into bureaucracy than to the things we want to pay tax for. (NO-29)

The unsustainability of current spending levels, acknowledged by a majority of participants:

I don't believe we can sustain the social security we have today, the way we do today. But I don't have the answer.... (NO-14)

This did not imply an abandonment of the welfare state. Several participants agreed that the current economic system will generate greater inequality so that more responsibility for meeting their own needs will fall on people's shoulders:

> I, unfortunately, am pragmatic enough to believe in capitalism, and in that respect every company will be profit maximizing. So within today's regulations one has to adapt.... (NO-21)
>
> There lies a big responsibility on the individual, because you cannot trust the government to the same degree. I believe the insecurity will be greater ahead than what it has been. (NO-22)

However, many Norwegian participants, unlike those in the UK, did not perceive neo-liberalism and individualism as inevitable, despite their awareness of the pressures on the welfare state and towards inequality. Instead, one group proposed more redistributive tax, though others disagreed as in the following discussion:

> many of them earn more than they should, compared to what they do to contribute. I'm not only thinking about salary, but share premium and the company's income. In that respect I feel one should tax them harder and distribute it to people who don't earn so much, but still make an effort. (NO-08)
>
> Macro-economically it will pay to make an extra effort and become a little richer for the whole of society to create more jobs.... Rather focus on everyone having an equal start, that you are paid equally later in relation to what effort you have put down in working life. (NO-10).
>
> I agree that it has to do with effort, but it isn't always about effort though, but I see what you mean. (NO-08)

An alternative was to promote private investment into projects of public benefit:

Motivation to pay tax has to be sustained, for example by making it easier to start and run a business yourself. We can have tax incentives for privately contributing to public jobs, like support for science, hospitals ... you get tax credit for donating a million for a new ward at the hospital. (NO-29)

The cost of healthcare in Norway, as in the UK, is seen to put an increasing strain on public spending. Several participants suggested that the private sector should play an expanding role in healthcare over the next 25 years:

In the future, I believe it will be more private healthcare than today. Also because the public health service is often behind. New treatments are most often introduced by the private market.... Takes time for public authorization and such to go through. So, you also have an upside to it that someone is willing to pay for it. (NO-11)
...
Everything we have discussed now are good ideas, but it costs. Struggles with not enough money, and then the private has to come into the picture, and we might have to cut treatments ... which are taken for granted today, but not lifesaving. I believe we will experience that [free] healthcare isn't so all-embracing in 30 years' time .... (NO-9)

As in the other countries, there was a strong emphasis on the contribution of welfare state professionals, teachers, doctors and nurses. Many participants believed these groups are underpaid:

I would be happy to lower my income to 500,000 to make sure [nurses] also had 500,000 ... I believe the government should regulate these things. (NO-08)

Interestingly enough and unlike Germany and (to a lesser extent) Slovenia, the issue of a Universal Basic Income (UBI) was not mentioned in the two days of discussion, even though plans to experiment with such a policy were under way in neighbouring Finland at the time. UBI is a benefit which all receive, whether in work or not, in order to create greater autonomy in work and training choices. There was also very little discussion of whether welfare benefits undermined work incentives and much more concern about wage inequalities:

My solution is the tax model to take away the high tops. (NO-31)

The low-paid should […] have a wage increase if possible. (NO-5)

There was also confidence in the country's investment in a positive activation and training approach to unemployment and job opportunities, but this was so deeply entrenched that people felt it unnecessary to lay weight on it.

To summarise, in Norway, neo-liberal and individualist ideas and concerns emerge in debate, but the majority supports the interventionist welfare state, wishes to see it continue and is prepared to increase taxes or make reforms to enable it to do so. Participants recognise many of the issues that dominate discussion elsewhere, but they value solidarity and believe their welfare state will be resilient.

Denmark

Participants in the Danish forums displayed strong commitment to the collectivist principles of state welfare in the opening plenary, with very little dissent:

Well, we talked about the welfare state on a theoretical level—it's so beautiful, it almost brings tears to your eyes. It is there for you if you fail, or if something happens in your life, and naturally we pay for that through tax. (DK-82)

We talked a lot about the basics of the origin of the welfare state and the way in which it was created. Our obligation to take care of the weakest. (DK-55)

A community where everyone contributes. (DK-65)

For many the welfare state was about shared and Nordic social values rather than a set of institutions. Trust was a central feature.

It's an institution that is unique to the Nordic countries.… It's all about trust. It's about certain values that we have in the Nordic countries.… (DK-59)

...trust ... is the key word for the welfare state. In Scandinavia we have this basic trust in each other. (DK-80)

However, individual responsibility was also seen as essential to solidarity, as can be seen in the following exchange, which took place shortly after a strong positive discussion of solidarity and the welfare state in the opening plenary:

I believe that one of the challenges is to preserve own responsibility for ourselves and others. (DK-69)

...another major challenge must surely must be financing, because if people are not willing to pay their taxes and if we do not maintain the high tax burden ... we will not be able to finance these welfare services.... (DK-85)

Those who feel weak should be lifted up, but they should not be given. (DK-84)

There are, however, real concerns about sustainability:

...things are going downhill today.... Our children cannot be looked after, our parents cannot be cared for properly, they wet themselves and are left like that all night ... And it gets worse and worse. (DK-72) [general assent followed]

This theme recurred during the two days of discussion leading to an emphasis on shifting investment from old to young in the final plenary.

We agreed on a proposal.... to continue to invest in education (DK-65, final plenary); *Moderator*: "Looking at it from a generational perspective ... we don't want the elderly to be given money at the expense of education."

The proposal was accepted unanimously.

There was minority support for the idea of cutbacks in state welfare to promote individual responsibility, but this was bound up again with the theme of trimming provision for older people to finance services for the young. For example:

You won't get anything from the state is a good starting point, because then you save up and you're not dependent…. I'm more interested in finding out how we're going to decide whether to put our efforts into older or younger citizens. (DK-62)

There was also some concern about welfare benefits eroding the work ethic and community solidarity, but this is a minority view and the principle of solidarity is basic to the debate, as this exchange in a group discussion on the safety net indicates:

I know several people, at least three, who cheat … and who don't bother to work. (DK-84)

I have no doubt that there are some who … would like to cheat the system. …I know from my work that when you scratch the surface of the people who seemingly can't be bothered there are so many other underlying reasons. (DK-75)

…a society will also be measured by how it treats those who struggle the most … The young people I work with every day, they become a strain for life. (DK-55)

They need to be supported! (DK-84)

Despite this sympathy for those facing social challenges, there was concern about welfare cheats:

those who really need help should get it while those who cheat or claim social benefits, early retirement or what have you, fraudulently, should not. (DK-87)

These issues were expressed within an overall valuing of a solidaristic welfare state, for example:

Looking forward to 2040, I can certainly imagine that the rules relating to how we contribute will change. … The starting point for the welfare society should be that all those who can do, should do. (DK-50)

The first conclusion stated in the final plenary was:

We started out talking about the whole concept of economic inequality in relation to the welfare state. We had some different thoughts on that but we agreed that it's all about revenue and transfers and an attempt to redistribute. ... We agreed on ... the need to safeguard the value of low incomes. ... That was our first priority. (DK-76)

This conclusion received unanimous approval. There was also strong support in the discussions of income inequality for fair pay and taxing higher incomes:

We've talked about financial income and we could tax that more. (DK-57)
...
The biggest problem is wage increases, right? If wages increase by 2 per cent for both high and the low-earners then that makes a big difference and this is why inequality increases. (DK-54)

However many participants were not willing to pay higher taxes to support state welfare:

We should not finance welfare benefits through a significant tax increase. There should be an incentive to work and pay tax in this country. (DK-81, final plenary)

This division over tax increases went along with opposition to further benefit cuts to support the maintenance of the status quo:

We also discussed the issue of undeclared work and the black economy ... people who'd come here because they'd been told that Denmark was this paradise where you could live it up without having to work. ... But ... the tightening measures that have been implemented over the last few years actually correct the problems.... We therefore recommend keeping benefits on the same level.... (DK-69 final plenary)

The debate in Denmark is broadly supportive of a solidaristic welfare state as the primary value (with some concerns about future sustainability, the level of taxes and welfare cheats). Within this framework, individualism becomes the commitment to act responsibly so as to support others in the community. It is recognised that some are unable to contribute as much as others and that the reasons why some do not succeed in maintaining themselves may not always be obvious. Individual responsibility is reinterpreted as part of a general community solidarity, not as the free-standing self-sufficiency of neo-liberalism.

Germany

In the German democratic forums participants also expressed favourable opinions towards neo-liberal and individualist policies, but to a much lesser extent than in the UK. Although there were some misgivings about the capacity and effectiveness of government, these did not lead to doubts about sustainability or support for greater individual responsibility but rather to suggestions for improving government services and a co-ordinated corporatist approach. Some participants believed that some claimers abused the welfare system:

> [t]here are plenty of people in our system who just take advantage … and this must be addressed. I know people who run small businesses, and they say that they have trouble getting trainees … because they don't want to get up and be at work at 7 a.m. I see many young couples who have children, because they will then get child benefits which they use to finance themselves. (DE-31)

Participants also expressed concerns regarding the role of the state in the labour market. Some of them argued that too much interventionism or labour regulations might hinder employment:

> It's always good if we can create good working conditions, optimal family-oriented jobs, gender equality and all of this, but you have to watch out, because if you bring too much of the state into business, then the employer is less likely to hire…. (DE-34)

This work ethic also included a commitment to valuing the individual for their contribution. As the spokeswoman for one of the discussion groups put it in the final plenary:

Our goal with regard to work and occupation was that work should always be worth it and achievement must also be worth it. The reason that is so important is that there is often an uncertainty that I can't afford to live my life or that I have to do several different jobs at the same time, and that certain occupations are not so recognized or appreciated. (DE-M2)

Individual responsibility was also stressed on several occasions, mostly in the context of healthcare and old-age pensions. While participants believe that the state plays an important role in providing basic protection (such as basic health insurance and the basic state pension), they stated that individuals should take more responsibility for improving their own lives:

We live in a performance-based society, and ... I feel that everyone has to take responsibility and see to it that they have a sufficient income in later life ... we can't cover all the costs later on for everyone, so you should build up funds for yourself. The state gives tax credits and advantages in order to encourage people to ... put aside some savings. It's very important for me ... because each person has to take care of this for him/herself and can't just expect the state or government to do it. (DE-22)

The positive argument for government interventions that support an active individualism encountered in the UK forums also appeared. Most people were confident in the quality of the existing apprenticeship system and focused more on educational opportunities. The concern in Germany was not so much to allow individuals to contribute to economic advance as to promote social equality:

better education opportunities ... a good education ... can only be afforded by the rich. (DE-5)

I'd say it begins with education, so that's most important. Qualification through education. (DE-26)

A fundamental basic requirement is having a good education, as that leads to ... well-paid work, which also leads to pension security in retirement. (DE-6)

There was lengthy and sympathetic discussion of the UBI. There was disagreement between those that favoured this approach (which would shift the balance more towards the state) and those who were concerned about giving a benefit which might erode individual responsibility.

> It should be something like an unconditional basic income. I don't think we can get around that, it's just a question of whether we can afford to do that alone here in Germany.... (DE-34)
> ...
> If my ex-husband, who was a manual worker, and I back then, if we'd been provided a basic income by the state in the same amount, then we'd only have had to decide which one of us works a bit extra, and I would not have had to go to work while still breastfeeding. ...if I have a living income basis that covered my basic needs, then I'm much more flexible in my additional options of how to work or run my life. (DE-05)
> ...
> Well, I have a completely different attitude toward this ... I know people in my circle of acquaintances, ... who receive social assistance and just waste it through smoking, alcohol and so forth. They buy the newest mobile phones, and then by the middle of the month, they have no money left and go to get additional state funds, because they can't just let them starve. I'm very much against the concept of unconditional.... (DE-32)

At the end of the event, participants voted on whether they would wanted UBI: 26 participants voted in favour, and 9 against, suggesting real but not overwhelming support for an approach that cuts against the conservative status-related tradition of German social insurance welfare and links individualist ideas with state welfare. Individualist and neo-liberal trends emerge elsewhere in German attitudes. These are strongest in relation to the work ethic and individual responsibility of unemployed people and also in support for private pensions, but the underlying commitment to the established welfare state is more powerful. The dominant framing of ideas links state provision to positive outcomes and is willing to pay the necessary tax and contributions, but includes some concern that benefits for unemployed people promote over-reliance on the system. The work-centredness of values entrenches support for apprenticeships and education as fundamental.

Slovenia

There is considerable dissatisfaction with public provision in Slovenia, focusing on the adequacy of services and benefits and on regulation and corruption. This does not lead in a market liberal direction and does not promote individualism but rather reinforces demands for the extension of state services and powers. The most important areas are the low level of healthcare spending, leading to long waiting lists; the low minimum wages and poor enforcement of labour market rights, leading to income and gender inequalities; the cost of care homes for older people; and the low level of pensions. The most important reason for the demand for a more extensive welfare state is to protect the weakest and most vulnerable and to create a fairer, more cohesive society.

> If there isn't any money for public healthcare ... You will have to pay for every service and think twice before signing your child up for a procedure. (SI-77)
>
> Let's see, the elderly home costs 1500 EUR for people who are chained to the bed. ... So the person should receive 1500 EUR pension, end of story. (SI-62)
>
> Perhaps it'd be best if they [pensions] were the same for everyone, that they'd enable you to lead a normal life. An old person needs to live also. (SI-81)

When asked in the final plenary what the most important issue was, the spokesperson for one group responded:

> We're talking about raising the minimum wage, right. We combine raising the minimum wage with lowering the pay ratios to 1:10.... (SI-61—also 62 and 88)
>
> And if the minimum wage is high enough, you'll go to work more, but it should provide at least something, because for the majority, if they don't have a place to live, you can't survive on minimum wage. (SI-88)
>
> That the wages will be fairer, that there won't be such differences between the rich and those that don't have anything. (SI-57)

Capitalism is stealing money from the weak. It's just the few on top who live well, the great majority of people—the middle class—is out of the game, it fell dramatically, disappeared.... (SI-81)

The emphasis in the discussion on inequality is striking, given that Slovenia has a relatively low level of inequality for an EU country, roughly equivalent to Denmark (see Chap. 4). However incomes are generally low and poverty widespread. Low pay and poor working conditions are also seen as responsible for the emigration of skilled people:

…the social aspect … matters, which means a decent pay check, a decent life standard and I think this would prevent so many people from moving abroad. (SI-57)

The incapacity of government is illustrated in the inefficient employment service and the ineffective gender equality laws:

I think that we've said a lot about the employment service. Here it should be reorganized.... (SI-85)

We probably have this apparent equality. Because if you look at it, when a woman is choosing a job … they give her a bunch of papers to sign; that she won't decide to have a child in 5 years, in 10 years, that she won't do this, that she won't do that … a bunch of demands. (SI-77)

There is support for UBI and for redistributive tax:

If we said all this income, all these reliefs would be suspended and everyone would be getting this basic universal income … it would all be more transparent … There'd be no more hiding, it wouldn't pay for that private business owner to hide, so that they'd have free kindergarten, and so on. (SI-69)
…
Because we all work together, right. In one state all of us are one body. And the body needs all the structures. All the structures need to survive, so that our little finger works normally, even the brain. And we all need that as a basis. And that's this basic universal income. … People also feel that taxation for ordinary people is too high and that the tax system is unfair. (SI-73, with agreement from SI-62, final plenary)

Taxes need to be relaxed because the employers are simply not hiring, the burdens are too big. (SI-85)

The cost and difficulty of getting access to healthcare, nursing homes and childcare leads to corruption, especially in health. Staff can practise privately as well as publicly, and have an obvious incentive to encourage state patients into the private sector. This damages social solidarity.

If you're private, you have a private practice, you shouldn't be working in public healthcare at the same time, which is the case now. (SI-82)

Similar issues emerge in education.

I'm again concerned about this relationship between the public and the private. Similar as in healthcare. As if the population were divided into two: poor, rich. So the rich people will have private healthcare, private schools, high quality. And the poor ones will be in public schools, public healthcare. (SI-not identified)

Social security cheating leads to unfairness and resentment:

...one files an application at the social work centre, for child allowance, whatever: all the applicants withdraw money from the accounts and hide their property. Which leads to the harder you work, the more the state will take from you. (SI-65)

There is also wider concern about corruption across society resulting from the weakness of government in relation to big business and the bribery of politicians:

A new scandal, not every day, sometimes multiple scandals per day, it's all a bit too much if you are hoping to educate good citizens. (SI-68)

The discontent with the ineffectiveness of government in regulating taxes and cheating resembles in some ways that in the UK, but is compounded by the poor quality of services and by corruption. The level of dissatisfaction is higher than elsewhere among our five countries, but does not generate a demand to move away from the state towards greater market and individual responsibility. Instead most people want more state spending on healthcare and older persons' homes and education, more regulation of the labour market to achieve more equality between better-off and worse-off and between women and men, higher taxes for the rich, a higher minimum wage and more support in finding jobs and for the general valuing of solidarity. There is strong support for UBI to allow people more opportunities to make choices, but other aspects of a social investment individualism were not discussed.

This leads to a framing of the state that points to inadequacy and low levels of provision that in turn generate corruption and use of private provision as people pursue all opportunities to meet their own needs. But this framing is coupled with a strong desire to improve state services and to ensure that outcomes become more equal. This is if anything a recognition of the pressures which elsewhere lead to neo-liberal responses, but a rejection of that route and enthusiasm for an expanded welfare state.

UK

Participants generally defended an individualist vision of society. The welfare state is widely seen as wasteful, unsustainable and grossly inefficient:

> I think there is a lot of waste in publicly funded things, because nobody feels that it's real money … accountability … goes out of the window. (UK-87)

Finance is the major issue in discussion of sustainability, with real concern that the state will be unable to fund key benefits and services, especially the NHS, as the population ages (see Chaps. 5 and 7). The weak capacity of government is shown in government's failure to control tax avoidance:

> These big companies that all aren't paying the taxes in this country and they're earning off of us like, and they're not paying the right taxes. They should be liable to pay taxes. (UK-48)

While the majority of participants did not believe that they should pay higher taxes to finance future welfare there was conflict between such commitments to property rights and support for an element of redistribution:

> I feel quite strongly, if you are bettering yourself, why should you pay twice as much tax as other people...? It's your money, you're earning it. (UK-44)
>
> ...
>
> I think I'm in quite a fortunate position in that I probably pay more tax than I get out of it ... that I know there are people who are worse off than me but I'm more than happy that my tax goes to make sure that they can eat. ... I think I pay enough tax and I think if that was to increase I think I'd feel a little bit miffed in that there are people that do take advantage of the system.... (UK-69)

Some participants also suggested offering specific tax breaks to individuals depending on their educational background or family situation:

> ...a system whereby when you pay taxes ... if you benefit from education ... and you've got a degree, then pay tax towards that. ... everybody pays tax don't they? Some people will never have kids but a lot of the tax that they pay is there to supplement people who do have children. ... voiding certain taxes for some people if they don't have children. (UK-67)

The failure of the benefit system to enforce a work ethic is seen as a key example of the general incapacity of government reflected in its ineffectiveness in promoting the individualist ethic of personal responsibility.

> It is too easy to remain unemployed. ... but there's plenty of jobs for people that could go out and work if they wanted to really, really hard. (UK-46)

Summing up the debate in the final session one respondent commented:

> We said the current system effectively encourages people to stay out of employment ... there should be equal opportunity, equal access to education, so perhaps more money invested in trained skills and apprenticeships, perhaps. (UK-67)

Much relevant discussion focused on the two most costly and popular areas of welfare state provision: the NHS and the basic state pension (see Chaps. 5 and 7). A majority argued that most individuals should be responsible for their own healthcare and pensions and should buy services privately, with means-tested public services:

> I think that's what people need to be encouraged to do, to plan for their own retirement, rather than relying on the state.… (UK-66)
>
> …
>
> The only way you are going to increase the amount of money we have got is to increase taxes. But as part of that, what if, say, the NHS was optional. So I can choose not to get free healthcare, but. I wouldn't pay as much tax. (UK-86)

The participants also endorsed the more positive aspects of individualism: the provision of services and support in areas like education, training and childcare (social investment) that helped people realise their potential as individuals:

> We need to think of some more long-term solutions.… Education … to try and combat unemployment. …retrain the youth … with apprenticeships to keep employment on a rolling scheme.… Cracking down on tax avoidance that we see in a lot of large companies.… (UK-64)

This would address the problem that current benefit policies are seen to promote dependency:

> …you can't have five or six kids or ten kids, unless you've got a good job and you work together with your partner but you see people who are on benefits with five, six, seven, eight kids. (UK-68)

And this led to an endorsement of workfare, though here the problem of government ineffectiveness in regulating business to provide jobs for British workers re-emerged. These comments fit together in a particular attitudinal framing of the liberal-leaning welfare state that supports many aspects of individualism but does so with little enthusiasm. The overall view is that the UK welfare state has many shortcomings, but the major services (the NHS in particular and state pensions) are highly valued. However it is simply impossible to sustain them into the future at anything like the current level without more effective government and higher taxes, which the participants will not pay. They see the state as weak in its failure to control tax evasion by big business and also in its oversight of both immigration and the benefits system, damaging work incentives. The failure to implement promised immigration reductions (they believe immigrants are a burden on the country and on themselves [see Chap. 3]) is yet further proof of the failure of government. This adds up to mistrust of government, which promotes an individualism that might be termed 'reluctant' (to parallel Keynes' 'reluctant collectivism').

At the same time there is a strong positive commitment to those aspects of individualism that involve state policies to promote opportunities in work and help people take responsibility for their own life-chances: education, training and childcare. The UK does not currently pursue effective policies in these areas. The upshot is that the country offers an example of what might be termed reluctant individualism. Policy follows the normal regime categorisation and the forum participants largely endorse liberal values, but do so for lack of an obvious alternative rather than through a vital commitment. They also aspire to a more interventionist government that might make a more positive social investment individualism work for younger citizens in the future.

Discussion

Looking across the five countries we can identify some common themes and some differences. Everywhere people value the main welfare state services (healthcare and pensions), everywhere they want greater equality and everywhere there is concern about the rising cost of the welfare state and about the capacity and accountability of government. The key differences are the enthusiasm or foreboding people feel regarding these issues and the ways in which they link them together. These emerge in the extent to which government policies undermine social values, the sustainability of the welfare state and enthusiasm for a move towards social investment policies (see Chap. 8).

While most people recognise limits to the size and scope of the state and the importance of ensuring that their national economy remains attractive to entrepreneurs, it is only really in the UK that people believe that current provision seriously threatens the work ethic. This leads to a division between two framings, one which sets individualism and the market against the interventionist state and one which believes that the welfare state is essential in market society. The first is dominant in the UK, the second in Germany and to a considerable extent in Slovenia and, emphatically, in Norway and Denmark (Table 2.2).

The conflict between these two approaches is reinforced by a division in attitudes to the capacity of government. While there is much complaint about the lack of transparency and accountability of both government and big business, and many demands for stricter regulation, most people in Denmark, Norway and Germany have confidence in the ability of the state to overcome these obstacles and expect the welfare state to continue indefinitely in a recognisable form. In Slovenia there is serious concern about corruption and about the current regulatory weakness of government, but there is still a strong desire for a reformed and fairer state. The UK again stands out in the number of forum participants who believe that state welfare will simply prove unsustainable.

The third framing concerns the more positive aspects of individualism. Here again there is considerable agreement. In all five countries most people support the idea that state intervention should be directed to help individuals to make the most of themselves. This conception is central to the Norwegian and Danish approach to the labour market and to education and to the German apprenticeship system. There is a strong demand in Slovenia and in the UK to develop training and childcare that allow people to grasp opportunities. The case for such approaches can be argued in terms of benefit to the economy or opportunities for parents or the child (see Chap. 8). While both aspects are seen as relevant, justification leans towards individual and social benefit in Norway and Denmark, is balanced in Slovenia, but more towards economic interest in Germany and much more in the UK.

Table 2.2 Individualism and neo-liberalism in attitudes to the welfare state

	Norway	Denmark	Germany	Slovenia	UK
Background					
Regime	Social democratic	Social democratic/ flexicurity	Conservative corporatist	Post-soviet welfare state	Liberal-leaning
Market centredness	Low	Low	Moderate	Moderate	High
Individual	Responsible participant in solidaristic community	Responsible participant in solidaristic community	Contributor/ consumer	Citizen expecting adequate provision	Self-sufficient actor
Overall theme					
State and market	Society faces challenges but state welfare is a core value and the state will prove resilient, with some shift from old to young	Society faces challenges but state welfare is a core value and the state will prove resilient with a greater role for the market	Market should expand, state services continue	Major problems (quality, benefit level, pensions and wages, inequality, corruption) but state must reform and improve provision	Workshy poor and state inefficiency real problems which govt. lacks capacity to overcome; decline of state, growth of private sector
Individual	Solidarity and state welfare will continue: some modifications needed	Solidarity will continue, but concerns about finance	Individual responsibility vital, but contribution must be valued	Current problems with state welfare	Self-sufficiency necessary; but state should provide support

(continued)

Table 2.2 (continued)

	Norway	Denmark	Germany	Slovenia	UK
Values	Primary values of solidarity and collectivism	Primary value of solidarity, perhaps with more enterprise	Individual contribution; fairness; equal provision	Equality and fairness	Work ethic and individual responsibility
Way forward Reforms required	Shift spending from old (pensions, healthcare) to young; increase taxes; tax MNCs better	Shift spending to young; Tax MNCs; some privatisation	Some privatisation of pensions and health; relax some labour market regulation	Eradicate corruption; improve services, employment protection; increase tax on better-off and MNCs	Privatisation of pensions and healthcare; extend means-testing; tax MNCs; regulate precarious jobs; more training and cheaper childcare
Rationale	Improve opportunities; older people well provided for; MNCs dodge tax	Enhance opportunities; older people well provided for; MNCs dodge tax; some waste	To contain costs; to improve work contributions and growth	All essential to ensure fairer, reasonable quality and adequately funded welfare state	Essential to meet challenge of sustainability; bottom-end jobs are increasingly ill-regulated

Conclusions

The core topics of this chapter, neo-liberalism and individualism, are attracting attention in discussion of the future of welfare as corresponding themes exert influence on European policymaking, especially after the Great Recession. They emerge with varying emphases in different countries and are associated with different policy directions and framings. The analysis of democratic forums in this chapter shows two things: neo-liberal individualism may play a powerful role in welfare state policies in Europe, but does not dominate attitudes and, more importantly, that individualism is understood in different ways and is linked differently to the nurturing role of government services and to the capacity of the market to guarantee self-sufficiency in different countries. Confidence in the capacity of government to manage difficult times is crucial.

Norway and Denmark stand out in their value-commitment to solidarity, with clear implications for the importance of individual recognition of an obligation to contribute to the community. Germany emerges as corporatist, strongly work centred and status oriented. Government must equip individuals to take their place and the labour market system must respect the value of their work. The UK is clearly the most liberal leaning with a strong current of neo-liberal individualism in attitudes to welfare, but also wants the government to provide the services (including adequate childcare and good quality training) that allow people to succeed in employment. Slovenian participants point to a wide range of problems with the current welfare state: low minimum wages, benefits and pensions, poor quality services, gross inefficiency and corruption at all levels. They recognise that state welfare faces the challenges of rising inequality and increasing demand. However, they are committed to welfare state reform and expansion, and (unlike the majority in the UK) they believe that this is possible.

While people judge the current achievements of their various welfare states differently and place different emphases on future challenges, they look to a state-centred rather than a neo-liberal future. The exception is the UK, where retreat from the state is bound up with mistrust in government. In most countries people value welfare state rights and want their governments to play the leading role in supporting individual development.

References

Andersen, J. G. (1999). Changing labour markets, new social divisions and welfare state support: Denmark in the 1990s. In S. Svallfors & P. Taylor-Gooby (Eds.), *The end of the welfare state? Responses to state retrenchment* (pp. 13–33). London: Routledge.

Arts, W., & Gelissen, J. (2001). Welfare states, solidarity and justice principles: Does the type really matter? *Acta Sociologica, 44*(4), 283–299.

Blekesaune, M., & Quadagno, J. (2003). Public attitudes toward welfare state policies. *European Sociological Review, 19*(5), 415–427.

Bolzendahl, C., & Olafsdottir, S. (2008). Gender group interest or gender ideology? *Sociological Perspectives, 51*(2), 281–304.

Bonoli, G. (2000). Public attitudes to social protection and political economy traditions in Western Europe. *European Societies, 2*(4), 431–452.

Burkhardt, C., Martin, R., Mau, S., & Taylor-Gooby, P. (2011). Differing notions of social welfare? In J. Clasen (Ed.), *Converging worlds of welfare?* (pp. 15–32). Oxford University Press.

Busemeyer, M., Garritzmann, J., Neimanns, E., & Nezi, R. (2017). Investing in education in Europe: Evidence from a new survey of public opinion. *Journal of European Social Policy, 27*(5). https://doi.org/10.1177/0958928717700562.

Cantillon, B. (2011). The paradox of the social investment state. *Journal of European Social Policy, 21*(5), 432–449.

Carriero, R. (2016). More inequality, fewer class differences. *Comparative Sociology, 15*(1), 112–139.

European Commission 2011 Linked to European Commission. (2011). *EU Economic governance "Six-Pack" enters into force*, Memo 11/898. Retrieved from http://europa.eu/rapid/press-release_MEMO-11-898_en.htm.

EC. (2013). *Towards social investment for growth and cohesion-including implementing the European Social Fund 2014–2020*. COM (2013) 83 final. Brussels: European Commission.

EC. (2015). *Results of the public consultation on the Europe 2020 strategy for smart, sustainable and inclusive growth*. Com 2015 100. Retrieved from http://ec.europa.eu/europe2020/pdf/europe2020_consultation_results_en.pdf.

Edlund, J. (1999). Progressive taxation farewell? In S. Svallfors & P. Taylor-Gooby (Eds.), *The end of the welfare state? Responses to retrenchment*. London: Routledge.

Ervasti, H., Andersen, J. G., Fridberg, T., & Ringdal, K. (2012). *The future of the welfare state*. Cheltenham: Edward Elgar Publishing.

Evans, D., Mariah, R., Kelley, J., & Breznau, N. (2014). *The welfare state and attitudes towards inequality and redistribution.* Paper presented at the ASA Annual Meeting, San Francisco, CA.
Ferrera, M. (1993). *EC citizens and social protection.* Brussels: European Commission.
Fong, C. (2001). Social preferences, self-interest, and the demand for redistribution. *Journal of Public Economics, 82*(2), 225–246.
Gough, I. (2011). From financial crisis to fiscal crisis. In K. Farnsworth & Z. Irving (Eds.), *Social policy in challenging times.* Bristol: Policy Press.
Hacker, J., & Pierson, P. (2010). *Winner-take-all politics.* New York: Simon & Schuster.
Hakhverdian, A., Van Elsas, E., Van Der Brug, W., & Kuhn, T. (2013). Euroscepticism and education. *European Union Politics, 14*(4), 522–541.
Higgs, R. (1997). The dream of the Mount Pelerin Society. *The Independent Review, 1*(4), 2–4.
Hobolt, S. (2016). The Brexit vote: A divided nation, a divided continent. *Journal of European Public Policy, 23*(9), 1259–1277.
IMF. (2017). World economic outlook database, October 2016. Retrieved from https://www.imf.org/external/pubs/ft/weo/2016/01/weodata/index.aspx.
Jessop, B. (2002). *The future of the capitalist state.* Cambridge: Polity.
Kaase, M., & Newton, K. (1995). *Beliefs in government.* Oxford: Oxford University Press.
Kiesi, J., Brähler, E., Schmutzer, G., & Decker, O. (2016). Euroscepticism and right-wing extremist attitudes in Germany. *German Politics*, online. https://doi.org/10.1080/09644008.2016.1226810.
Knijn, T., & Komter, A. E. (2004). *Solidarity between the sexes and the generations: Transformations in Europe.* Cheltenham: Edward Elgar Publishing.
Knijn, T., & Van Oorschot, W. (2008). The need for and the societal legitimacy of social investments in children and their families. *Journal of Family Issues, 29*(11), 1520–1542.
Kriesi, H., Grande, E., Dolezal, M., Helbling, M., Hoglinger, D., Hutter, S., & Wuest, B. (2012). *Political conflict in Western Europe.* Cambridge: Cambridge University Press.
Larsen, C. A. (2008). The political logic of labour market reforms and popular images of target groups. *Journal of European Social Policy, 18*(1), 50–63.
Linos, K., & West, M. (2003). Self-interest, social beliefs, and attitudes to redistribution. *European Sociological Review, 19*(4), 393–409.
Likki, T., & Staerklé, C. (2014). Welfare support in Europe: Interplay of dependency culture beliefs and meritocratic contexts. *International Journal of Public Opinion Research, 27*(1), 138–153.

Mau, S. (2003). *The moral economy of welfare states: Britain and Germany compared*. London: Routledge.
Meier Jæger, M. (2006). What makes people support public responsibility for welfare provision? *Acta Sociologica, 49*(3), 321–338.
Meuleman, B., & Chung, H. (2012). Who should care for the children? In H. Ervasti, J. G. Andersen, T. Fridberg, & K. Ringdal (Eds.), *The future of the welfare state* (pp. 107–133). Edward Elgar.
Mewes, J., & Mau, S. (2012). Unraveling working-class welfare chauvinism. In S. Svallfors (Ed.), *Contested welfare states: Welfare attitudes in Europe and beyond* (pp. 119–157). Stanford, CA: Stanford University Press.
Morel, N., Palier, B., & Palme, J. (2012). *Towards a social investment welfare state? Ideas, policies and challenges*. Bristol: Policy Press.
Nolan, B. (2013). What use is 'social investment'? *Journal of European Social Policy, 23*, 5.
OECD. (2011). Fiscal consolidation: Targets, plans and measures. *OECD Journal on Budgeting, 11*(2). https://doi.org/10.1787/budget-11-5kg869h4w5f6.
Pederson, J. (2014). Where should the money go? *International Journal of Social Science Studies, 2*, 1.
Pierson, P. (Ed.). (2001). *The new politics of the welfare state*. Oxford: Oxford University Press.
Piven, F. (2015). Neoliberalism and the welfare state. *Journal of International and Comparative Social Policy, 31*(1), 2–9. https://doi.org/10.1080/21699763.2014.1001665.
Roosma, F. (2016). *A multidimensional perspective on the social legitimacy of welfare states in Europe*. Tilburg: Tilburg University.
Roosma, F., Gelissen, J., & van Oorschot, W. (2013). The multidimensionality of welfare state attitudes: A European cross-national study. *Social Indicators Research, 113*(1), 235–255.
Sen, A. (1977). Rational fools: A critique of the behavioural foundations of economic theory. *Philosophy and Public Affairs, 6*(3), 317–332.
Springer, S., Birch, K., & MacLeavy, J. (Eds.). (2016). *The handbook of neoliberalism*. London: Routledge.
Staerklé, C., Likki, T., & Scheidegger, R. (2012). A normative approach to welfare attitudes. In S. Svallfors (Ed.), *Contested welfare states: Welfare attitudes in Europe and beyond* (Vol. 81). Stanford, CA: Stanford University Press.
Stiglitz, J. (2016). *The Euro and its threat to the future of Europe*. London: Allen Lane.

Svallfors, S. (1997). Worlds of welfare and attitudes to redistribution. *European Sociological Review, 13*(3), 283–304.
Taylor-Gooby, P. (1982). Two cheers for the welfare state. *Journal of Public Policy, 2*(4), 319–346.
Taylor-Gooby, P. (2002). The silver age of the welfare state. *Journal of Social Policy, 31*(4), 597–622.
Taylor-Gooby, P., & Martin, R. (2010). Fairness, equality and legitimacy. *Social Policy & Administration, 44*(1), 85–103.
Taylor-Gooby, P., Leruth, B., & Chung, H. (Eds.). (2017). *After austerity: Welfare state transformation in Europe after the great recession*. Oxford: Oxford University Press.
Ullrich, C. G. (2002). Reciprocity, justice and statutory health insurance in Germany. *Journal of European Social Policy, 12*(2), 123–136.
van der Waal, J., Achterberg, P., Houtman, D., De Koster, W., & Manevska, K. (2010). 'Some are more equal than others': Economic egalitarianism and welfare chauvinism in the Netherlands. *Journal of European Social Policy, 20*(4), 350–363.
Van Oorschott, W. (2006). Making the difference in social Europe. *Journal of European Social Policy, 16*(1), 23–42.
Vandenbroucke, F., Hemerijck, A., & Palier, B. (2011). *The EU needs a social investment pact*. OSE Paper Series, Opinion paper 5. Observatoire Social Europeene, Brussels.
Von Hayek, F. (1973). *Law, legislation and liberty*. Chicago: University of Chicago Press.

3

European Welfare Nationalism: A Democratic Forum Study in Five Countries

Christian Albrekt Larsen, Morten Frederiksen, and Mathias Herup Nielsen

Introduction

Immigration potentially places stress on public support for inclusive welfare policies. Majority reluctance to grant immigrants access to social rights may be explained in terms of self-interest or national identity. We add a further explanation, people's understanding of national interest, and provide new evidence for it from our Democratic Forum (DF) methodology. The context is that a number of European countries have experienced an increased inflow of immigrants. This is both immigration from outside Europe, for example Syrians fleeing from civil war around 2015, and from other European Union (EU) countries, for example Eastern Europeans looking for better living standards and job opportunities. These developments have shaped public debates about immigration and about the role and scope of the welfare state.

C. A. Larsen (✉) • M. Frederiksen • M. H. Nielsen
Aalborg University, Aalborg, Denmark
e-mail: albrekt@dps.aau.dk

One of the early predictions was that increased ethnic diversity would make Europeans less supportive of welfare states' arrangements (for example Alesina and Glaeser 2004; Larsen 2011). The background for this prediction was the American experience where ethnic diversity, especially the presence of a deprived black minority, has been decisive for public resistance towards poverty-relief programs such as the former social assistance program for single mothers (Aid to Families with Dependent Children), Medicaid and food stamps (Gilens 1996, 2000). A number of studies have tried to verify or falsify this prediction connecting stocks or flows of immigrants to general public attitudes to European welfare states. The results have been inconclusive. At the aggregated national level, it is hard to find any significant relationships (Brady and Finnigan 2014; Mau and Burkhardt 2009), while a growing body of literature points to a negative relationship at more disaggregated levels (Eger 2010; Eger and Breznau 2017). Our interpretation is that the result at least demonstrates the absence of a general law-like connection between ethnic diversity and public support for state welfare, as implied for example by Alesina and Glaeser (2004). In the European context, with a popular welfare state already in place (in contrast to the United States [US] case) and with a multi-party system making it possible to combine anti-migrant, anti-EU and pro-welfare attitudes (in contrast to the two-party system of the US), ethnic diversity is more likely to lead to what has been labelled welfare chauvinism. The chapter will use the more encompassing term 'welfare nationalism'.

This 'welfare for our own kind' has been a winning political formula in a number of European countries, for example the United Kingdom (UK) case, where the social rights of immigrants were central to the debates leading up to the Brexit referendum in 2016. The 'welfare for our kind formula' was pioneered in Denmark and Norway in the late 1980s by the so-called progress parties (Andersen and Bjørklund 1990) and refined by the Danish People's Party. With roots in the former Progress Party, the Danish people's party developed a new anti-migration, pro-welfare and anti-EU platform. According to Schumacher and van Kersbergen (2014, p. 300).

this party's electoral success and influence on government policy has motivated diffusion of welfare chauvinism to the Dutch Freedom Party and to a lesser extent to the Sweden Democrats, The Finns and the French National Front.

Working on party manifesto data, Eger and Valdez (2014) show how 'welfare for our own kind' has become a pivotal element among the populist right parties in Europe. As the populist right parties successfully exploit these European political opportunity structures, their position is likely to influence the position of mainstream political parties and actual policies. There are a number of examples of national legislation that limit the social rights of immigrants while maintaining rights for natives (Sainsbury 2006). National parliaments are free to do so in the case of non-EU immigrants, whereas the EU treaties (and their interpretation by the EU court) protect some of the social rights of EU immigrants. Whether populist right parties are the cause or the product of public welfare nationalism is virtually impossible to determine; the most plausible answer is that causality goes in both direction.

The chapter contributes to the emerging literature on welfare nationalism by analysing data from Democratic Forums. As discussed in Chap. 1, Democratic Forums are a major advance that takes us beyond the quantitative survey methodology used in most previous studies. Survey data is typically unable to show whether the questions most relevant to the respondents' understanding have been asked, why people reply as they do, and what would citizens agree upon if they were able to discuss the issue with each other. These limitations lead us to ask the following three research questions:

- Do welfare nationalist attitudes emerge in public deliberation on immigration and the future of the welfare state in Europe?
- What types of rationales are employed in justifying welfare nationalism in public deliberation in Europe?
- What policy suggestions and consensus positions emerge from public deliberation on immigration and the future of the welfare state in Europe?

Theories About the Micro-Level Rationales of Welfare Nationalism

The study of attitudes to the social entitlements of immigrants stands at a crossroads between the many studies of attitudes to immigration and immigrants and the many studies of attitudes to welfare schemes/redistribution. Both strands of literature have been used to theorise the background for welfare nationalist attitudes, which leave us with large number of macro-, meso- and micro-level theories. One way to provide an overview is to look at the rationales theorised as underpinning welfare nationalist attitudes at the micro-level. We distinguish broadly between self-interest, lack of solidarity with immigrants and sociotropic (common interest) concerns for the nation state.

Following a long tradition both in studies of general attitudes to immigration and general attitudes to welfare schemes, reluctance to grant immigrants social rights could be rooted in self-interest. The main argument is that welfare nationalist attitudes derive from competition (imagined or real) for scarce resources (jobs, benefits and services) between natives and immigrants (Scheve and Slaughter 2001). In this setup, welfare nationalism is believed to be strongest among those who stand to lose the most if immigrants are granted social rights. This is often operationalised as the lower strata of society: those in precarious jobs, unskilled workers or those living on welfare benefits. These groups are believed to face the strongest competition from immigrants in the labour market (that could be attracted by generous social rights) and have the strongest self-interest in not sharing limited resources (if immigrants become unemployed and claim benefits). This would lead lower strata of society to reject granting social rights to immigrants. In contrast, the upper strata are believed to have less to lose as they face weaker labour market competition, are less dependent on welfare benefits and stand to gain from cheaper labour.

The second main explanation for welfare nationalist attitudes has been the lack of shared identity with immigrants. The argument is that support for social policies is rooted in a feeling of mutual shared identity among the members of a given nation state (e.g. Miller 1993). The nation state formed the boundaries of the democracy, the political mobilization and the class compromises that fostered the modern welfare state. In a simple sense, everyone is a welfare nationalist; no one seems to imagine that the Norwegian people's pension should be paid to a Malaysian woman who has never been to Norway. Welfare states are systems of reciprocity and are constituted by mutual obligations among those who belong to that particular (nation) state. This intersection between national identity, social rights and obligations creates a strong division in perceived entitlement. Thus, immigrants constitute a grey zone between those who are included and excluded from the nation. In this framework, variations in welfare nationalism could reflect:

- How the majority think about their national identity—for example in civic or ethnic terms;
- How distant the identity of immigrants are believed to be from the identity of the national in-group e.g. in religious terms; or
- How deserving immigrants are believed to be on non-identity criteria such as need or work ethic.

The common dominator in this line of reasoning is that it is the presence or absence of solidarity with immigrants that shapes welfare nationalist attitudes.

To these two main lines of theorising the micro-level rationales of the public, one can add a third framing, which we label sociotropic reasoning. The argument is that welfare nationalism could (also) be rooted in concerns about the overall functioning of society. Within election research, voting rooted in the overall (perceived) needs of the national economy rather than one's own pocket book is labelled sociotropic voting (e.g. Kinder and Kiewiet 1981). This perspective is also found in studies of general attitudes to immigration (see Hainmueller and Hopkins 2014 for an excellent metastudy). The basic argument is that welfare nationalism might not (only) be rooted in the calculation of self-interest or the absence of feelings of recipient-focused solidarity, but also in perceptions of immigration as dysfunctional for the overall society. There is an element of self-interest and identity in such sociotropic rationales (what is *best* for *us*), but it makes a difference that the yardstick is societal—collective concerns and not individual concerns. In such a framework, variations in welfare nationalism have mainly been theorised as rooted in the perceived costs or benefits of granting social rights to immigrants for society overall. These costs and benefits can be strictly economic. Several international surveys ask about perceived economic net gain or loss caused by immigration, but might also include costs and benefits for the broader social order within the nation state. For example, some surveys ask how immigration is likely to influence the crime level. However, as we shall see, sociotropic justifications of welfare nationalism can take a number of other forms, as is the case when citizens are asked to justify their general opinions about the welfare state (Frederiksen 2017; Nielsen 2018; Taylor-Gooby and Martin 2010).

Empirical Findings from Survey Methodology

Previous studies of welfare nationalist attitudes among the public have almost exclusively been based on quantitative surveys (Gerhards and Lengfeld 2013; Mewes and Mau 2012, 2013; Reeskens and van Oorschot 2012; van der Waal et al. 2010; van Der Waal et al. 2013). In the European Values Study (2006), Europeans were asked about whose living conditions they were more concerned about. In all countries, the public were more concerned about the elderly, the sick and handicapped and the unemployed than they were about the living condition of immigrants. Van Oorschot's (2006) conclusion was that it is lack of shared identity that makes immigrants the least 'deserving' for support. One of the key findings from the many studies based on the 2008 European Social Survey (ESS) is that the vast majority in most European countries support what can be labelled *conditional access* for immigrants.

The question had the following wording: '*Thinking of people coming to live in [country] from other countries, when do you think they should obtain the same rights to social benefits and services as citizens already living here?*' Very few support giving the same rights 'immediately on arrival', but only a minority would 'never' give immigrants the same rights. The other predefined answer categories in the ESS were length of stay in the country (at least one year), tax payment (at least one year) and citizenship.

Another key finding from these studies is that persons in lower socio-economic strata are indeed more reluctant to give immigrants access to social benefits and services than are persons in higher socio-economic strata. This methodology gives an excellent overview of welfare nationalist attitudes throughout Europe, but the ability to understand the answers is limited: regression techniques can be used to sort out the relative strength of various variables, but with cross-sectional data this is by no means a bulletproof method. For example, the fact that lower strata in society hold stronger welfare nationalist attitudes may be rooted in self-interest, in more ethnic nation-perceptions, in prejudices against outsiders and/or in stronger sociotropic concerns.

The classic survey methodology has been supplemented by studies that include survey experiments designed to isolate causal mechanisms. The typical methods have been to use vignettes to vary the characteristics of receivers and afterwards measure welfare attitudes. In general, these studies find that ethnicity cues matter. In Sweden, Hjorth (2015) measured attitudes to the amount of child benefit given to immigrants after varying by 'Dutch immigrant' or 'Bulgarian immigrant' (and the number of children). He finds that Swedes will give a lower amount to Bulgarian immigrants. In the UK, Ford (2016) measured attitudes to the current levels of housing benefits and disability benefits. In the former, he demonstrated that more British (white) respondents found the level of housing benefits to be too high when exposed to an Asian Muslim rather than a native-born or a black Caribbean unemployed male living in London. In the latter experiment, Ford finds that more respondents judge the level of disability benefit for a person injured in a car accident to be too high when the recipient is a Muslim Asian immigrant, a white immigrant or a Muslim Asian native (in this rank order) than when he/she is a white native. This leads to the conclusion that both ethnicity and immigrant status matters. In the US, Canada and the UK, Harell et al. (2016) measured attitudes to five different benefits (in a merged measure) after varying both verbally and non-verbally by white, black, Hispanic, Asian, South Asian and Aboriginal ethnicity. The main effects are surprisingly modest in the US but somewhat stronger in Canada and the UK. The experimental effect tends to be strongest for subgroups that indicate racial prejudices in the survey. Finally, Kootstra (2016) measured attitudes to financial support from the government after varying not only by ethnicity but also by gender, job, family status, level of need, job search effort, work history and immigration status. She found that by taking the cues of effort, work history and migration status into account, the effect from ethnicity largely disappears. However, she also finds that when given a negative cue, such as little effort to search for work, non-native groups are punished harder than ethnic groups.

The DFs provide a more exploratory design. The material is extremely well suited for studying how citizens frame and actively justify welfare state nationalism—including the institutions, persons, objects and narratives they refer to while doing so (Boltanski and Thévenot 2006).

The Democratic Forums, Case Selection and Initial Attitudes

In all five countries included in this study, participants were tasked to select five themes for discussion during the first day, as mentioned in Chap. 1. The immigration issue was chosen in Germany and the UK but not in Denmark, Slovenia and Norway. Before the second day, participants were given basic written information about the size and character of immigration and the main conclusions were summarised on the second day, where the immigration issue was forced onto the agenda. As part of the pre- and post-survey the participants were also asked three of the ESS questionnaire items related to welfare nationalism: the dependent variable used in many of the previous studies (see above), a Likert scale question about perceptions of whether social benefits attracted immigrants and an 11-point scale about the perception of immigrants' net gain/contribution in relation to social benefits and services.

The ESS (2008) data indicated a clear potential for welfare nationalism in all five countries, as illustrated in Fig. 3.1. Average agreement or disagreement with the statement that social services and benefits in each of the 28 ESS countries encourage people from other countries to come and live here is shown on the x-axis (Likert scale from 1 'strongly disagree' to 5 'strongly agree'). Fig. 3.1 indicates large variation. In most of the Eastern

European Welfare Nationalism: A Democratic Forum Study... 71

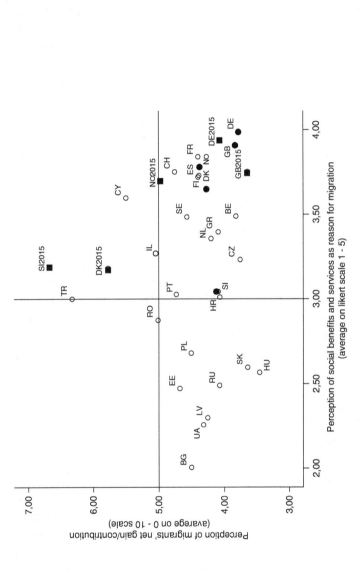

Fig. 3.1 The welfare state encourages immigration and immigrants' net gain/contribution to the welfare state (2008 ESS and 2015 Democratic Forums pre-survey). *BE* Belgium, *BG* Bulgaria, *CH* Switzerland, *CY* Cyprus, *CZ* Czech Republic, *DE* Germany, *DK* Denmark, *EE* Estonia, *ES* Spain, *FI* Finland, *FR* France, *GB* United Kingdom, *GR* Greece, *HR* Croatia, *HU* Hungary, *IL* Israel, *LV* Latvia, *NL* Netherlands, *NO* Norway, *PL* Poland, *PT* Portugal, *RO* Romania, *RU* Russian Federation, *SE* Sweden, *SI* Slovenia, *SK* Slovakia, *TR* Turkey, *UA* Ukraine

European countries, the public tend to disagree with the statement that the social benefits and services of their country encourage people from other countries to come and live there. The most extreme case is Bulgaria. In all Western European countries, respondents tend to agree with the statement. Germany and the UK are the most extreme cases. The Norwegians and Danes also tend to agree that their level of social benefits and services encourages immigration. Slovenia is found at the borderline with an average a little above three. Average public perception (in answer to a different survey question) of whether immigrants receive more social benefits and services than they pay in taxes is shown on the y-axis. Here the cross-country variation is smaller. The typical response, apart from a few cases (Turkey, Cypress, Israel and Romania), is that immigrants receive more than they contribute. The most extreme case was Hungary. By combining the two axes, Norway, Denmark, Germany and the UK are found in the lower-right quadrant where the public both see their welfare states as a reason for immigration and think of immigrants as net gainers from the welfare state. Slovenia is also located in this quadrant but more on the borderline due to the uncertainty about their welfare state being a reason for inflow of immigrants.

Figure 3.1 also includes the average position of the answers given by the DF participants to the survey just before the forums took place. On these two items the average position of the German and British participants resembles the attitudes of Germans and Britons interviewed in the ESS in 2008. They are positioned in the lower right quadrant. Norwegian participants are on average also located in this quadrant though they are less certain that immigrants have a net gain from social benefits and services than were Norwegians interviewed in 2008. The Danish and Slovenian participants, however, are on average located in the upper-right quadrant. Thus, at least in the pre-survey, these participants saw their welfare state as an encouragement to immigration, but at the same time they thought—on average—that immigrants actually contributed more to the welfare state than they took out.

There is no one-to-one relationship between perception of welfare magnetism and net contributions of immigrants and willingness to give access. Fig. 3.2 shows the proportion believing that immigrants should 'never' have the same rights or only 'once citizenship' is achieved. Measured this way in 2008, Cyprus, Hungary and Slovenia had the highest proportions that would more or less unconditionally restrict social rights to

European Welfare Nationalism: A Democratic Forum Study... 73

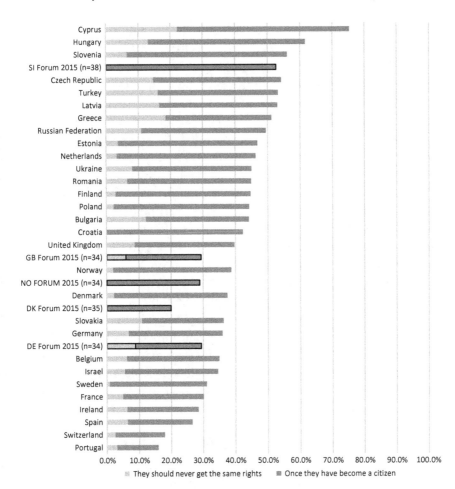

Fig. 3.2 Attitudes to granting immigrants equal social rights across 28 countries (2008, ESS)

natives. In Slovenia it was about half of the respondents. Measured this way, the share of welfare nationalists in the UK, Germany, Norway and Denmark were lower than that found in Slovenia. In the ESS in 2008, the share was between 35 and 40 percentage points giving one of the two answers. Fig. 3.2 also includes the proportion in the pre-survey among the DF participants in 2015. The general pattern is that the welfare nationalists are slightly under-represented in the DFs if the ESS 2008 results are used as baseline. This is especially the case in Denmark, where none of the participants indicated 'never' in the pre-surveys and only seven out of the 35 participants agreed that citizenship should be required. This indicates an absence of 'hard-core welfare nationalism' in the DFs, which should be remembered in the interpretation of the data.

Our qualitative analysis is based on two rounds of coding. In the first, we thematically coded all the material, isolating all statements about immigration. In the second round, we coded all these statements, distinguishing between rationales of self-interest, identity and sociotropic concerns. As a guideline, all statements on increased competition (for example for jobs, hospital beds, welfare benefits) were classified as rationales of self-interest, whereas all statements referring to the deservingness of the immigrant were classified as rationales of identity. For sociotropic rationales we coded a range of statements referring to the assumed societal gains or losses resulting from immigration. It is important to notice that apart from the qualitative differences between countries, important quantitative differences emerged as well. The topic was more salient in the UK and Germany, which resulted in more data from these two countries. It should also be noted that the design implicitly encouraged participants to activate sociotropic concerns. The material therefore offers rich insights into the rationales of sociotropic welfare nationalism whereas rationales of self-interest are less likely to appear in this kind of setting.

The Rationales of Welfare Nationalism

In the DFs we conducted, there were significant differences between countries on the topic of immigration and the welfare state.

United Kingdom

The UK data includes a number of statements that point to the importance of self-interest. In terms of competition in the labour market, the reference point is the hard-working Polish men who

> "work really hard, they will do the hours, they will do the jobs but we won't" (UK-88).

Some respondents also found competition by higher-skilled immigrants intensified due to the increased costs of education in the UK. Highly educated immigrants who received free education in their country of origin competed with natives with fewer educational opportunities. In terms of competition for welfare benefits and services, British participants were mainly concerned about immigrants' access to the universal healthcare system, the National Health Service (NHS), and education. One basic argument was that if

> you allow immigration more and more and more, the Government have to spend more money on benefits for them instead of putting the money into education and social care and other kind of stuff. You need to control the immigration (UK-61)

In addition some believed that the free NHS attracted immigrants to the UK. A small number linked the competition issue to housing and even prisons. The underlying logic was that immigrants increased existing strains in these areas.

The UK data also contains a number of statements that point to the importance of deservingness. As elsewhere, a clear distinction emerged between immigrant outsiders and the more deserving native insiders. Homeless ex-soldiers were a reference point: if the UK cannot support this highly deserving group, there is no sense in helping immigrants. The least-deserving immigrants were those so-called scroungers attracted by the NHS and other benefits and services, typically unspecified. It was especially degrading if British benefits were sent to persons living outside the UK or used to buy real estate outside the UK:

> There are people in this country that claim child benefit, three or four children and they get the benefit and the children are not living in this country, they are living in where the people came from. (UK-45)

However, the status of 'true refugee' could potentially make the 'immigrants' more deserving: 'you have people who are running from torture and killing. Then you have people just coming because of the easy life and [inaudible] the benefits. So the government need to look at the people in crisis' (UK-89). Thus, the UK participants operated in various places with a distinction between 'real refugees' that should be entitled to some rights, 'immigrant-scroungers' that should be entitled to no rights at all and 'hard-working immigrant workers' who could earn rights through insurance and years of tax payment. European citizenship did little to increase the deservingness; on the contrary the EU-citizens' right was seen as a particular problem (especially in NHS treatment). What could lower the deservingness of natives—typically in comparison with the 'hardworking immigrant worker'—was the status of being a native welfare scrounger (either found among young unemployed or among single mothers). Thus, the British were unique in suggesting that the 'hardworking immigrant' is sometimes seen as a person that could teach the native scroungers an important lesson about how to behave (for a similar finding in mass media content see Larsen 2013).

The main sociotropic concerns of British respondents were about fiscal sustainability:

> Okay, it's an issue because we know that there is overcrowding, there will be. The strain on the NHS, housing, and education. What the problem is now but tenfold, okay? (UK-44)

Immigrants were mostly considered as a strain on the future of the British economy and welfare state leading to discussion of a points-based system modelled on Australia. Another proposed solution was an annual immigration cap. No one argued that immigration might help solve future fiscal problems by providing more taxpayers, and there was little recognition of the value of largely working-age immigrants to an ageing population. In contrast, a number of respondents discussed the lack of space and overcrowding caused by immigration. The sociotropic concern about maintaining authentic British culture was also absent. A number of respondents stated sociotropic concerns for the current and future social order:

> There's going to be a lot more people coming in, and there's going to be a lot more people getting annoyed and to stand up so, there's going to be a lot more riots. There's going to be a lot more trouble and conflict. (UK-24)

Concerns were raised about criminals and even terrorists among immigrants, leading to arguments for stricter screening of immigrants before entry. The migrant camps in Calais in France were used as a reference point in some of these discussions. Finally, a number of respondents were worried about the social order in more abstract terms. Thus, concerns were raised about future riots and even internal war.

Germany

The high inflow of Syrians set the context for the discussions of immigration and the welfare state in the German DF. The government was almost unanimously criticised in regards to the lack of planning and funding of the efforts to receive, distribute and integrate refugees:

> The state started this whole thing by bringing them in, and now the state must deal with this themselves. (DE-18)

Mostly, the influx of refugees was seen to result from a government decision for which government is unwilling to take responsibility. The most prominent topics are the general lack of trust in government management of the issue and an apparent absence of planning. The need for volunteers and the lack of coordination between the organizations involved was also criticised. There were a number of statements within these discussions about the current refugee crisis that point to competition for scarce resources:

> I'd like to make a comment on that. I have heard from friends that they signed their child up for daycare, but then they received a call from the administrator saying that they can't take their child, because they have to have enough space for the refugee children they have to take on. I think this is a negative aspect. (DE-12)

The other two areas mentioned were shortage of housing and of special support in school classes: if the state cannot even provide decent childcare, schooling and housing before the Syrian crisis, the inflow would only makes things worse. There was also a more general discussion about funding, for example whether immigrants' needs were to be funded by higher taxes or lower benefits and services. Besides a single statement about a lack of jobs in Germany, there was no discussion about competition for jobs in the labour market.

Discussion of the deservingness of immigrants was briefer in the German DF than in others. This might partly be explained by the focus on the current refugee crisis. Participants discussed the war zones in Syria and former war zones in Kosovo. The moral right of these persons to have protection was more or less unquestioned, though there was a discussion about whether the burden should be more equally distributed across European countries. Some participants made the distinction between 'economic' and more deserving 'war refugees':

> Well, and also differentiating between those refuges who are just deciding to come here for economic reasons and those refugees for whom it's really about life and death; also between those who really want to work hard here, and those who just want to show up and get a handout. (DE-03)

Finally, there were concerns that the recent inclusion of Bulgaria and Romania in the EU could bring more of the less deserving 'economic refugees'.

The key topics in Germany were sociotropic concerns for cultural and socio-economic integration. As far as socio-economic integration is concerned, participants reflected and debated on the possibilities of refugees and immigrants becoming productive participants in the labour market—in particular through education. A prominent concern is the educational level of immigrants and the distinction between refugees with good education—for example from Syria—and with little education, and whether the latter should be turned away or offered training. More prominent in discussions, however, was the issue of cultural integration. This debate revolved around two interlinked issues: the appropriateness, willingness and possibility of refugees and immigrants adapting to German culture, practices and values; and the impact on German culture. On the first, there was much discussion on how far immigrants should become Germans in culture, summed up by the moderator as follows:

So how are we to address this, how do you get the tradition or the culture across, so that they adjust relatively quickly to life here and can work here?

Some argued that it is both appropriate and necessary that people retain their cultural roots, while others argued that they must adhere to Germany culture. The strongest consensus was over the need to learn and speak German. Education should be used, it was argued, to bestow a respect for common principles of mutual respect, democracy, the rule of law and hygiene on refugees and immigrants. Another central issue is that refugees and immigrants should become part of communities and society in general—not packed away in ghettoes or camps.

Some argued that the German language, main religion and values will change due to the influx of immigrants:

> We'll die out, and the Muslims will take over. That's the way it will be. (DE-23)

Others saw this position as exaggerated and argued that education will help immigrants adapt to German culture. Fear and conflict were also common topics discussed throughout the forum. Fear of immigrants and refugees was thought to have increased in Germany due to the increased levels of crime, immigrants' (perceived) lack of gratitude, their (again, perceived) proneness to Islamic extremism and terrorism, and the lack of public debate on these issues. Some participants argued that programmes to limit the number of immigrants and integrate those already in Germany would lead to greater safety in schools and a reduced risk of drug crimes. There are, however, many who reject this view, arguing that the increase in societal conflict levels is created by both residents and immigrants, and exploited by the far right.

Denmark

Danish participants said virtually nothing about direct competition between natives and immigrants. Instead, the group discussed immigration policies and the overall principles of welfare policies. In terms of the welfare state, the two main issues addressed were whether immigrants and refugees should gain access to welfare benefits and services and the impact on work incentives:

> Immigrants come here voluntarily. They shouldn't get benefits because they have a reason for being here, presumably in order to work. On the other hand, I think that if you've obtained Danish citizenship and you've contributed for a certain a period of time then you shouldn't get kicked out if you suddenly become unemployed after 5 years. Then you've been a part of society and should have the same rights as the rest. (DK-65)

The issue of work incentives was connected with welfare magnetism, which was not framed as a competition issue. Neither did Danish discussions include deservingness, apart from using refugee status to pinpoint a more deserving group. Participants argued that welfare entitlements depend on when immigrants and refugees had proven sufficiently that they were willing to integrate and contribute to society. This discussion connected a set of important issues: integration, work, self-sufficiency and deservingness to the issue of contribution.

Sociotropic concerns were pivotal. The dominating focus was whether immigration and immigrants' welfare entitlements were good or bad from a societal perspective. Costs and benefits revolved around the framing of immigrants as not only an expenditure but as a potential gain for the Danish economy:

> If we just look a little selfishly on the refugees ... it's super, super awesome that we have well to do, well-educated people who have been able to raise enough money to travel ... here. They can be a huge resource. I'm more worried about the migrants who come here looking for work, because they're the ones who can't make it work at home. (DK-62)

What was emphasised was the need for labour and in particular highly qualified labour. Many participants further discussed better selection of qualified and productive immigrants. A distinction was made between 'qualified Western' and 'unqualified non-Western' immigrants and between 'qualified refugees' and 'unqualified spouses and parents' arriving through family reunification. The discussion considered costs as an investment in a future social return from increased immigration. These ideas seemed to unite the group of participants inclined to look more critically on immigration. Many participants brought up the notion of 'integration' and argued that lack of integration led to different kinds of social pathologies:

> Permanent residence and then willingness to integrate and cultural affinity.... Because it's a big problem at the moment that people come here without intending to adopt the Danish ways. (DK-79)

The integration concept itself was used very broad way by most participants, but it emerged that integration means contributing to society through labour market participation and self-sufficiency, which some saw as the key requirement for obtaining permanent residency and access to family reunification.

Norway

The discussions in the Norwegian forum resemble those in the Danish forum. As in Denmark there were almost no references to direct competition for scarce resources. There was a single statement that Norwegian young people are unable to get apprenticeships because foreigners have entered the job market, but other participants called it a 'system mistake' and did not continue the discussion. There was one general statement about immigrants taking jobs in the future. An older participant provided a flashback to the 1970s where unemployment caused a conflict between Pakistani workers and Norwegians. The underlying logic was that the current situation is different. The problems of welfare magnetism and the work incentives of immigrants were presented, but as in Denmark these issue were discussed in sociotropic terms, as either a potential future socio-economic problem—'many people don't take jobs because the social benefits are so good that there is no need to work' (NO-30)—or a problem for the integration of immigrants:

We do get many Muslims now. Some are Shia and some are Sunni. There have been conflicts in other places and we could risk having conflicts here too. (NO-31)

The solidarity and deservingness rationales were more prominent in Norway than in Denmark. The status of 'refugee' was categorised as the most deserving. Refugee status was not only linked to current conflicts, for example in Syria, but also to environmental issues, and was seen as likely to increase due to climate change. As for the broad category of 'immigrants', including 'refugees', the dominant argument was that labour market integration and a broad willingness to 'integrate' made a person more deserving:

I have interviewed immigrant women myself to get them apprenticeships and possibility for a long-term job. Then many of them say, "No, I can't wear trousers because I wear a long dress". Then I have made adjustments as to how people can do things, but many say no, culturally. I think Norway has to be harsher in those cases. You have to work, and actually say yes to what is offered to you. (NO-10)

Some agreed with statements that suggested greater conditionality in receiving benefits while others disagreed. The discussion was especially linked to Roma beggars in the streets of Oslo. Some participants questioned the deservingness of this current 'problem' group with reference to a lack of reciprocity in the form of tax payment and general lack of integration into Norwegian society. Finally, a number of participants claimed that (other) Norwegians are outright racists. This was more or less unchallenged by the other participants. This diagnosis led to sociotropic concerns for 'social cohesion' (see below) but probably also drew on moral rationales for what immigrants should or should not expect in Norway. The underlying logic was that some of the current problems experienced by immigrants were not due to lack of effort by immigrants, but to Norwegian racism.

The Norwegian discussions were dominated by sociotropic concerns. The general positive attitudes to both refugees and immigrants were mostly connected to the current and future need for labour in Norway:

We will be needing manpower, at least in healthcare with the elder boom coming. We don't have enough people to care for the old people. (NO-12)

Many stated that both refugees and immigrants hold valuable qualifications. Therefore the lack of labour market integration was perceived as something that needs to be fixed through various means, such as reducing discrimination in recruitment procedures, better acceptance of foreign skills and diplomas, and compulsory language courses. The minority position questioned whether Norway really would be short on labour in the future. This led to a consensus position about a need for a selection of 'immigrants' but not 'refugees'.

As in Denmark, there was also a sociotropic concern for broader social cohesion. There were no references to the need to protect an 'authentic' Norwegian culture. What comes closest was a statement about not bringing foreign flags to the parade of the 17th of May when Norwegians celebrate their constitution. Otherwise the coherence debate was framed around the maintenance of gender equality, violent young immigrants and the problem with extreme right-wing nationalism. As in the Denmark, the somewhat fuzzy concern for 'coherence' is linked to the fuzzy concept of 'integration'. In Norway a number of specific state policies were suggested, especially compulsory language programs. This led to a discussion about the balance between the responsibility of the state and the individual for 'integration'.

Slovenia

The Slovene DF also contains few statements about direct competition for jobs, benefits and services between natives and immigrants. Syrian refugees were perceived to have no intention to settle, though the number of refugees was discussed. In contrast, attracting highly qualified immigrants was the main issue, since well-educated Eastern European migrants tend to depart for Northern Europe (see below). Deservingness did not generate discussion because there is little 'welfare nationalism'. Some argued that welfare rights should not be granted to 'immigrants' when Slovenia was still building a decent welfare state for its own citizens.

The most prominent sociotropic topic was the issue of attracting qualified labour while retaining cultural integrity. The issue of attracting qualified labour and much-needed experts was even framed by some of the participants as a question of how to retain refugees and immigrants currently moving through southern Europe and on to central and northern Europe. Slovenia was seen as less attractive to qualified immigrants than Germany, for example. More generally, the lack of highly qualified experts and skilled and unskilled labour is seen as a potential economic threat:

> Since our country is lacking certain profiles of people, for example in health care, and even our people are running to other countries, I guess— OK ... we could possibly attract these profiles with ... benefit bonuses, to come from abroad and work here ... not Northern countries, but the south and the Middle East. (SI-55)

Much of the discussion revolves around creating the right incentives to attract qualified immigrants, for example tax exemptions and various services or benefits.

The issue of cultural integrity emerged as a concern; the entry of immigrants with different cultural values was seen by some as threatening to Slovenian society, identity and language:

> We'll end up losing our own identity, if we allow them to bring their entire culture here and continue to follow it.... (SI-58)

The inflow of different cultural values was seen as a cause of conflict and as threatening principles such as tolerance and equality. In particular, Muslims and the practice of wearing veils were mentioned by some as representing a different and incompatible pattern of cultural values; this position was contested by others, however. The issue of cultural integrity was primarily framed as an issue of integration or assimilation, emphasising the need both to accept the majority way of life and in particular learning the Slovene language as part of becoming a citizen:

> Now if it's happening, I just see that, that the problem is public use of Slovenian language.... (SI-76)

Citizenship also played an important role in the discussion of integration and citizenship requirements such as language skills and employability.

Policy Proposals and Attitude Consensus

The content of the discussions in the DFs allows us to (partly) answer the first research question about whether and how welfare nationalist attitudes emerge and the second question about how these attitudes are justified. However, an additional advantage of deliberative forums is the possibility of studying how discussions enlightened by contrasting opinions and basic information about the subject at hand affects participants' agreement with particular ways of framing the issue. The pre-and post-survey results can describe forum dynamics and potential consensus positions. As expected, the data indicates a move towards fewer 'don't know' answers as well as middle-position answers (five on an 11-point scale or neither agree nor disagree). The participants developed their opinions as the forums progressed. There is, however, little evidence that this dynamic of opinion formation leads to fewer welfare nationalist attitudes. This is somewhat surprising, as we would expect the process of rational deliberation to temper more extreme attitudes.

In the Slovenian case, the pre- and post-survey comparison indicates that the participants came to hold more welfare nationalist attitudes. Twenty-seven of the 37 Slovenian participants answered in the post-survey that equal social rights to immigrants should require citizenship, reflecting a reduction in those answering that equal access should be given after tax payment for a year or more (from 17 participants to eight participants). No one came to think that entitlements should be given immediately on arrival or independently of work. This harder attitude was formed despite a majority perception (both in the pre- and post-survey) of immigrants being net contributors to the Slovene welfare state and the discussion about ways of increasing immigration of the higher-skilled workers. In the voting process at the end of the second day of discussion five consensus positions emerged: 'Reducing the brain drain'; 'Attracting immigrants for shortage professions'; 'Assimilation of immigrants'; 'Foreign investments'; and 'Internationalisation of education'.

In the British case the pre- and post-survey also indicates more welfare nationalist attitudes. Twenty-four of the 34 British participants answered in the post-survey that equal rights should only be granted after at least a year of tax payment. No one continued to defend the view that rights should be granted immediately on arrival or independently of work. Those answering 'never the same rights' as denizens increased from two to five participants. In the post-survey more British participants also indicated that the welfare state encouraged immigration (21 participants out of 34), while they became a little more polarised on the issue of net contribution. The consensus positions which emerged at the end of day two were: 'introduce a points-based system' as 'incomers need to bring something to the system'; 'no benefits should be given to immigrants before residing in the country for a period of minimum two years'; 'immigrants' employers should pay for their healthcare for a period of two years'; 'an ID card system should be introduced so that immigrants using the National Health Service can be tracked down and pay for the use of such services'; 'immigrants committing crimes should be deported'.

In the Danish case there was almost no change between pre- and post-survey on the question about welfare nationalism. Four more participants came to see social benefits and services as an encouragement to immigration, and four more came to see immigrants as net receivers. In Denmark seven consensus positions emerged from the voting procedure at the end of day two: 'refugees should not sit in camps but should be subject to swift case work'; 'everybody should contribute, nobody should receive passive benefits'; 'selection of qualified immigrants that can contribute to society'; 'immigrants should be seen as an equal resource, which should lead to an attitude change among politicians'; 'similar rules in all of EU plus benefits adjusted to living costs'; 'family reunification only in case of economic self-sufficiency'; and 'immigrants should demonstrate willingness to integrate and there should be a wish to learn the language and abide by the laws'.

In the German case the participants became a little more polarised on the question about net receiver or contributor, but otherwise the pre- and post-surveys indicate no overall change in welfare nationalist attitudes. In Germany three consensus positions emerged from the discussion: 'there should be clear guidelines for refugee policy'; 'refuges should be integrated via access to education, labour market and housing; and 'immigration, including refugees, should be lowered in number and a global distribution of refugees should be made'.

Only in the Norwegian case did the pre- and post-survey indicate a change to less welfare nationalist attitudes. In the post-survey 22 of the 32 Norwegian participants indicated that equal rights should be given after minimum a year of tax payment; six fewer participants indicated that citizenship should be a central criterion. Norwegian participants did not change their attitude that social benefits and services encouraged immigration, but more participants came to see immigrants as net contributors to the Norwegian welfare state. In Norway five consensus positions emerged from the voting procedure: 'intensified training in language, culture and laws and regulations'; 'more use of temporary residence permits and work permits (to get immigrants into the labour market faster)'; 'long-term job creation for those with permanent residence'; 'campaigns aimed at employers to hire immigrants'; and 'linguistic and cultural integration of immigrants through mandatory Norwegian language courses, requirements for work and self-sufficiency for economic immigrants'.

Conclusions

The DFs provide a qualitative insight into the framing of welfare nationalism. This was especially salient in UK, where it was linked to Brexit discussions, and in Germany, where it was linked to the exceptionally high inflow of Syrian refugees in 2015. As for our first research question (*Do welfare nationalist attitudes emerge in public deliberation on immigration and the future of the welfare state?*), the DFs show that when asked openly to reflect upon the future of the welfare state and immigration, the issue of migrants' entitlements to social rights emerged as a salient issue in the UK, Germany, Norway and Denmark, while the issue of how to attract highly qualified labour dominated in Slovenia. As for the second research question (*What types of rationales are employed in justifying welfare nationalism in public?*), the forums demonstrate that a number of different rationales were employed in the justification of welfare nationalism. As expected, the purely self-interest rationales were rarely used in the DFs. This is not to say that the prominent role of self-interest explanation applied in previous survey studies is wrong. However, the forums demonstrate that self-interest rationales are rarely applied when people are required to justify their views in a DF. There seems to be a norm, at least in the DFs, that welfare nationalism rooted in pure self-interest arguments is unacceptable. The exception was the UK. A possible interpretation is that the acceptance of self-interest rationales is enhanced by what has become a residual welfare state. Scarcity of public benefits and services probably makes such justifications more common and acceptable. This interpretation is supported by the complete absence of these rationales in the more generous Danish and Norwegian welfare states.

The perspective that theorised welfare nationalism as rooted in the absence of shared identity and solidarity with immigrants was highly relevant in all five countries. At a very basic level, the participants in all five countries used and implicitly accepted terms such as 'native' and 'immigrant', showing that for them the boundaries of nation states were self-evident. There were no statements about support for the social rights of fellow EU- or world-citizens. This supports the general findings from the vignette studies that 'native-status' matters. The idea of an ethnic hierarchy, suggested by some vignette studies, is more questionable. In the deliberative forums the distinction most used was between the deserving 'refugees' and other groups of immigrants. Not giving social rights to refugees is hard to justify in an open democratic discussion. The category was especially present in Germany and Norway. It was less clear-cut in the UK as there was a distinction between the deserving 'true refugee' and 'the scroungers'. In Denmark deservingness discussions were shaped by the distinction between 'Western' and 'non-Western' immigrants and the willingness to integrate, which point to sociotropic concerns. In the Slovenian case, the 'deserving refugee' was not salient in the discussions. Furthermore, even in Germany and Norway, where questioning the social rights of the self-evidently deserving refugee seems to be unacceptable, the category of the deserving immigrant might implicitly make it more acceptable to question the rights of the others.

As expected, sociotropic rationales and justifications of welfare nationalism were present in all five forums. The social rights of immigrants were discussed in relation to what was good or bad for British, German, Norwegian, Danish and Slovene society overall. These rationales and justifications clearly dominated the debate in Germany, Norway,

Denmark and Slovenian, while the discussions in the UK were more mixed. The economic sociotropic rationales were highly salient in the UK, Denmark, Norway and Slovenia. In the UK, the main topic was the (perceived) economic strain immigrants put on the British welfare state. In Denmark and Norway, the main theme was how immigrants could be (or be made) an economic net gain for society. Thus, in all three countries, the idea of a better selection of economically attractive immigrants was salient. In Slovenia, it was a matter of beginning to attract highly skilled immigrants. The economic sociotropic concerns were less present in Germany. Cultural sociotropic rationales about preserving an authentic national culture were absent in the British discussions and virtually absent in the Danish and Norwegian discussions. These rationales were more prominent in Germany and Slovenia. One interpretation could be the presence of a more ethnic nationalism in the latter two countries and a more civic nationalism in the former three. However, in the UK, Denmark and Norway the discussions did include rationales about the overall social order: a fear of racism among (other) Norwegians, a fear of riots in the UK and a fear of parallel societies in Denmark.

According to the post-surveys, deliberation in the DFs did not lead to a decline in welfare nationalism. Only in Norway did deliberation lead to greater willingness to give immigrants social rights, which was primarily rooted in a consensus that immigrants were needed in the labour market. Our findings are an antidote to the idea that welfare nationalism is something simply created by populist right-wing parties which can be counteracted by deliberation among enlightened citizens.

References

Alesina, A., & Glaeser, E. (2004). *Fighting poverty in the US and Europe: A world of difference*. Oxford: Oxford University Press.
Andersen, J. G., & Bjørklund, T. (1990). Structural changes and new cleavages: The progress parties in Denmark and Norway. *Acta Sociologica, 33*(3), 195–217.
Boltanski, L., & Thévenot, L. (2006). *On justification: Economies of worth*. Princeton, NJ: Princeton University Press.

Brady, D., & Finnigan, R. (2014). Does immigration undermine public support for social policy? *American Sociological Review, 79*(1), 17–42.
Eger, M. A. (2010). Even in Sweden: The effect of immigration on support for welfare state spending. *European Sociological Review, 26*(2), 203–217.
Eger, M. A., & Breznau, N. (2017). Immigration and the welfare state: A cross-regional analysis of European welfare attitudes. *International Journal of Comparative Sociology, 58*(5), 440–463.
Eger, M. A., & Valdez, S. (2014). Neo-nationalism in Western Europe. *European Sociological Review, 31*(1), 115–130.
Ford, R. (2016). Who should we help? An experimental test of discrimination in the British welfare state. *Political Studies, 64*(3), 630–650.
Frederiksen, M. (2017). Varieties of Scandinavian universalism: A comparative study of welfare justifications. *Acta Sociologica, 61*(1), 3–16.
Gerhards, J., & Lengfeld, H. (2013). European integration, equality rights and people's beliefs: Evidence from Germany. *European Sociological Review, 29*(1), 19–31.
Gilens, M. (1996). Race coding and white opposition to welfare. *The American Political Science Review, 90*(3), 593–604.
Gilens, M. (2000). *Why Americans hate welfare: Race, media, and the politics of antipoverty policy*. Chicago, IL: University of Chicago Press.
Hainmueller, J., & Hopkins, D. J. (2014). Public attitudes toward immigration. *Annual Review of Political Science, 17*, 225–249.
Harell, A., Soroka, S., & Iyengar, S. (2016). Race, prejudice and attitudes toward redistribution: A comparative experimental approach. *European Journal of Political Research, 55*(4), 723–744.
Hjorth, F. (2015). Who benefits? Welfare chauvinism and national stereotypes. *European Union Politics, 17*(1), 3–24.
Kinder, D. R., & Kiewiet, D. R. (1981). Sociotropic politics: The American case. *British Journal of Political Science, 11*(2), 129–161.
Kootstra, A. (2016). Deserving and undeserving welfare claimants in Britain and the Netherlands: Examining the role of ethnicity and migration status using a vignette experiment. *European Sociological Review, 32*(3), 325–338.
Larsen, C. A. (2011). Ethnic heterogeneity and public support for welfare: Is the American experience replicated in Britain, Sweden and Denmark? *Scandinavian Political Studies, 34*(4), 332–353.
Larsen, C. A. (2013). *The rise and fall of social cohesion. The construction and de-construction of social trust in the USA, UK, Sweden and Denmark*. Oxford: Oxford University Press.

Mau, S., & Burkhardt, C. (2009). Migration and welfare state solidarity in Western Europe. *Journal of European Social Policy, 19*(3), 213–229.
Mewes, J., & Mau, S. (2012). Unraveling working-class welfare chauvinism. In S. Svallfors (Ed.), *Contested welfare states: Welfare attitudes in Europe and beyond*. Stanford, CA: Stanford University Press.
Mewes, J., & Mau, S. (2013). Globalization, socio-economic status and welfare chauvinism: European perspectives on attitudes toward the exclusion of immigrants. *International Journal of Comparative Sociology, 54*(3), 228–245.
Miller, D. (1993). In defence of nationality. *Journal of Applied Philosophy, 10*(1), 3–16.
Nielsen, M. (2018). Four normative languages of welfare : A pragmatic sociological investigation. *Distinktion : Scandinavian Journal of Social Theory, 7*(3), 1–25.
Reeskens, T., & van Oorschot, W. (2012). Disentangling the "new liberal dilemma": On the relation between general welfare redistribution preferences and welfare chauvinism. *International Journal of Comparative Sociology, 53*(2), 120–139.
Sainsbury, D. (2006). Immigrants' social rights in comparative perspective: Welfare regimes, forms of immigration and immigration policy regimes. *Journal of European Social Policy, 16*(3), 229–244.
Scheve, K. F., & Slaughter, M. J. (2001). Labor market competition and individual preferences over immigration policy. *Review of Economics and Statistics, 83*(1), 133–145.
Schumacher, G., & van Kersbergen, K. (2014). Do mainstream parties adapt to the welfare chauvinism of populist parties? *Party Politics, 22*(3), 300–312.
Taylor-Gooby, P., & Martin, R. (2010). Fairness, equality and legitimacy: A qualitative comparative study of Germany and the UK. *Social Policy & Administration, 44*(1), 85–103.
Van Oorschot, W. (2006). Making the difference in social Europe: Deservingness perceptions among citizens of European welfare states. *Journal of European Socail Policy, 16*(1), 23–42.
van der Waal, J., Achterberg, P., Houtman, D., De Koster, W., & Manevska, K. (2010). 'Some are more equal than others': Economic egalitarianism and welfare chauvinism in the Netherlands. *Journal of European Social Policy, 20*(4), 350–363.
van Der Waal, J., De Koster, W., & van Oorschot, W. (2013). Three worlds of welfare chauvinism? How welfare regimes affect support for distributing welfare to immigrants in Europe. *Journal of Comparative Policy Analysis: Research and Practice, 15*(2), 164–181.

4

Attitudes to Inequalities: Citizen Deliberation About the (Re-)Distribution of Income and Wealth in Four Welfare State Regimes

Jan-Ocko Heuer, Steffen Mau, and Katharina Zimmermann

Introduction

Inequality is back! At least since Thomas Piketty's (2014) bestseller *Capital in the Twenty-First Century*, economic inequalities are back on the political agenda. In many advanced economies, inequalities of income and wealth have increased over the past decades, spurred by and spurring changes in other dimensions of social inequality, such as housing or education (OECD 2008). Economic inequalities have grown in both good and bad economic times, driven primarily by surges in the incomes of high earners, with much lower growth, or even declines, in the incomes of the middle class and especially low earners (OECD 2011). Studies also suggest that increasing inequalities have negative effects on economic growth,

---

J.-O. Heuer (✉) • S. Mau • K. Zimmermann
Humboldt University of Berlin, Berlin, Germany
e-mail: jan-ocko.heuer@hu-berlin.de

financial stability, social cohesion and political participation (Cingano 2014; Erikson 2015; OECD 2015a; Ostry et al. 2014). Hence, for many observers the containment and reversal of rising economic inequalities is one of the most important challenges of our time (Atkinson 2015).

Among the causes of rising inequality are not only technological developments and economic transformations, but also political choices and institutional changes, such as the weakening of collective bargaining and the restructuring of regulatory frameworks, tax systems and welfare states (Atkinson 2015). Accordingly, a return to lower levels of inequality would involve more state intervention in the distribution of income and wealth, which, in turn, would require support from the population—but do citizens want a revival of interventionism and a stronger welfare state?

In this chapter, we examine the attitudes of citizens in four European countries representing distinct regimes of inequality and welfare provision—Denmark, Germany, Slovenia and the United Kingdom—towards the distribution and redistribution of income and wealth. We answer the following questions:

- How do citizens perceive and assess economic inequalities and their development?
- What do they assume to be the causes and consequences of changing inequalities?
- What do they think about government measures that could influence the distribution of income and wealth?

To examine citizens' views on inequalities and their causes, consequences and countermeasures, we use a unique data source: Democratic Forums that brought citizens together to freely and openly discuss the welfare state of the future (see Chap. 1). While this approach cannot offer the representativeness of population surveys, it has two advantages. First, it allows us not only to touch upon people's attitudes but also to delve deeper into their understandings and framings of inequalities. And second, from a comparative perspective, we can obtain hints and clues about how inequality and welfare regimes shape citizens' attitudes towards inequalities and whether there are country-specific perceptions and discourses that extend across social groups and socio-economic strata.

We will first outline the literature on the relations between welfare regimes, economic inequalities and citizens' attitudes towards inequalities and redistribution (section "Linking Inequality and Welfare Regimes to Citizens' Attitudes") and describe levels of income inequality and review public opinion on inequalities as measured by population surveys for the four cases (section "The Cases in Context: Economic Inequalities and Public Opinion"). We then introduce our approach for analysing citizen deliberation about economic inequalities and present our findings (section "Citizen Deliberation About Inequalities in Four Welfare State Regimes"). Finally, we summarise the results and discuss implications for comparative research on welfare regimes and attitudes towards inequalities (section "Comparative Discussion: How Welfare Regimes Shape Inequality Attitudes").

Linking Inequality and Welfare Regimes to Citizens' Attitudes

There is a large quantity of research linking inequality and welfare regimes to citizens' attitudes and mass opinion (Svallfors 2010). One strand takes self-interest as starting point and views attitudes as mainly determined by people's relative position in the distributional order and the way they are beneficially involved in the tax and transfer system. The basic idea is that discontent arises from a relatively skewed income distribution with few people at the top and many at the bottom, as the position of the median voter counts (Curtis and Andersen 2015; Meltzer and Richard 1981). By and large, however, it became clear that self-interest cannot fully grasp people's inequality assessments and their demand for redistribution, and that values and beliefs about distributional justice also play a role (Fong 2001). Thus, another strand of the literature starts from the assumption that welfare regimes embody (different) normative principles and that there is a nexus between these principles and people's attitude patterns (Mau 2003). While attitudes might shape welfare regimes, welfare arrangements might also influence attitudes (Jordan 2013; Kumlin and Stadelmann-Steffen 2014). Using Esping-Andersen's (1990) well-known typology of social democratic, corporatist and liberal regimes, one would expect citizens in Scandinavian countries to exhibit more egalitarian attitudes, citizens in Anglo-Saxon countries to be more accepting of market-generated inequalities, and continental Europeans to prioritise status maintenance over equality and emphasise meritocratic as well as paternalistic principles.

However, empirical studies come to somewhat inconclusive findings. While it has been shown that attitudes towards inequalities and redistribution are affected by the type of welfare regime, this relationship is not straightforward and not very pronounced (Andreß and Heien 2001; Arts and Gelissen 2001; Jæger 2006; Svallfors 1997). Some authors are rather sceptical about welfare regimes as a factor in explaining differences in the demand for redistribution (Schmidt-Catran 2016). Others suggest a focus on how normative principles are applied to different social risks and find that policy designs in specific areas, such as old-age pensions, are linked to redistributive preferences (Reeskens and van Oorschot 2013). Still others argue that perceived fairness in the procedural distribution of social positions goes along with acceptance of inequality (Larsen 2016).

In a longitudinal perspective and against the background of increasing economic inequalities, one would expect that people become more critical of inequality. The median-voter hypothesis suggests that higher market inequality leads the median voter to favour more redistribution, so that democratic elections mitigate rising inequalities (Meltzer and Richard 1981). While longitudinal studies show that demand for redistribution is indeed positively related to levels of inequality (Schmidt-Catran 2016), this relationship is—again—not straightforward. One aspect is that people might have inaccurate perceptions of the level of inequality and its development (Gimpelson and Treisman 2015; Kenworthy and McCall 2008; Niehues 2014). Another is that with rising inequalities people might get used to higher levels of inequality, so that growing inequalities might go together with higher tolerance for inequality (Kerr 2014; Medgyesi 2013). Also, broader societal transformations linked to individualisation and people's stakes in labour and financial markets may have facilitated the willingness to accept higher inequalities than in the past (Mau 2015). Another argument holds that people might become more accepting of inequalities if they assume that their society is moving forward and thus they or their children will have better lives in the future (Larsen 2016).

What complicates matters more is that people's attitudes towards inequality are often ambivalent or even contradictory. For example, a French survey found high levels of inequality rejection and inequality affirmation at the same time, often expressed by the same people (Forsé and Galland 2011). People might also deem inequalities too high, but view income differentials based on differences in skill, training or job responsibility as legitimate (Gijsberts 2002; Kelley and Evans 1993). Pierre Rosanvallon (2013) argued that behind prevalent criticisms of inequalities, there is an implicit 'consent to inequality', resulting in widespread affirmation of market-generated inequalities in practice.

These inconclusive findings point to the need for qualitative cross-country research on people's attitudes towards inequalities. While studies based on survey data can offer a broad picture of inequality perceptions and assessments, they can account only to a limited extent for the complexity and potential ambivalence of attitude patterns as well as for contextual factors that influence how these factors are framed and shape people's answers to a survey questionnaire. Qualitative studies can explore themes, understandings and lines of reasoning (Sachweh 2012). Also, using a comparative framework can show if and how inequality and welfare regimes shape people's attitudes and if similarities in public opinion extend to underlying understandings of inequalities. Democratic Forum research across a range of countries is a promising way to advance research on welfare regimes and inequality attitudes.

The Cases in Context: Economic Inequalities and Public Opinion

This chapter focuses on four cases representing different types of welfare regimes: Denmark, Germany, Slovenia and the United Kingdom (UK). Looking at inequalities, *Denmark* has one of the lowest levels of income inequality in the world, but inequality in this country rose in the past three decades at about the same pace as the OECD average due to increased earnings dispersion, rising capital incomes and changes in household structures (Causa et al. 2016). *Slovenia* closely trails Denmark in the low level of income inequality, due to relatively high levels of government redistribution via taxes and transfers (OECD 2015a). Income inequalities have been rather stable since the country's independence in 1991, and poverty levels have been contained by the introduction of a minimum wage in 1995 (Hrast and Ignjatović 2013). By contrast, the level of income inequality in the *United Kingdom* has been well above the OECD average in the past three decades, and the average income of the richest ten per cent is almost ten times as large as for the poorest, with the lowest ten per cent having recently experienced losses in real incomes. The effects of taxes and benefits on inequalities in disposable incomes are lower than in other European countries, partly as the marginal top income tax rate has been cut and benefit levels have been reduced (OECD 2015b). Finally, *Germany* is located between Denmark and Slovenia on the one hand, and the UK on the other, but it has also experienced increases in income inequality, especially in the early 1990s and early 2000s. Since the early 1990s, the growth in real incomes lags behind GDP growth, and the lower 40 per cent of the income distribution did not experience increases in real incomes (Grabka and Goebel 2017).

If we combine these country characteristics with the arguments and findings outlined in section "Linking Inequality and Welfare Regimes to Citizens' Attitudes", one would expect a higher acceptance of inequalities in the UK than in Germany, Slovenia and Denmark. Given welfare regime theory, Denmark should stand out as the country where people have the strongest 'taste for equality', although the good economic standing of Denmark might also make citizens more accepting of inequalities. Slovenia might still bear the legacy of the past and its moderate path of transformation towards a market economy. Earlier research has found that people in post-socialist countries are more egalitarian than their Western counterparts (Delhey 1999), but there is also a partial alignment of attitude patterns in East and West (Cebulla 2011). Germany should stand in the middle of this rank order, which would fit its self-characterisation as a 'social market economy'.

Yet data from public opinion surveys on citizens' attitudes towards inequalities reveal some of the puzzles and inconsistencies indicated in the section "Linking Inequality and Welfare Regimes to Citizens'

Attitudes to Inequalities: Citizen Deliberation... 99

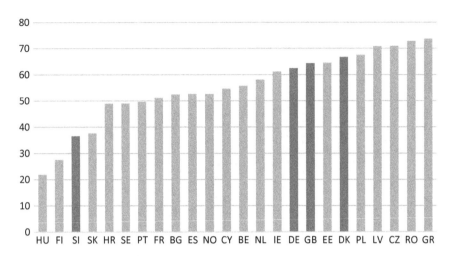

Fig. 4.1 Percentage of people who agree/strongly agree with the statement 'large differences in income are acceptable to reward talents and efforts' (2008, ESS)

Attitudes". We use two variables from the European Social Survey 2008 to measure attitudes towards inequalities. The first asks if large differences in income are acceptable to reward talents and efforts (Fig. 4.1). While the low rate of agreement in Slovenia and the high rates of agreement in Germany and the UK are broadly compatible with theoretical assumptions, it is surprising that the people in Denmark show one of the highest rates of agreement with meritocratic principles.

Figure 4.2 shows the level of agreement to the statement 'for a fair society, income differences in standard of living should be small', which can be understood as a general egalitarian attitude. Again to our surprise, we find in all four country cases relatively low support for egalitarianism, at least compared to other European countries. Especially noteworthy is that Denmark ranks lowest of all countries, with only about 32 per cent of people favouring small income differences.

The interpretation of these findings is not easy. Partly they contradict theoretical assumptions and partly they do not match with observed levels of inequality. For example, although Denmark has the lowest level of income inequality within the OECD world, people seem to be quite posi-

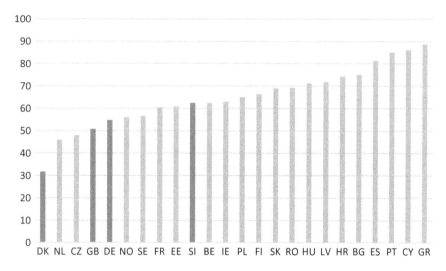

Fig. 4.2 Percentage agreeing/strongly agreeing with the statement 'for a fair society, income differences in standard of living should be small' (2008, ESS)

tive about inequalities and meritocratic principles. This could point to the aforementioned economic optimism and the feeling that differences in income do not derive from unfair and fraudulent advantages. Another explanation might be that survey respondents do not relate to abstract principles but to the inequality they experience, so that reluctance to support egalitarian statements might be caused by the belief that the level of inequality is already low. This would indicate a 'ceiling effect' rather than an anti-egalitarian stance. Survey data are largely silent about people's reasoning and its context, pointing again to the need to explore citizens' attitudes towards inequalities from a qualitative-comparative perspective.

Citizen Deliberation About Inequalities in Four Welfare State Regimes

To explore citizens' understandings of economic inequalities, we use data from Democratic Forums (DFs) conducted as part of the NORFACE WelfSOC-project (see Chap. 1 for details). Based on the literature, a coding scheme with basic questions and categories was developed (see

Table 4.1). This was extended, revised and refined during the coding process and was accompanied by coding notes capturing general observations, differences between breakout groups, degrees of agreement and disagreement, interpretations, and comparative assessments. To expand the range of insights into the DFs and make our interpretations comprehensible, we collected statements in comprehensive tables that are included in Table 4.3 at the end of this chapter. These should be read in conjunction with the following analyses, as they exemplify our empirical basis and illustrate our main findings.

A first result of our analyses is that major differences in understandings and framings of economic inequalities exist between countries. In other words, although within each country there were obviously differences of opinion and disagreements between the DF participants, citizens in each country thought and talked about inequalities in a specific way. They shared understandings and this extended across all three breakout groups, ruling out the possibility that initial framings were producing these commonalities. In this section, we focus on the main perceptions and arguments within each country, starting with Denmark and followed by Germany, Slovenia and the UK. We will provide a cross-country comparison and discussion of the implications in the final section.

Denmark: Support for Rising Income Differentials and Criticism of Progressive Taxation in a Universal Welfare State

DF participants in Denmark expressed a high level of general satisfaction with the welfare state, and some praised it as an institution unique to the Nordic countries or even singled out the Danish welfare model among the Scandinavian ones (see DK-1, Table 4.3). The Danish welfare state was lauded for protecting against numerous social risks, ensuring a decent standard of living for everyone and thus preventing poverty, and fostering economic productivity and growth. Most importantly, the welfare state was described as a community, and some participants thus preferred the term 'welfare society' to capture the notions of comprehensiveness, sense of community and generalised trust. Moreover, people showed a high inclination to discuss general purposes and problems of the welfare state

Table 4.1 Basic coding scheme for analysis of attitudes towards economic inequalities

Main aspect	Questions and possible concepts
How much discussed?	**How much were inequalities discussed in the DF?** (Compared to other topics and given the pre-determination of themes on day 2)
Types of economic inequalities	**What types of economic inequalities were discussed?** Examples: wages, earnings, incomes; wealth; poverty, affluence/luxury; consumption; debt, over-indebtedness
Perceptions, assessments and rationales/justifications	**How were economic inequalities perceived?** Current situation; changes over time; compared to other countries; e.g.: high, low; higher/lower than prior/elsewhere **How were economic inequalities assessed/judged?** Currently; over time; compared to other countries; e.g.: (much) too high, about right, (much) too low **What were rationales/justifications for the judgments?** Examples: High/low inequality is positive/negative because…; Inequality is too high/low because…; economic aspects (e.g. economic growth, productivity), social-political aspects (e.g. poverty, social exclusion), moral/ethical aspects (e.g. values, norms, ideologies)
Causes	**What were presumed causes of economic inequalities and their development?** Macro-level (capitalism, states; e.g. globalisation, deregulation, financialisation, retrenchment, austerity) vs meso/micro-level (behaviour of organisations, companies, households, elites); economic, technological, political, social changes; focus on economic systems, welfare states, labour markets, financial markets etc.
Consequences	**What were presumed consequences of economic inequalities and their development?** Examples: impact on living standards, well-being, health/healthcare, housing, education, labour market participation, old-age pensions, social mobility, social participation (exclusion), social cohesion (conflicts), political participation, economic growth, gender relations, public revenues; impact on economy, society, groups, individuals
Countermeasures	**What were attitudes to measures that could influence economic inequalities?** Examples: state intervention yes/no (with justification); degree of intervention: hard (law/regulation) vs. soft (incentives, campaigns); area of intervention: e.g. taxes (income, wealth, inheritances), education (investments, vouchers), social benefits and services (pre-/redistributive) in various social policy areas

instead of specific social policy fields, which might be due to the universalist nature of the Danish welfare state and its financial foundation in general taxes rather than field-specific social insurance contributions.

Given this willingness to discuss broader themes and given that Denmark has one of the lowest levels of economic inequalities globally (see previous section), it is noteworthy that inequalities and redistribution were not much of a topic in the DF. In all breakout groups, the dominant topics were labour market policies, intergenerational issues, welfare state financing, and immigration, and participants also rarely discussed inequalities regarding these topics. Instead, people often referred to a collective 'we', possibly reflecting the universalist structure of the Danish welfare regime. Thus, economic inequalities were primarily discussed on day two of the DF, when the topic was introduced by the research team as one of the five predetermined topics.

The discussions about economic inequalities were similar to those in the other countries in three respects. First, people focused primarily on inequalities of income (not wealth) and agreed that inequalities had increased in the recent past:

> If we are to be able to have a welfare state in 2040 then income inequality needs to be regulated in one way or another. The insane things that are happening in the US are also happening in Denmark to a lesser extent. In the United States income inequality is constantly increasing. I don't believe in holism and that everyone should earn the same, in order to ensure that there's greater incentive to make money, but regulation is important in order to ensure that we can have a tax basis and to prevent unrest. If only a small percentage have money, then that will create social unrest. (DK-80)

Second, people criticised the high earnings of some occupational groups—such as politicians, managers, bankers or professional footballers—and contrasted these with the low earnings of the 'working poor', although, in contrast to other countries, the emergence of in-work poverty was described as a future threat, not a present reality:

We must just avoid a situation where you have working poor, like in Germany, the US and England. It's not okay to slave away working two to three jobs and still be unable to afford basic things such as education for your children and food to eat. (DK-74)

And third, people highlighted the negative effects of (increasing) inequalities on health, individual opportunities for upward mobility and economic development:

I wouldn't say it's important to balance inequality 100 per cent. But it is important to combat the major inequalities in society. Studies have shown that the more inequality there is in a society, the poorer it becomes. So the more equality there is in a society, the richer the society will be, and that also benefits those who have come here from other countries. (DK-62; see also DK-4 and DK-5, Table 4.3)

However, in line with results from population surveys (see previous section), several citizens also opposed criticisms of rising economic inequalities and supported (high) income differentials. The main justifications were that high incomes and income differentials are necessary to attract top performers and businesses, create incentives for innovation and job creation, and reward talent and effort (see DK-5, DK-6 and DK-7, Table 4.3). While these arguments were put forward in other countries as well, it is remarkable that the Danish DF had probably the highest number of people arguing in support of income inequalities (matched only by the UK, where discussions about inequalities were framed in a completely different way; see section "UK: The Main Divide Is Seen to Lie Between (Hard-)Working People and (Lazy) Welfare Recipients"). How can this support for (rising) inequalities in one of the world's most equal societies be explained?

The DF discussions suggest three answers. First, low levels of economic inequality seem to make people more ready to accept (limited) increases in inequality. In line with this, a DF participant argued that it is easy to support (rising) inequalities in a relatively equal society such as Denmark, indicating that people base their judgments not on absolute inequality levels but on the inequality context they experience (see DK-2, Table 4.3).

This is also suggested by the arguments of several supporters of (rising) inequalities, who stressed that they do not advocate inequality levels as high as in other countries (with the United States used as the main cautionary example by many DF participants; see DK-2, DK-4, DK-5, Table 4.3). However, the Slovenian case shows that low inequality levels do not necessarily lead to acceptance of higher inequalities, so this explanation is not sufficient.

A second answer is that (rising) inequalities seem to be accepted when people believe that they are the result of procedural fairness and meritocratic principles instead of corruption or nepotism (see the contrasting Slovenian case). Thus, both supporters and critics of rising inequalities stressed that they approve of high incomes if these can be ascribed to contribution, innovation, production or value added (see DK-3, DK-5 and DK-7, Table 4.3).

The third answer requires a deeper look at the supporters' line of reasoning. It turns out that rising income inequalities were usually understood in terms of rising incomes among high earners, not as a fall for low earners. Thus, people argued that rising incomes at the top are acceptable if people at the bottom can retain their (decent) standard of living, either via adequate wages or via social benefits and services (see DK-5, DK-6, DK-7, Table 4.3). This means that people understood the distribution of incomes not as a distributional conflict between different social groups (which would imply that rises at the top involve falls at lower levels), but as a dynamic process in which rises at the top are unrelated to developments in the lower-income strata. This line of reasoning is best exemplified by a participant who argues that:

> If we lowered the minimum wage, then yes. Then I would agree that we would be affecting the welfare state. But if we keep the service level—the basic level—the same or increase it, then what's the problem with those who earn more earning even more? It's a moral and ethical discussion, not a welfare problem. (DK-69; see also DK-6, Table 4.3)

Thus people accepted rising incomes at the top by disconnecting them from the overall (re-)distribution of incomes and pointing to a rather high level of (minimum) wages, social benefits and services. This line of reasoning seems to be based on the existence of a universalist welfare state that ensures a decent standard of living for all citizens. In this view, rising inequalities might also signal that the society is moving forward and that in the future all citizens will participate in the economic gains.

While economic inequalities in general were not a prominent topic, in all breakout groups there was a lot of criticism directed at the income and business tax regime. People demanded more transparency, simplicity and fairness, and criticised (excessively) high taxes on (high) incomes and businesses, claiming that this would stifle effort, productivity and innovation and result in capital flight and tax evasion. Thus, in all breakout groups—but especially in the self-employed group—participants proposed replacing the progressive (state) income tax by a proportional 'flat tax', arguing that this would increase productivity, transparency and fairness and result in greater tax compliance. Yet, overall the DF participants remained ambivalent about this idea: in the final voting about policy priorities, there was broad support for a proposal not to tax people 'who create value in society', but also for a proposal to keep the redistributive balance in the tax regime as it is. However, a proposal for more redistribution was rejected, suggesting that the universalist Danish welfare regime has reached its redistributive limits.

Germany: Criticisms of Social Inequalities Abound, but Also Scepticism Towards Government Intervention

In the German DF, social inequalities were a prominent—or even the prevalent—theme. The topic 'inequalities' was not only already chosen by the participants as a topic for discussion on day one, but inequalities were also a regular theme in discussions about other topics and policy fields, such as education, healthcare, old-age pensions, housing or labour markets. In other words, the DF participants exhibited a high sensitivity towards inequalities and often highlighted (perceived) unfairness and injustice. This related not only to the fate of the poor but was a widespread sense of unfair treatment within all social strata—or, as the participants put it (here regarding the income tax regime):

For those who earn very little, they see it as unfair, and for those with a lot of money.... (DE-53)

They also think it's unfair. [Laughter] (DE-44)

Inequalities of income and wealth were an important aspect in these debates. The general impression was that economic inequalities had increased in the past, and many participants argued that inequalities are too high (see DE-1, Table 4.3). Also, especially the incomes of some occupational groups—such as managers, bankers, politicians, public officials or professional sportspersons—were criticised as too high. This was combined with demands for appreciation of necessary but low-paid or unpaid work, such as childrearing, care or traditional crafts, and with debates about how to reward high individual performance. Generally, numerous kinds of wage inequalities were noted, such as inequalities between East and West Germany, men and women, old and young employees, managers and workers, or for public employees between different federal states (see DE-2, Table 4.3). Also, wealth inequalities were more often discussed and criticised than in other countries, possibly reflecting the relatively high level of wealth inequality in Germany.

Economic inequalities were also seen as one cause of inequalities in several social policy areas. People criticised the fact that high earners can buy better education, healthcare or old-age pensions (e.g. DE-3). Yet, financial aspects were seen as only one contributing factor to inequalities in these areas, as people also highlighted that inequalities were produced by labour market policies and the (divided) structure of social insurance schemes, with high-earning individuals or certain professions benefitting from separate health insurance or old-age pension schemes:

For me with the subject of retirement, I think of injustice. For instance, paying into the lawyers' retirement fund, which is unjust, because later I'll get a higher pension than the normal BfA [former German federal pension fund] federal pension, because mine doesn't need to cover unemployment factors and absenteeism, inability to work insurance, etc. There are also the architects, the doctors, etc. They all have their own pension organisations, which are very privileged. The other alternative would be that everyone pays into the federal pension fund. It's similar with regard to the distinctions in health insurance. It would be sensible that everyone pays into one fund. (DE-54; see also DE-4 and DE-5, Table 4.3)

Yet, despite criticism of economic and other inequalities, most DF participants were sceptical about the welfare state's ability or willingness to mitigate inequalities and about the desirability of state intervention and government redistribution. In fact, many participants expressed a preference for a basic level of social security provided by the state (which was usually envisaged as higher than the current level) and the possibility of additional private provision for old-age pensions or healthcare as well as for private schools. The general image conveyed was that of a society torn between (returning to) public protection and (proceeding to) private provision.

This ambivalence about government intervention and redistribution was reflected in the policy priorities proposed and how people voted on them. On the one hand, a policy priority proposing 'lower taxes for lower incomes, higher taxes for higher incomes' received 23 'yes' votes and only 2 'no' votes. On the other, the taxation of wealth—which was especially promoted by a group of well-earning individuals from the self-employed group—was opposed by many DF participants. Opponents argued that wealth taxation would result in capital flight, generate only small revenues and be unfair because wealth had already been taxed as income. Accordingly, a policy priority proposing 'one-time taxation of (high) wealth' received only 2 'yes' and 12 'no' votes.

By contrast, participants favoured less conventional measures of government intervention. One very controversial issue was the introduction of an unconditional basic income to replace the traditional welfare state. This was extensively discussed in the German DF and presented by its proponents (mostly progressive, well-educated and high-earning people from all breakout groups) as a solution for several problems, including not only increasing inequalities but also precarious employment, lack of jobs, low or no pay for socially valuable work, decreasing pension levels, and poverty (see DE-7, Table 4.3). Yet, a policy priority proposing the unconditional basic income to combat poverty and inequalities in old-age remained controversial and received 28 'yes' votes but also a high share of 'no' votes.

More—in fact, unanimous—support came for the idea of using education to combat inequalities. Education was presented as a universal remedy against all kinds of social inequalities (DE-8), and a policy priority demanding 'fair/equal educational opportunities' to combat inequalities received not only the most 'yes' votes of all policy guidelines but also no 'no'-votes; it was thus the most-supported and only consensual policy priority. However, the popularity of the idea of education as a remedy for economic inequalities might be partly because this does not interfere with current economic inequalities and defers the (presumed) decline of inequalities into the distant future.

Slovenia: Perceptions of Income Polarisation and Crony Capitalism Trigger Demand for Redistribution

Despite the relatively low levels of economic inequality in Slovenia (see section "The Cases in Context: Economic Inequalities and Public Opinion"), wage inequalities were a much-discussed and criticised issue in the Slovenian DF. People argued that income differences are high and had increased, and participants assessed this development as negative (see SI-1, Table 4.3). Justifications for this negative assessment of inequalities revolved around the term 'fairness', which often alluded to the notion that income inequalities in a society should be small. In marked contrast, the Slovenian society was described as consisting of—or developing towards—two classes: the wealthy few, and a struggling lower-class majority, with a disappearing middle class (see SI-2, Table 4.3). Participants also expected that the rise of inequalities will continue and expressed doubt that state intervention would be able to change this (see SI-3, Table 4.3). In short, the dominant notion was an ongoing polarisation of incomes between 'the rich and those that don't have anything' (SI-57; see also SI-1, Table 4.3).

The participants highlighted several negative consequences of (increasing) economic inequalities, especially in the areas of education, health/healthcare, elderly care, pensions and living standards in old age:

I'm again concerned about this relationship between the public and the private. Similar as in healthcare. As if the population were divided into two: poor, rich. So the rich people will have private healthcare, private schools, high quality. And the poor ones will be in public schools, public healthcare. (SI-86, see also SI-4, Table 4.3)

Aside from these effects in various social policy areas, it was argued that rising inequalities and poverty undermine social values and lead children to judge people only in terms of their economic value. When determining causes of the (perceived) rise of economic inequalities, participants mainly emphasised two factors. On the one hand, they argued that increasing inequalities and polarisation are defining characteristics of capitalism (see SI-5, Table 4.3). On the other hand, they highlighted opportunity structures for political and economic elites in Slovenian 'crony capitalism' to (ab)use their power for private gain and to divide the national wealth among themselves. In line with this, people often criticised (perceived) high levels of corruption, lack of integrity, and low social trust and depicted the Scandinavian countries as positive examples of more just, equal and transparent societies (see SI-6, Table 4.3).

In general, the perceptions and assessments of economic inequalities among the DF participants were very similar. This is also indicated by the fact that the three breakout groups came up with similar policy priorities to counter increasing inequalities and that in the subsequent voting procedure most priorities received support from almost all participants. The proposed policy priorities were 'classic' measures of redistribution via taxes, labour market regulations, and pension, healthcare and elderly care policies. All three breakout groups considered an increase in the minimum wage to be the most important measure, arguing that this would result in a reduction of poverty, more equality, stronger work incentives, lower welfare spending, more consumption and economic growth, and a larger middle class (see SI-7, Table 4.3). Other priorities were the determination of a maximum ratio of pay differences between the workers and the management of a company (see SI-8, Table 4.3); higher taxes for the wealthy and on high incomes and luxury goods (see SI-9, Table 4.3); tax relief for the middle class by creating a more graduated income tax scheme; and the creation of a basic pension.

In sum, economic—and especially wage and income—inequalities were a much-debated issue in the Slovenian DF, with the participants agreeing that inequalities had risen and are too high, and thus favouring redistribution by the welfare state. What is surprising here is that the actual level of economic inequalities in Slovenia is among the lowest worldwide, and we will come back to this discrepancy between perceptions and statistical measurements in section "Comparative Discussion: How Welfare Regimes Shape Inequality Attitudes".

UK: The Main Divide Is Seen to Lie Between (Hard-) Working People and (Lazy) Welfare Recipients

The debates about economic inequalities in the UK differed from those in the other countries in one fundamental respect. While in other countries inequalities between the better-off ('the rich'), the middle class and the lower classes were at the centre of debates, in the UK the debates revolved around a perceived antagonism between '(hard-)working people' and '(lazy) welfare benefit recipients'. While the stigmatisation of welfare recipients as a result of 'liberal' welfare regimes' targeting of (means-tested) benefits on the poor has been noted before (for example Rothstein 1998), it is still surprising that the topic of economic inequalities triggered these perceptions, and that in all three breakout groups this framing overshadowed all other aspects of economic inequalities. One participant expressed this view quite clearly:

> The divide isn't between the rich and the poor. I think the divide is between the working class and the benefits people. That's where the divide is. (UK-80; see also UK-1, Table 4.3)

Another stated:

> It's literally, as we said earlier, there's going to be a war soon amongst us in this country because [unclear]. I'm going out there working hard and someone is just sitting there, not doing anything, earning more than what I'm earning in my wages, that really gets to me, it really does get to me. (UK-89; see also UK-6, Table 4.3)

To be fair, some statements focused on the whole spectrum of income and wealth inequalities, for instance by arguing that poverty is 'increasing daily I think, from what I see' (UK-n.i.) and that 'the rich [are] getting richer and the poor [are] getting poorer' (UK-n.i.) (both statements from the general discussion before any breakout group interactions in the first plenary on day one), and that 'if you look at the gap [between rich and poor], the gap is huge' (UK-45). Yet, participants often found justifications for the legitimacy of these phenomena and then returned to discussions about the (presumed) privileges of benefit recipients. Also, while inequalities in the labour market were acknowledged and criticised, especially the problem of zero-hour contracts (see Chap. 8), these inequalities seemed to foster aversions against benefit recipients, who were construed as the exact opposite to the 'deserving' working poor. In line with this, many issues were framed not in terms of different social strata, but in terms of a collective 'we' and the benefit-receiving 'other'.

The prevalent reasoning in the UK about economic inequalities was roughly as follows: high inequalities are legitimate, because they are the result of voluntary contractual agreements and individual effort and performance (see UK-2 and UK-3, Table 4.3). The causes of inequalities are (lack of) access to education, but also different parenting styles, implying poor parenting in the lower classes (see UK-4, Table 4.3). On the other hand, the rich have legitimately earned their fortune and should thus either not pay higher taxes or even pay lower taxes. The main injustice is that below a certain financial threshold people receive many allowances from the government, so that they ultimately have more than working people (see UK-6, Table 4.3); welfare recipients also exploit their privileges by bearing more and more children and teaching them to live off benefits (see UK-5 and UK-8, Table 4.3). Yet, most people can work and contribute to society, and thus people should not receive benefits if they do not contribute (see UK-7 and UK-8, Table 4.3). In some cases, people explicitly noted that their images of welfare recipients were based on depictions in the media, particularly the press (see UK-5, Table 4.3).

This line of reasoning also resulted in some policy priorities that differed markedly from the ones in other countries, as they focused on support for working people at the expense of benefit recipients. One such priority was to reform the amount and taxation of welfare benefits (see UK-9 and UK-10, Table 4.3): the group argued that there should be a difference between the level of welfare benefits and the minimum wage to reward employment, but that raising the minimum wage would put a strain on businesses; thus, they developed the policy priority that welfare benefits should be cut and the money go to businesses to pay higher wages. In addition, they decided to put a tax on welfare benefits—purportedly all for the sake of reducing inequalities.

In short, the issue of economic inequalities was framed mainly in terms of an antagonism between the working class and welfare recipients, which also led to presumptions about the causes and consequences of inequalities that differed from those found in other countries and resulted in policy priorities designed to increase the income gap between working and non-working people by reducing welfare benefits.

Comparative Discussion: How Welfare Regimes Shape Inequality Attitudes

From a comparative perspective, the perceptions and assessments of economic inequalities in the four countries under study were in a few respects relatively similar. Most importantly, in all countries there was agreement that inequalities had increased in the past, and many participants saw them as too high. However, our analyses of the main arguments have also shown that behind these few commonalities were many differences in understandings and framings of economic inequalities and their causes, consequences and countermeasures. Table 4.2 summarises our findings by mirroring the main categories of the initial coding scheme in Table 4.1.

In this section, we discuss how these understandings of economic inequalities relate to inequality and welfare regimes. However, we want to stress that the following ideas and implications cannot be strictly deduced from our findings, as our analyses can only offer some general insights into inequality assessments within the countries. It is not possible with the data available to isolate specific explanatory factors or to generalise to the level of welfare state regimes. The main aim of this section is to provide some comparative assessments and generate ideas and hypotheses for further research.

Table 4.2 Comparison of attitudes towards economic inequalities in four welfare state regimes

	Denmark	Germany	Slovenia	UK
Welfare regime	Social democratic	Conservative	Post-socialist	Liberal
Level of income inequality	Relatively low, increasing	Average, increasing	Relatively low, increasing	Relatively high, increasing
Overall theme	Acceptance of (limited) rises in top incomes (if these are effort-based), as the welfare state safeguards the bottom	Widespread notions of unfairness and injustice, but also scepticism towards state intervention and redistribution	Criticism of crony capitalism and income polarisation and demands for state intervention and redistribution	Seeing 'the real divide' between working people and benefit recipients, leading to demands for welfare cuts
Focus on type(s) of inequality	Wages/incomes: rises at the top acceptable if decent level at the bottom	Wages/incomes: many inequalities; also, criticism of wealth inequalities	Wages/incomes: wage differentials; prevalence of low wages	Wages/incomes: (low) wages versus welfare benefits
Perception	Low inequalities; have increased	High inequalities; have increased	High inequalities; have increased, will further increase	Small differences between wages and benefits
Assessment	Not too high; rises in top incomes are acceptable	Too high; 'unfair'; countermeasures controversial	Too high; 'unfair'; countermeasures will be ineffective	Benefit recipients get more than working people
Rationales/justifications	Inequalities can be fair and harmless	Produce unequal opportunities in life	More equal wages required	Work should pay off

	Causes	Consequences	Countermeasures	Degree of (dis-)agreement
	Meritocratic principles, contributions, innovation, productivity, value added, etc.	Negative effects on health/healthcare, educational opportunities, economic growth	Preservation of high level of (minimum) wages, social benefits and services	Disagreement if causes apply
	Education; divisions created by labour market policies and social insurance schemes	Negative effects on health/healthcare, educational opportunities, old-age pensions, labour market participation, housing	Educational opportunities; controversial: unconditional basic income, taxes	Disagreement about main inequalities
	Capitalism creates inequalities; political and economic elites taking advantage	Negative effects on health/healthcare, access to education, pensions; negative effects on social bonds and values	'Classic' state intervention: taxes, social policies	Very high agreement
	Differences in (access to) education; bad parenting by welfare recipients	Negative effects on access to education	Reductions in welfare benefits; taxes on benefits	Some disagreement

The most distinct case in our sample was the United Kingdom, as citizens framed inequalities not in terms of rich versus poor people or different social classes, but in terms of (hard-)working people versus (lazy) welfare benefit recipients. This confirms the finding of comparative welfare state research that the targeting of means-tested benefits towards the poor in 'residual' liberal welfare states contributes to a stigmatisation of welfare recipients (Rothstein 1998). Yet, it is surprising that even after a decades-long dismantling of the welfare state in the UK, benefit recipients were still at the centre of critique of the DF participants—unless one assumes that the dismantling of the welfare state promotes exactly these attitudes. The lack of discussions about high and rising levels of economic inequality in the UK suggests that after four decades of neo-liberal policies people have got used to high inequalities and tolerate them. Also in line with neo-liberal tenets, the DF participants saw individuals and families as mainly responsible themselves for their social position and ascribed a low social standing at least partly to bad parenting (see also Chap. 2). Overall, the UK case contradicts the strand of welfare attitude research that focuses on economic self-interest and argues that high and rising inequalities would lead the median voter to support more redistribution. By contrast, high and rising inequalities in the current economic and political context seem to have a self-perpetuating character resulting in more positive views of inequality and of the rich, and more negative views of those left behind. Hence, there are no signs that a reversal of rising inequalities in the UK is likely.

Denmark and Slovenia exhibited similarly low levels of economic inequalities, but differing—or even contrasting—perceptions and assessments of inequality and government redistribution. In Denmark, a high proportion of DF participants was accepting of (higher) income differentials, which is broadly in line with the results of population surveys. The discussions in the DF point to three possible explanations: first, the debates in Denmark seem to confirm the argument that people referred in their inequality assessments not to global differences or absolute levels of inequalities but to the inequality context they experienced, as even proponents of greater inequality stressed that they do not necessarily advocate high levels of inequality. Second, people were ready to accept inequalities when they had the impression that these were based on individual effort and contributed to economic development; by contrast, they criticised inequalities when they believed that these were not reflecting individual performance or were of little value for society. This relates to, and extends, arguments emphasising the importance of procedural fairness and meritocratic principles for acceptance of inequalities (Larsen 2016). A third factor seems to be that people did not think that rises in top incomes might have a negative impact on those at the bottom, as the welfare state ensures a decent standard of living for all.

In sum, the existence of a universalist welfare state seems to be a precondition for the acceptance for rising inequalities in Denmark, as it creates the conditions that people referred to: it conveys a sense of fairness and thus provides legitimacy for higher incomes; due to its redistributive impact, it makes sure that inequality levels are limited; and it offers a high general standard of living, thus eliminating concerns about poverty. It is also noteworthy that both the residual British and the universalist Danish welfare state seem to be conducive to acceptance of inequalities, although via different mechanisms and to different degrees.

By contrast, Slovenia exhibits levels of income inequality similar to those in Denmark, but fundamentally different perceptions and assessments. The DF participants criticised a (perceived) polarisation of incomes between the wealthy few and a growing lower class, with the middle class disappearing. Preferences for low inequality levels and the (mis-)perception of high levels of inequalities led participants to favour several measures of government intervention and redistribution, including a higher minimum wage, a maximum pay ratio, and higher taxes for the wealthy and on luxury items. The explanation for these perceptions and preferences might be partly based in the considerations advanced for the Danish case—but now for a case in which the universalist welfare state is absent and overall standards of living are lower. In other words, people might have been critical of inequalities because they had the impression that these were not the result of procedural fairness and meritocratic principles, but of 'crony capitalism', corruption and nepotism. Moreover, people might not have had the impression that their society is moving forward and that rises in top incomes might ultimately benefit all citizens, but that a political and economic elite is keeping the welfare gains. Another important factor seems to be the historical legacy and the transformation from socialism to capitalism in Slovenia. This might explain that economic inequalities were interpreted in terms of labour exploitation, societal polarisation, and alliances between economic and political elites at the expense of the rest of the population.

While the attitudes towards economic inequalities in these three countries pointed in a specific direction, the German case is more opaque. On the one hand, there was a widespread sense among DF participants of inequalities and unfair treatment in various social areas, generated by economic inequalities and by divisions in the labour market and the welfare state. On the other hand, there was considerable scepticism about the positive effects or even desirability of government redistribution, with people expressing preferences for less conventional measures to combat inequalities, such as investments in education or an unconditional basic income. Two developments might have contributed to these ambivalent attitudes: the partial departure from the principle of status maintenance in the German welfare state, and the partial turn from state support to private provision in healthcare and old-age pensions. In combination with the inequalities produced by the German labour market and welfare state, these new inequalities and insecurities seem to have created a general sense of unfairness and injustice that extends far into the middle class (see also Heuer and Mau 2017).

Two main conclusions for research on welfare regimes and attitudes towards inequalities can be drawn from this study. First, despite all disagreements, citizens in a country seem to share certain lines of reasoning about and framings of inequalities. And second, these understandings seem to be shaped by both institutional legacies of the past and recent social policy changes—possibly by a combination of these two, as short-term changes were often assessed in the light of long-term paths and legacies. These conclusions point to the need for further exploration of citizens' attitudes towards and framings of inequalities via qualitative methods within comparative settings.

Table 4.3 Quotations used in this chapter

Attitudes towards economic inequalities in Denmark

DK-1 **The (Danish) welfare state as great achievement and modern version of the community:** [Pl1] **82**: Well, we talked about the welfare state on a theoretical level—it's so beautiful, it almost brings tears to your eyes. It is there for you if you fail, or if something happens in your life, and naturally we pay for that through tax. [...] **59**: It's an institution that is unique to the Nordic countries, and we agreed that we would like to support it going forward. [...] **65**: We talked a lot about the welfare state as a community where everyone contributes. It's not just about who gets something and who the weak ones are or how much they should get, but about a community. A community, both in terms of tax for road maintenance and libraries and in terms of looking after sick people and all sorts of things that make it all work.—[Pl2] **69**: We agreed that the structure of our current social safety net is sound. No one in our group expressed a wish to change it in any radical way. We can all identify elements which could be better and which obviously aren't functioning optimally today. I think we could all identify an area where we would like to see improved quality or transparency, but fundamentally we think that the system that we have today is working.—[Se2] **67**: It's proven to be the best system in the world. [...] I struggle to imagine a better society than the Danish. The Swedes are destroying theirs and the Norwegians have always been skewed. Denmark is one of the world's best countries to live in and we must keep it that way. That's why we should only make small adjustments to our model.

DK-2 **The level of inequalities is low, but it has increased and might further increase:** [Ue1] **68**: [Participant 57] said that it doesn't matter how much inequality there is, that it's perfectly fine. That's where I reacted strongly and said that of course it matters. It's easy for us to say that here in Denmark where the level of inequality is very minor. An associate high school lecturer gets DKK 45,000 per year and the lowest-paid teacher maybe 25,000. That's a very small pay gap globally speaking.—[Se2] **80**: If we are to be able to have a welfare state in 2040 then income inequality needs to be regulated in one way or another. The insane things that are happening in the US are also happening in Denmark to a lesser extent. In the United States income inequality is constantly increasing. I don't believe in holism and that everyone should earn the same, in order to ensure that there's greater incentive to make money, but regulation is important in order to ensure that we can have a tax basis and to prevent unrest. If only a small percentage have money, then that will create social unrest.

DK-3 **There are considerable income differentials among occupational groups and sectors:** [Min2] **69**: The area where I see the greatest economic inequality, and I know we'll deal with gender later, but the fact that we value our workforce so differently, depending on whether you're employed in the public health care sector or in the world of finance. I think they do what they can, a lot of hard work, but the pay is different.—[Se2] **74**: We must just avoid a situation where you have working poor, like in Germany, the US and England. It's not okay to slave away working two to three jobs and still be unable to afford basic things such as education for your children and food to eat.

(continued)

Table 4.3 (continued)

DK-4	**(Rising) inequalities have negative effects on health, social mobility and economic growth:** [Se1] **56**: Fundamentally there is inequality in terms of health. Rich people are healthier. When your working conditions are poor you don't have the same ability to save up and pay for extra medication etc. […] **61**: My worst-case-scenario is the US model, where only the privileged can afford insurance. That requires you have a job, and the beauty of our welfare state is that it's not a question of what you earn.—[Se1] **65**: […] I think everyone should have the same opportunities. You need to be able to go to university even if your parents aren't academics. I think it's important that we, as a society, take responsibility to make sure that children can achieve to the best of their ability. I think it's a shame that a lot of talent is lost.
DK-5	**(Rising) inequalities are acceptable if they are based on production, value added etc.:** [Ue2] **62**: I wouldn't say it's important to balance inequality 100 per cent. But it is important to combat the major inequalities in society. Studies have shown that the more inequality there is in a society, the poorer it becomes. So the more equality there is in a society, the richer the society will be, and that also benefits those who have come here from other countries. **57**: I don't agree that inequality is a problem. It's only a problem if the poor get poorer. The richer can get richer, that's not a problem. […] **68**: It becomes a problem if the inequality becomes too great because the poor get poorer! There's less distribution and the rich can decide everything in society; we see that happening in the US. There should be allowed to be some inequality, if it's based on production and value. Where it's gone completely off the rails is salaries. Back in the 1970s in the United States, the richest earned 10–20 times as much as the poorest and now they earn 76 times as much. And on top of that they make completely absurd amounts off financial capital, based solely on speculation. None of the major companies pay taxes. Differences should be allowed to exist in terms of production so those who contribute more are rewarded more. In the US, the rich don't contribute to society.
DK-6	**Rises in high incomes are acceptable if there is a basic level of wages, social benefits and services:** [Min2] **60**: Inequality is usually seen as something negative, but there needs to be a certain degree of inequality. **69**: We agree on that. I just don't see any contradiction between economic inequality and the welfare state. If we lowered the minimum wage, then yes. Then I would agree that we would be affecting the welfare state. But if we keep the service level—the basic level—the same or increase it, then what's the problem with those who earn more earning even more? It's a moral and ethical discussion, not a welfare problem.—[Se2] **67**: […] I believe that there needs to be inequality. There needs to be an incentive to make us all want to contribute more financially. And people mustn't be punished through excessive taxation. It needs to be the same as today; we have the top tax rate which dampens the max. I'm a big believer in that. Equally, I would like to elevate the bottom level so that people on the bottom can have a decent standard of living. The fact that there are multi-billionaires doesn't much matter. Our income distribution ensures that the weakest have a decent standard of living and those at the top shouldn't feel compelled to move their money.

DK-7	**The rich and businesses should not pay (too) high taxes:** [Se2] **74**: [...] We mustn't hinder or take from successful or income-generating people simply to reduce the relative inequality. As long as everyone's basic needs, such as health and education, are safeguarded then I don't have a problem with people not being able to go to the Bahamas. [...] **71**: I agree with participant 74. Those who come up with good ideas such as Skype shouldn't be hindered by high taxes. Those in the bottom just need to have a decent living standard. Everyone should have something to eat and a place to live. You can get by without working your ass off, and quietly and calmly save up for a car or a trip. Years ago a president from the Danish Confederation of Trade Unions said that we have prevailed by having a good labour market. Everyone's basic needs are met so there's nothing left to fight for, and that's maybe where we're at now.—[Min2] **69**: Maybe we're shooting ourselves in the foot here, because last time we talked about how we wanted a more transparent tax system. One thing we've focused on a lot in Denmark is creating a system which ensures redistribution. Maybe we've gone too far, it has become too complicated. If we made it easier for the richest, would that create more jobs?—[Min2] **60**: What's the objective? That inequality mustn't be allowed to increase? I don't necessarily think it's a problem that it increases. What's the inequality level now? Is it acceptable or too high or low? I don't think there should be massive inequality, but on the other hand, if you increase the tax on the rich, the result will be that they move to another country.
DK-8	**Policy priority: replacement of progressive by proportional income tax:** [Pl2] **68**: I would like to specify things bit. All the groups talked about the issue of progressive and proportional taxation as two opposing systems. I would like to say briefly how much easier it would be if it was proportional. You can create a tax-free allowance which makes up to 100,000 tax-exempt. That would benefit low-income earners the most and then the rest, that is to say above that, is taxed at 50 per cent and then all those marginal tax rates and expense claims are gone. Then it's very easy to grasp; we give 50 per cent, meaning that the richest are going to contribute a lot more in terms of money, but not as a percentage. A very simple system and fair in principle. To the left this is tantamount to slaughtering a sacred cow, but it's high time to do so. I'm left-leaning myself, but it makes sense to slaughter it for the sake of having a clear and simple as well as a fair system.

Attitudes towards economic inequalities in Germany

DE-1	**Economic inequalities are (too) high:** [Se1] **27**: If you think about the obligation of the government and how some people are earning 9.50 euros per hour if they're lucky and others earn 10 million, then you have to think about taxing that higher to 50 per cent or something, because what do they need the other 5 million for? The state should change things like that. Also wealth tax for instance. There are people who don't work at all but simply live off their interest or off their wealth, and they don't do anything to earn it. They may have just inherited it. There needs to be a change there too in my personal opinion.

(continued)

Table 4.3 (continued)

DE-2	**Numerous kinds of wage inequalities:** [Se1] **M**: What else about the point of wage inequality? That was mentioned early on. **20**: I mentioned it, because I've had experience with East/West inequality. Not so much men versus women, but in general. In the East, wages are lower than in the West. **M**: What do the rest of you feel with regard to wage inequality? **29**: For instance, emigration of qualified personnel, teachers for instance, or doctors who want to leave their federal state to go live in other federal states, because the conditions are better there, or the fact that small towns are dying out, because the young people leave to find jobs in other places. **24**: When I think of Winterkorn, the VW manager who stepped down, who earned 16 or 17 million in one year—that is completely out of proportion with the workers who are employed there in the company and manufacture the cars. Those differences have grown from three or four times to over thirty times the amount. This differential gap has gotten too large. **20**: It's the case in some companies where you have older people with many years of experience and really know what they're doing, and they've worked there for twenty years, and then new young people come in fresh out of university or whatever, and this new person gets twice as much money, because he's new so to say. **17**: Then you can talk about gender in this discussion as well, because there are still too few women in certain job positions, even though more girls than boys are taking the 'Abitur' test [matriculation exam] and there are more women than men at university. How can that be?
DE-3	**Inequalities in education:** [Se1] **17**: There is no equality with regard to education opportunities. It depends on what family background you come from. […] **27**: It depends on what you're born into. If it's a wealthy family, then the children will have much better chances than those who have to fight for everything and who have little time to help support the children's learning themselves.—[Ue1] **M**: Education and school. We said that has to do with inequality—how does that relate? **14**: That depends on where you grow up, in which area and what schooling and education you receive. **M**: Do you have experience with that in your daily life? **14**: Yes, I come from Berlin-Wedding myself, and there the schools have a very high percentage of foreign students, so the standard is relatively low, because they can't all really speak German, and so they can't start as early with reading and writing, because the basic skills are not yet in place. Or maybe they don't have good behavioral examples with regard to social life. So you have to teach them that in the first grade on. **M**: How do the rest of you see that with regard to inequality in education? **53**: Then we come to the question systems, public schools and private schools, and there too there is a differentiation. **31**: There are two of income, because this difference you've mentioned is based on income. If I want to send my child to a private school, then I have to earn enough money to pay for this, and that is unevenly distributed.

Attitudes to Inequalities: Citizen Deliberation... 123

DE-4 **Inequalities in old-age pension schemes:** [Se1] **34:** Injustice, because the younger people pay in, but they'll only get a small percentage of what we're getting in pension payouts.—[Se1] **24:** For me with the subject of retirement, I think of injustice. For instance, paying into the lawyers' retirement fund, which is unjust, because later I'll get a higher pension than the normal BfA [*former German federal pension fund*] federal pension, because mine doesn't need to cover unemployment factors and absenteeism, inability to work insurance, etc. There are also the architects, the doctors, etc. They all have their own pension organizations, which are very privileged. The other alternative would be that everyone pays into the federal pension fund. It's similar with regard to the distinctions in health insurance. It would be sensible that everyone pays into one fund.

DE-5 **Inequalities in healthcare:** [M1] **M:** The next [topic] we talk about is health. What comes to mind with that? [...] **21:** Premiums. **32:** And two-class medicine. **51:** That's right. **M:** [...] What is the problem there? **21:** The difference between private and state-insured. **06:** You have two different rooms at the same doctor's office, one for private patients which is empty, and one for state-insured. **03:** They ask what kind of insurance you have, and that determines the attention you get. **26:** Right, come tomorrow, I'll have time. **06:** My husband is a public official, and he's privately insured, so when he calls somewhere, he gets an appointment right away, and when I call the same doctor, I have to wait four or five weeks. Even though the politicians say there's no difference. Our children are also privately insured. **21:** They pay more. It's logical.

DE-6 **Policy priority: wealth tax:** [Pl2] **31:** In the green group, we talked about how a kind of wealth tax for wealthy citizens could be created. [laughter] **M:** Is that a possibility? Who would be against that idea, and why? **21:** There is already a graduated tax scheme. You can't drive these people out of the country that way. Many are already leaving. **28:** I'm of the same opinion. There are already maximum tax rates, and would taking a bit more from the super-rich really bring us what we need? I don't think that that would help. [...] **M:** Who is for wealth taxation? **22:** What I want to mention is that we should differentiate between income where there is a top tax rate, and wealth. With regard to wealth, there is a difference where there is an inequality which has in the past few years become even more pronounced, and therefore I think it's completely legitimate to at least mention the option of distributing some of this cream off the top so to say. Just saying there is a top tax rate, that is not enough in my view. **24:** I think that's good. I also think there should be a wealth tax with a limit of one million, that is justifiable in order to use these so-called strong shoulders to help bear the costs that we all have to share, because through redistribution and taxation it's easier to maintain certain social programs and realities, and at least leave them in place. I think that people who have a million in income or wealth, they would not notice this. It would only be a limit of 10 per cent from one million. That is not very much. But as he said, the wealth gap is getting larger and larger. The number of billionaires has gone through the roof, and there are more and more millionaires in Germany, and they should do their part to make sure that the schools and streets are maintained here.

(*continued*)

Table 4.3 (continued)

DE-7	**Policy priority: unconditional basic income:** [Se1] **31**: It's like what you were saying with the difference between rich and poor. This would still exist, because some people would have no urge to work and would say the 1000 euros is enough for me, and someone else is a machine and works like crazy and gets much more money than everyone else. **34**: That's OK. **24**: Yes. **31**: But wait, we're talking here about the divide between rich and poor that is always becoming bigger. But now that we have [an unconditional] basic income, the divide between rich and poor is OK? **27**: Well, because no one is poor anymore. **34**: We've taken the steam out of the boiler.—[Se2] **04**: I have a problem with these drawers we keep opening and closing so to say. We had these topics that were announced and as one of the subordinate points was this unconditional basic income that we discussed. If we were to take that as a main topic, then many of these other topics would be obsolete and would no longer play a role. We would no longer have any at-risk people, because those issues would simply be solved. Then we have all these issues of limited and part-time work, atypical workers, etc. But none of that would be important if we had this basic income.
DE-8	**Policy priority: educational opportunities:** [Pl2] **24**: We had educational opportunities. We had a good group for that, because we have a lot of children at school ages, and we came to the point that educational chances also have to do with the parents' income. It starts with tutoring and so forth, private school, public school for those who can't afford to send their children to a private school, and who has to go to public school, whose conditions are always lesser. Then seeing this as a fundamental state responsibility, because the state depends less on raw materials and more on the raw materials in people's minds, and therefore education chances for children are absolutely necessary, and they must be financed. They can really only be financed via taxes, and then we came to the point that, if it's necessary to raise taxes, we crossed the bridge to wealth tax and the advantage of taxes, and where we are to set our priorities.—[Pl4] **16**: Above all, I think it's very important that children are independent from their parents' financial circumstances and all get the same education, regardless of whether one earns more or less, and we can't deal with everyone, but you try as a teacher to help and support every child. I think that's very important.

Attitudes towards economic inequalities in Slovenia

SI-1	**Economic inequalities have been increasing and are (too) high:**	[PI1] **57**: The wage system. **M**: I see. In what sense? **57**: That the wages will be more fair, that there won't be such differences between the rich and those that don't have anything.—[PI1] **56**: There's enough money, it's just not distributed correctly. Stolen. Let them bring back what they've taken out and we'll all live like in Switzerland, I guarantee.—[PI1] **81**: I'd like to really suggest something important and that's that at that time, in that many years, right, really fairness, so that this mass of wages would be fairly distributed according to a ratio, the ratio of wages is minimal and fairly high, there's nothing in between, you know, like it used to be, when we were all satisfied with our wages.—[Se1] **81**: That's why in these companies ... we are talking about the economy, right? Basically, we, the older generation, this was unknown to us, we just knew that the ratio was 1:3, I knew exactly how much the manager, my boss, earned, that was public, a 1:3 ratio. **88**: 1:5, rather. **81**: Yeah, OK, even if it was 1:5, but I want to say ... **82**: Now it can be 1:100 ... **81**: Basically, at the time, I felt as a member of that team and we were fighting to be successful, because we knew that the differences in wages were not such, everyone contributed something to our work and that's why the achievements were visible. That's why it's important for this wage ratio to be transparent.—[Ue2] **55**: Well, I guess there will always be inequality, nothing more to say. But it is true, that it is getting increasingly bigger, increasingly bigger.
SI-2	**Some people are extremely wealthy and live in abundance, while the lower class is expanding and the middle class is vanishing:**	[PI1] **58**: Luxury tax [as a topic for discussion], some have so many things, and the state doesn't benefit from it at all.—[Min2] **72**: A handful of the richest are holding up above the water, while the poorer classes, the lowest class is expanding.—[Ue2] **60**: Just one thing. I have heard about it here, and in general there has been talk about this recently, that the middle class is really struggling. While it is actually the very middle class that is the most crucial. Because it's the most numerous, two it spends the most ... **56**: Yes, because it is the most numerous. **55**: It is the most numerous. **60**: Yes. One, it is the most numerous, it's only the lower class that will remain, which can barely make ends meet, which cannot afford anything apart from the very basic things. Then on the other hand, the luxury class, which, as it is (points hand high in the air), right. **51**: Today there is no, we have the lower class that will vanish soon. **50**: And now, if it gets too pressured, it's only the lower class that will remain, which can barely make ends meet, which cannot afford anything apart from the very basic things. Then on the other hand, the luxury class, which, as it is (points hand high in the air), right. **51**: Today there is no, we have the lower class that will vanish soon. **50**: It will soon vanish. Yes, it will vanish soon. **50**: And now, if it gets too pressured, it's only the lower class that will remain, which can barely make ends meet, which cannot afford anything apart from the very basic things. Then on the other hand, the luxury class, which, as it is (points hand high in the air), right. **51**: Today there is no, as people say these days, you either have something or nothing, right. That is all that is left. **60**: I would, well, yes. We're not there yet, but the middle class is vanishing.

(continued)

Table 4.3 (continued)

SI-3	**Further increases in inequalities are expected in the future and political measures will probably not change this:** [Se1] **M**: What can happen to us in the future, I mean long term consequences…? **78**: Even bigger differences. **88**: Low and high class. But that's already happening anyway. **M**: What would need to be done for this not to happen? **82**: We would have to curb this differentiation as much as possible, focus our powers as much as possible for everything that's public to retain its quality.—[Ue2] **M**: Which priority tasks, priority duties, urgent measures are we going to highlight on the subject of the last topic, income inequality, in order for our country to go in the right direction in 25 years' time? **56**: It won't. [laughter] **53**: We're so pessimistic. **56**: Well, that's how it is.
SI-4	**Negative effects of inequalities on healthcare, education, living standards in old-age, elderly care:** [Se1] **86**: So, someone who can afford to go to private practice will receive a higher quality of service than someone who can't afford that. And I see this here as quite a problem.—[Se1] **86**: I'm again concerned about this relationship between the public and the private. Similar as in healthcare. As if the population were divided into two: poor, rich. So the rich people will have private healthcare, private schools, high quality. And the poor ones will be in public schools, public healthcare.—[Se1] **82**: Private schools are an issue. Because there money practically enables you to pass the exams, to get your hands on a degree easily. Private schools should be more closely controlled. I know parents with money who enroll their child into a private school and the child has practically bought that education. I'm talking of higher education also, not just high school.—[Se1] **88**: There'll be more and more of us [pensioners]. **77**: And they're more and more ill. **81**: And more and more poor. **M**: I see. Why is that the biggest problem, that they're more and more poor? **81**: Low pensions. **84**: Because the wages are low, and consequently the pensions are low as well. **88**: And illness goes hand in hand with poverty, I suppose.—[Se1] **83**: Because at the moment, assisted living apartment are for those with means. **78**: Those that can afford them.—[Min1] **72**: They have calculated that my pension would amount to 618 euros, and I don't dare apply for any elderly homes, because I could hardly afford any care services there. **67**: You simply cannot afford to go to the home for the elderly. **72**: Thank you for comforting me. **69**: Perhaps to have a bed in a sort of a dorm room.

SI-5	**Capitalism increases inequality, and capitalism and inequality negatively affect social values:** [Se1] **81**: Capitalism is stealing money from the weak. It's just the few on top who live well, the great majority of people—the middle class is out of the game, it fell dramatically, disappeared, and that's the thing, this higher class needs to … **88**: But the point of capitalism is to have as many as possible working for minimum wage, that's the point.—[Se1] **77**: I think that we shouldn't just let this capitalist selfishness to expand indefinitely and destroy everything that can be destroyed, but that we need to go back a bit to those socialist, positive, human values; capitalism has … it encourages that work ethic, but perhaps we could take that from capitalism and everything else from socialism, these relationships somehow, so that you help. (…) **86**: Also at home, if the child sees at home that the family barely manages and that the parents say, damn, how are we going to pay for that, and the taxes, and we'll do this and push this scholarship through somehow, then it's difficult for a child to have certain values.—[Ue1] **62**: All in all, the thing is that the privileged few who profit on the shoulders of others should be stopped, the big bosses, you know. Nowadays workers in the production sector are no longer seen as part of the company's staff and collective, but as a cost, and such thinking should be stopped. One has to work on values, human values and not the value of profit.
SI-6	**In Slovenian capitalism, the elites are (ab-)using their power for their own benefit:** [Min2] **72**: Our capitalism is still being shaped and our current capitalists are only interested in making quick profits. Western capitalists, however, know very well that if they lose a good employee, they lose a lot. Yes. They have a tradition and things are done quite differently there. **65**: Yes. And they also give adequate pay to good workers…, unlike in our country.—[Pl2] **83**: I'd like to know, how many people step down voluntarily, without being convicted of anything? We have that issue here, while abroad, regardless if it's the German president, where there was just the suspicion of doubt, they want to step down. Just because of suspicion. They step down just because of suspicion, while in Slovenia, we hide behind legislation and say, until you've been convicted by final judgement, and even then. Well, that's a different story.
SI-7	**Policy priority: raising minimum wage:** [Se2] **88**: Raising the minimum wage. Because if the minimum wage were to be raised, the other wages would need to be raised as well, and probably as a consequence, not everyone would be in the lowest pay grades, as it says here.—[Min2] **69**: Raising the minimum wage. **72**: And make it threefold. [laughter]—[Ue2] M: Any other specific, any specific priorities? **57**: Raising the minimum wage. M: Raising the minimum wage. **55**: [Ue2] M: Any other specific, any specific priorities? **57**: Raising the minimum wage. M: Raising the minimum wage. **55**: Oh my, look at how social we are.—[Ue2] M: Any other measure for the state? **58**: Yes, definitely, in order to balance income inequality, as we have already mentioned, raise of the minimum wage. **62**: Yes, it belongs to this topic, of course. **50**: Yes, right. **51**: Yes, right, the minimum wage plus the costs of transport to work, the lunch and so on.

(continued)

Table 4.3 (continued)

SI-8	**Policy priority: setting maximum pay ratios between managers and workers:** [Ue2] **58**: Also on the subject of inequality, in a, in a company. Certain proportions need to be established. The director cannot have a huge pay check, if the workers in the same company are receiving minimum wage. More just ratios should be established, because today they are collapsing completely. The director earns 15,000 euros, while the worker earns 500 euros. This just should not be. **62**: That's exactly right. **M**: If we are more specific, what sort of ratios could still be acceptable? **57**: Maximum one to three, one to three. **56**: One to one hundred. **55**: One–ten, I think that for a while it was one–ten, one–ten. I think it is one–ten. **60**: One–ten, yes. **58**: One–ten. Then if this was the case, then nobody would be forced to stuff the pockets and the workers would still be earning more.
SI-9	**Policy priority: higher taxes for the wealthy and on high incomes and luxury goods:** [Se2] **83**: Taxation of the wealthy. Higher taxes for the wealthy.—[Min2] **65**: I think that those who have very high pay checks should perhaps be taxed a little more, as well as luxury items, luxury in general. **M**: You mean taxation of higher pay checks. **67**: That's the thing.—[Ue2] **55**: Taxation of luxury. **51**: Yes, exactly. **53**: What is considered a luxury then? **55**: Luxury from A to Z. From individuals and single people owning huge apartments to, I don't know … **58**: To yachts. **50**: Owning four cars. **55**: To yachts, four cars, to, I don't know … **50**: Having two weekend houses.

Attitudes towards economic inequalities in the United Kingdom

UK-1	**The divide is not between rich and poor, but between the working class and benefits recipients:** [Se1] **80**: Benefits money is going up to cover the cost of living, but our wages aren't going up to cover the cost of living. So that's the divide. The divide isn't between the rich and the poor. I think the divide is between the working class and the benefits people. That's where the divide is.
UK-2	**Individuals are self-responsible for their status and should not complain of the richer:** [Se1] **M**: So, this is the gap between rich and poor, so do people see this as an issue? [Unknown]: A big issue. **80**: I think poverty is an issue. If I go back to my dad, he'd be kind of lower to middle class. We had an outside toilet and everything and I've worked my way up to middle. I'm hoping, I'm pushing my children and educating them so they do go into the higher class but to me it's down to the individual. So if I push my children into a higher class I'd be [inaudible] because people who sit on their butts don't want to educate themselves … **85**: Hear, hear. **80**: … and moan about the people who are getting richer.

UK-3 **It is legitimate that people earn a lot of money; thus higher earners should not be taxed higher:** [Ue1] [**Unknown**]: If you look at the gap, the gap is huge. [**Unknown**]: It's about income equality, and I think frankly, people [unclear] for that gap to change. **44**: Yes, but I don't have a problem if somebody is going to work and they are earning the money and the company they're working for is prepared to pay them an extortionate amount of money; okay, fair enough. Footballers are completely off the scale, but if somebody goes to work and earns what I consider to be an extortionate amount of money, which isn't probably a lot to some people but if they're going to work and they're earning it and the company they're working for wants to pay it, then why shouldn't they take that home? **46**: But why then should they be paying a monstrous amount of tax? **44**: Exactly! It's their money but can you go back on that now? In 2040 can you say, well everybody will be paying the same percentage of tax? **M**: So, in terms of priorities, thinking about 2040, are you saying that actually you shouldn't be taxing the rich? **44**: You shouldn't be taxing high earners higher—no!

UK-4 **Causes of inequality are (lack of) access to education and (bad) parenting:** [Se2]: **81**: I think things like university costing so much and individuals working full-time and not being able to go to university when they quite easily be earning in that higher tax bracket and they're not given the opportunity to do so. **M**: So access to education is one of the things that creates inequality. Is there anything else that people think creates that sort of gap? [**Unknown**]: It's ... **86**: Poor parenting. [...] **86**: I think it says, in education I think people from richer families are more likely to do well at school and achieve better and that's down to obviously the quality of the schools in inner cities. The inner city schools are obviously not as good as the suburbs if you're in a village in Little Aston. **80**: I don't know, [inaudible] have to disagree with that. **86**: It is facts. It's in there that pupils from middle of the road families to rich are doing better in education than those in areas from lower income families. Obviously [voices overlapping]. **80**: I wouldn't put that down to the schooling though. **88**: No, it's down to the parents, isn't it?

(continued)

Table 4.3 (continued)

UK-5	**Welfare recipients get boosted by the government and bear children to get more benefits:** [Ue1] **51**: If you're below a certain income then you get boosted by the government, they give you sort of allowances for [unclear], allowances for this, allowances for that (…)—[Se1] **83**: [Unclear] these benefits that people who are on benefits, apparently the more children that they seem to have, the more benefits they're going to get, so therefore more children are being born and the population is growing again, so we're going to have overcrowding, so the benefits issue is [unclear]. **84**: [Unclear] but what, so that what you've just said, which I think is true, the poor children being born into a society that encourages financially the mother to have another child because she gets paid more benefits, what sort of chance are they going to have with life and role models, that is parents that have had kids to pay the bills if you know what I mean. So they, I know it sounds terrible, but they are the kids that are being born into the problem situations, you know what I mean?—[Min1] **68**: And then you have still got this money that most people that work 40 hours a week don't even earn that amount. I mean I could be on benefits and I hear some people having 6, 10, 12 kids. A working person couldn't afford that.—[Pl2] **[Unknown]**: So if, yes but if, if the government's going help with apprenticeships instead of giving money for people being on the dole and having five or six kids because if you work you can't have five or six kids or ten kids, unless you've got a good job and you work together with your partner but you see people who are on benefits with five, six, seven, eight kids even. I read in the paper the other day, one's on her twelfth child, and she's on benefits. It's not right. How can someone on benefits be earning, be getting £40,000 a year and the average person is probably getting around £21,000–£22,000 a year, working hard, and they're getting double the amount. It's not fair.

UK-6	**It is not fair that welfare recipients receive more money than working people**: [Se1] **84**: But what is fundamentally wrong, what is it, its craziness, like the gentleman there said if you can earn more money getting benefits than actually going to work for 40 hours a week [unclear], do you know what I mean, that is just wrong. **89**: It's a big problem, big problem. **84**: Massive. […] **80**: [Unclear] but benefits dictate this country and that's where the problem is, and its predominantly the lazy people that are sitting on the benefits, that are sitting there, saying oh they get more money than us, you're making us poverty, we want this, we need this and that's basically [unclear]. **89**: It's literally, as we said earlier, there's going to be a war soon amongst us in this country because [unclear] I'm going out there working hard and someone is just sitting there, not doing anything, earning more than what I'm earning in my wages, that really gets to me, it really does get to me.
UK-7	**Everybody can work and contribute**: [Min1] **69**: Circumstances will dictate how an individual, how much they can contribute to society but the bottom line is everybody can contribute to society if they worked or wanted and as long as they understand that and they provide people those opportunities, there shouldn't be any reason why people can't earn their benefit. […] **63**: They should look at the people who are unemployed. They should look at the reason each person's unemployed and then help fix that problem. Like I think most people can work and make up excuses and they should look at the excuse and see how they can … what sort of job they can do. Like if they can't walk or something, they could do a job where they're sitting down.
UK-8	**People must contribute—or they should not receive any benefits** [PI2] **[Unknown]**: I think if you can't feed your kids then you're going to work, aren't you? So, as well, either work for your benefits or you get no money. So if you've got no money, you can't feed your children. That's my opinion. I think you should work for, even if it's community service, bring something into the country so that when you get in, because it's not fair that the average person working 40 hours a week, don't get as much money or can't live as comfortable as the person that's not working at all and wants to play on a PlayStation for how many hours and drink all night and smoke cigarettes. It's not fair. It's not, and they're just going to be teaching their own children the same thing. It's just going to keep going over and over and over.

(continued)

Table 4.3 (continued)

UK-9	**Policy priority: reducing welfare benefits to give the money to businesses for their employees:** [Se2]: **80**: You've got to be paid more than somebody on benefits. **84**: You've got have … the minimum wage has got to be 25 per cent more than people on benefits. That's either (a) by bringing benefits down or (b) by bringing the minimum wage up. **88**: Well, the thing is they can't bring the minimum wage up any more though, because business is going to struggle. I work for HSBC and obviously I deal with a lot of customers and I know a lot of businesses now are going to struggle next year with the minimum wage going up, so it's a vicious circle if you ask me. **80**: How can they struggle when they've earned so much throughout the [voices overlapping]? **84**: Yes, but it's not on about Amazon and stuff like that, it's on about Joe Bloggs the plumber who's got four or five staff who he's got to spend an extra thousand pound a month on wages that he can't [voices overlapping]. **88**: Well, that's another employee, isn't it? He could employ somebody else. **84**: Exactly but that's where the government money … take 25 per cent from benefits and give it to those small businesses to pay people. **86**: But these people on benefits [voices overlapping]. **88**: [Inaudible] and stuff like that, it pisses me off. **89**: This is a shame to know people on benefit getting, some people, more than what I earn, tax them, tax them. **M**: So it sounds then … just to sum up the first policy … **89**: Tax their benefit. **M**: … that does everyone feel the first policy, a decent sum up is, the government should, the policy should be people in work should always earn more than people on benefits … **89**: Yes. **80**: Yes. **88**: Absolutely. **M**: … and that should be achieved by reducing benefit levels, then placing that cost savings towards employers to then also help raise the minimum wage.
UK-10	**Policy priority: require welfare recipients to pay taxes on benefits:** [Se2] **80**: Rather than, as you say, reduce the benefits, you could make them pay tax on the benefits, that's the same as reducing it, but it means they're coming into the system, so … **M**: Okay, so … **89**: You can't get fairer than that, because how could somebody not working, I'm working and they're getting more money than me who is working. How does that make me feel? **83**: It comes back down to equality at the end of the day; everybody is paying tax whether it be via benefits or by … it's equal, isn't it? Everyone's paying tax. **M**: So do we want to have that as the third policy for the group? People paying, the policy is paying tax on benefits for the third main policy. **83**: Yes.

[Abbreviations used in all four tables: *Pl1* Opening plenary session on day 1, *Pl2* Closing plenary session on day 1, *Pl3* Opening plenary session on day 2, *Pl4* Closing plenary session on day 2, *Se1* Breakout group with self-employed persons on day 1, *Se2* Breakout group with self-employed persons on day 2, *Ue1* Breakout group with unemployed persons on day 1, *Ue2* Breakout group with unemployed persons on day 2, *Min1* Breakout group with persons from ethnic minorities on day 1, *Min2* Breakout group with persons from ethnic minorities on day 2, *M* Moderator]

References

Andreß, H.-J., & Heien, T. (2001). Four worlds of welfare state attitudes? A comparison of Germany, Norway, and the United States. *European Sociological Review, 17*(4), 337–356.

Arts, W., & Gelissen, J. (2001). Welfare states, solidarity and justice principles: Does the type really matter? *Acta Sociologica, 44*(4), 283–299.

Atkinson, A. B. (2015). *Inequality: What can be done?* Cambridge: Harvard University Press.

Causa, O., Hermansen, M., Ruiz, N., Klein, C., & Smidova, Z. (2016). *Inequality in Denmark through the looking glass*. OECD Economics Department working papers 1341, Paris.

Cebulla, A. (2011). A convergence of attitudes? Perceptions of social inequality and work in post-communist and 'traditional' European market economies. *Sozialer Fortschritt, 60*(3), 43–51.

Cingano, F. (2014). *Trends in income inequality and its impact on economic growth*. OECD Social, Employment and Migration working papers 163, Paris.

Curtis, J., & Andersen, R. (2015). How social class shapes attitudes on economic inequality: The competing forces of self-interest and legitimation. *International Review of Social Research, 5*(1), 4–19.

Delhey, J. (1999). *Inequality and attitudes: Postcommunism, western capitalism and beyond*. Berlin: Wissenschaftszentrum Berlin für Sozialforschung.

Erikson, R. S. (2015). Income inequality and policy responsiveness. *Annual Review of Political Science, 18*(1), 11–29.

Esping-Andersen, G. (1990). *The three worlds of welfare capitalism*. Princeton: Princeton University Press.

Fong, C. (2001). Social preferences, self-interest, and the demand for redistribution. *Journal of Public Economics, 82*(2), 225–246.

Forsé, M., & Galland, O. (2011). *Les Français face aux inégalités et à la justice sociale*. Paris: Armand Colin.

Gijsberts, M. (2002). The legitimation of income inequality in state-socialist and market societies. *Acta Sociologica, 45*(4), 269–285.

Gimpelson, V., & Treisman, D. (2015). *Misperceiving inequality*. IZA Discussion Paper 9100, Institute for the Study of Labor, Bonn.

Grabka, M. M., & Goebel, J. (2017). Realeinkommen sind von 1991 bis 2014 im Durchschnitt gestiegen—erste Anzeichen für wieder zunehmende Einkommensungleichheit. *DIW Wochenbericht, 2017*(4), 71–82.

Heuer, J.-O., & Mau, S. (2017). Stretching the limits of solidarity: The German case. In P. Taylor-Gooby, B. Leruth, & H. Chung (Eds.), *After austerity: Welfare state transformation in Europe after the great recession*. Oxford: Oxford University Press.

Hrast, M. F., & Ignjatović, M. (2013). Growing inequalities and their impacts in Slovenia. GINI Country Report Slovenia, Amsterdam Institute for Advanced Labour Studies (AIAS), Amsterdam.

Jæger, M. M. (2006). Welfare regimes and attitudes towards redistribution: The regime hypothesis revisited. *European Sociological Review, 22*(2), 157–170.

Jordan, J. (2013). Policy feedback and support for the welfare state. *Journal of European Social Policy, 23*(2), 134–148.

Kelley, J., & Evans, M. D. R. (1993). The legitimation of inequality: Occupational earnings in nine nations. *American Journal of Sociology, 99*(1), 75–125.

Kenworthy, L., & McCall, L. (2008). Inequality, public opinion and redistribution. *Socio-Economic Review, 6*(1), 35–68.

Kerr, W. R. (2014). Income inequality and social preferences for redistribution and compensation differentials. *Journal of Monetary Economics, 66*, 62–78.

Kumlin, S., & Stadelmann-Steffen, I. (Eds.). (2014). *How welfare states shape the democratic public: Policy feedback, participation, voting, and attitudes*. Cheltenham: Edward Elgar.

Larsen, C. A. (2016). How three narratives of modernity justify economic inequality. *Acta Sociologica, 59*(2), 93–111.

Mau, S. (2003). *The moral economy of welfare states: Britain and Germany compared*. London: Routledge.

Mau, S. (2015). *Inequality, marketization and the majority class: Why did the European middle classes accept neo-liberalism?* Basingstoke: Palgrave Macmillan.

Medgyesi, M. (2013). *Increasing income inequality and attitudes to inequality: A cohort perspective*. GINI Discussion Paper 94, Amsterdam Institute for Advanced Labour Studies (AIAS), Amsterdam.

Meltzer, A. H., & Richard, S. F. (1981). A rational theory of the size of government. *Journal of Political Economy, 89*(5), 914–927.

Niehues, J. (2014). *Subjective perceptions of inequality and redistributive preferences: An international comparison*. Cologne: Cologne Institute for Economic Research.

OECD (2008). *Growing unequal? Income distribution and poverty in OECD countries*. Paris: OECD.

OECD (2011). *Divided we stand: Why inequality keeps rising*. Paris: OECD.

OECD (2015a). *In it together: Why less inequality benefits all*. Paris: OECD.

OECD (2015b). *Income inequality data update and policies impacting income distribution: United Kingdom*. Paris: OECD.
Ostry, J. D., Berg, A., & Tsangarides, C. G. (2014). *IMF Staff Discussion Note SDN/14/02, Redistribution, inequality and growth*. International Monetary Fund, Washington.
Piketty, T. (2014). *Capital in the twenty-first century*. Cambridge: Belknap Press of Harvard University Press.
Reeskens, T., & van Oorschot, W. (2013). Equity, equality, or need? A study of popular preferences for welfare redistribution principles across 24 European countries. *Journal of European Public Policy, 20*(8), 1174–1195.
Rosanvallon, P. (2013). *The society of equals*. Cambridge: Harvard University Press.
Rothstein, B. (1998). *Just institutions matter: The moral and political logic of the universal welfare state*. Cambridge: Cambridge University Press.
Sachweh, P. (2012). The moral economy of inequality: Popular views on income differentiation, poverty and wealth. *Socio-Economic Review, 10*(3), 419–445.
Schmidt-Catran, A. W. (2016). Economic inequality and public demand for redistribution: Combining cross-sectional and longitudinal evidence. *Socio-Economic Review, 14*(1), 119–140.
Svallfors, S. (1997). Worlds of welfare and attitudes to redistribution: A comparison of eight western nations. *European Sociological Review, 13*(3), 283–304.
Svallfors, S. (2010). Public attitudes. In F. G. Castles, S. Leibfried, J. Lewis, H. Obinger, & C. Pierson (Eds.), *The Oxford handbook of the welfare state*. Oxford: Oxford University Press.

5

Intergenerational Solidarity and the Sustainability of State Welfare

Mi Ah Schøyen and Bjørn Hvinden

Introduction

This chapter considers the sustainability of European welfare states through the lens of intergenerational solidarity. The welfare state may be conceived as an implicit contract between generations. It institutionalises intergenerational solidarity through transfers and services to the young and even more so to the old. People of working age support (non-working) dependent groups at early and later life stages (Svallfors 2008). For example, Kohli (1987, p. 128) speaks of a 'normative system of mutual obligations' in relation to pensions in Germany, thereby linking retirement income to the moral economy.

Against the backdrop of intensified competition over public resources and population ageing, it seems naïve to assume that the implicit intergenerational contract on which modern welfare states were constructed, will persist in its current form. While policies that make it easier to

M. A. Schøyen (✉) • B. Hvinden
NOVA Norwegian Social Research, Oslo Metropolitan University,
Oslo, Norway
e-mail: miah.schoyen@nova.no

combine work and bringing up children could mitigate the demographic challenge, such efforts 'would have to be financed (at least partly) out of current outlays for pensions, in the form of either longer working life or cutbacks in pension levels' (Svallfors 2008, p. 381). These structural pressures render the 'working conditions' of modern welfare states very different from the post-war era when European welfare states were developed. Population ageing under austerity places a greater load on the shoulders of the working-age population and we cannot rely on economic growth to solve current financial challenges.

The chapter uses the Democratic Forum data (see Chap. 1) to examine the strength and nature of intergenerational solidarity in modern welfare states. It considers whether there is evidence of new age-based tensions or conflicts among ordinary citizens and whether we can identify new expressions of intergenerational solidarity resulting from the abovementioned structural pressures. Is the public (or collective) intergenerational solidarity around which the welfare state was constructed being replaced by private forms of intergenerational solidarity? Or do people embrace both forms of solidarity at the same time following separate and not necessarily coherent framings (see Chap. 6)? Here we assume that future welfare politics and policies will be heavily influenced by people's attitudes towards the intergenerational contract. Conversely, we expect that such attitudes are influenced, at the macro level, by a combination of already existing welfare policies and institutions as well as by the national socio-economic context.

In the next section we outline the main channels through which modern welfare states allocate resources to age groups at different stages of the life course, distinguishing age groups from generations. We also present comparative data on three broad age categories (children, working-age population and elderly) in the five country cases discussed in Chap. 1. We hypothesise about the direction of people's attitudes with regard to different kinds of age-based allocations of resources. Next, the chapter moves on to chart differences and similarities in public and family-based forms of intergenerational solidarity as expressed by people's attitudes across the five cases. We assess our hypotheses against empirical evidence from the Democratic Forums. The chapter concentrates on the future of *state* welfare—cash transfers and social services provided or mandated by the state. For reasons of space we pay less attention to occupational or market-based institutional arrangements (see Chaps. 2, 6 and 7 for a discussion of welfare mixes and the role of occupational and private provisions).

Age and Generations in Modern Welfare States

Age is an important criterion for the allocation of state welfare. First, in all welfare states the elderly receive cash transfers in the form of old-age pensions (Ebbinghaus 2011; Immergut et al. 2007). The other category of age-related cash benefits is child and family benefits; most modern welfare states recognise the importance of supporting families with children (particularly low-income families).

The second branch of age-related support is care services. Entitlements to elderly care services are generally triggered by a combination of advanced age and documented care needs: home or residential care. Modern welfare states also offer childcare support to families: day care and sometimes after-school childcare, whether publicly or privately provided and financed through grants or tax credit. Childcare is considered beneficial for the child's development (see Chaps. 2, 6, and 8) and allows parents, especially mothers, to (re-)enter the labour market after having a child.

It is important to distinguish analytically between *age groups* and *generations*. Within the family, generation is related to kinship and refers to position in the line of descent. At the societal level *generation* refers to 'the aggregate of persons born in a limited period who therefore experience historical events at similar ages and move through the lifecourse in unison' (Kohli 2005, p. 518; Pampel 1998). The concept of *age group* refers to the specific age held by a group of persons at a given point in time. Hence, 'age groups are to be viewed not as entities with fixed membership but with regularly changing membership, with all individuals progressing through the life course from one to the next according to an institutionalized schedule' (Kohli 2006, p. 458).

It follows from the above that all persons belong to the same generation or *birth cohort* throughout their lives, whereas they enter different age groups as they move through the life course. Unequal treatment of age groups may in some instances make perfect sense on justice grounds. Age groups sometimes have different needs or risk being disadvantaged economically or socially in the absence of targeted special treatment—for example, old-age pensions help smooth income over the lifecycle. This distinction is relevant to understanding interest: while different age groups have different interests (in working-age benefits and pensions, for example), a generation will progress through age stages and has an interest in its own future prospects. Need and equality are two of the commonly applied principles—along with merit—according to which we justify interventions in the lives of citizens through social policy. In addition, we may invoke these principles to judge the fairness of distributive outcomes (Kohli 2008).

As the above conceptual distinction suggests, intergenerational fairness may relate to the economic and social position of young and old at a given point in time or to the position of successive cohorts (Lindh et al. 2005). A simple measure of how welfare states treat different age groups is given by data on public expenditure. Previous research has shown that there is a considerable age bias towards the elderly in most welfare states (Esping-Andersen and Sarasa 2002; Lynch 2006). Despite cost-containing old-age pension reforms, population ageing is causing continued upwards pressures on public spending. In 2013 the OECD countries spent on average 7.7 per cent of their GDP on transfers (cash and in-kind) to the elderly but only 5.6 per cent on the working-age population (Fig. 5.1). Unemployment benefits, active labour market policies, family benefits and services (including paid parental leave and early childhood education and care) and incapacity-related transfers (such as sick pay and disability pensions) are included in transfers to the working-age population. Since children tend to live with their parents, most support aimed at the working-age population, and not only that classified as family benefits and services, may potentially improve the welfare of children and young people.

Figure 5.1 shows that, as expected, spending on the elderly increased between 2007 and 2013 in all countries except Germany. With the exception of Norway, the same is true for spending on the working-age population. There is a considerable difference, especially in Germany and Slovenia, in the amounts spent on the elderly compared with the working-age population.

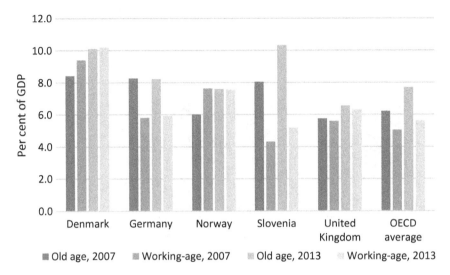

Fig. 5.1 Public social expenditure: elderly and the working-age population, in 2007 and 2013. Source: OECD Social Expenditure Database

Opinions about which age groups should get what from the welfare state may be affected by judgements of vulnerability or need. Comparing children (aged 18 or younger), the working-age population (aged 18–64) and the elderly (aged 65 or older), Fig. 5.2 shows that in the EU as a whole, children were at a greater risk of poverty or social exclusion than the total population. The situation worsened between 2007 and 2015. The working-age population moved from a position that was slightly better than the population as a whole in 2007 to exceed the 'at risk of poverty and social exclusion' (AROPE)[1] rate for the total population in 2015.

Cross-country variations emerge in average AROPE levels, as well as across age groups. Concentrating on 2015, Slovenia is the only country in which the elderly appear more vulnerable than the overall population. In the other countries, the elderly are clearly less at risk than children and working-age people. A comparison of the situation in 2007 with that in 2015 suggests that the global financial and economic crises have had more severe consequences for young people than for the elderly. With the exception of Norway, which was left relatively unharmed by the international economic turbulence (see Andersen et al. 2017), there was a notable

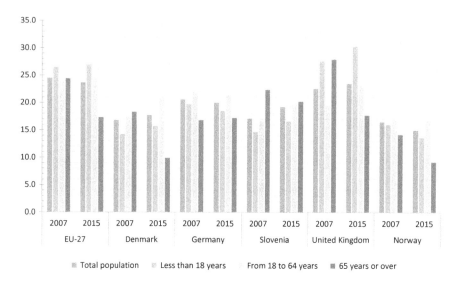

Fig. 5.2 At risk of poverty and social exclusion (AROPE) by broad age group. Source: Eurostat [ilc_peps01]

increase in AROPE rates for the working-age population and children between 2007 and 2015. The level of poverty among children in the United Kingdom is particularly worrying. In 2015 it exceeded 30 per cent.

Population ageing puts pressure on the working-age population throughout the developed world. Figure 5.3 shows old-age dependency ratios—a common indicator of population ageing—for 2015 and as projected for 2050. The comparison demonstrates clearly that even though population ageing occurs in all five countries, it does not take place at the same pace. It is particularly rapid in Slovenia, but also fast in Germany and slowest in Norway.

Based on the above outline of age-based state welfare, we advance three hypotheses:

1. *Old-age pensions*: Given the difficulties many young people have in the transition to the labour market, we hypothesise that young people question whether they will receive the same treatment as their parents' generation when they reach retirement (the intergenerational contract

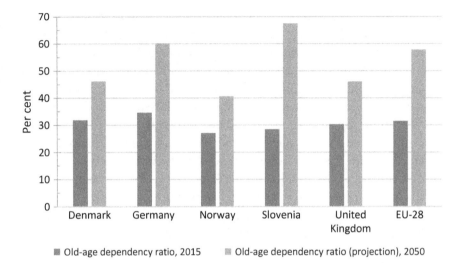

Fig. 5.3 Level and expected pace of population ageing by country. Note: Old-age dependency ratio is the number of persons age 65+ as a share of the working-age population (age 20–64). Source: European Demographic Datasheet 2016, Wittgenstein Centre (IIASA, VID/OEAW, WU), Vienna

in practice). We expect younger people to be more sceptical than older people towards public pensions and express a lower degree of acceptance to finance public (pay-as-you-go) pensions, a system within which one generation of workers pays for the currently retired generation, for two reasons.

First, young people today know that they will have to pay for an increasing share of older people, something which has forced policy-makers in most European welfare states to reform public pension systems by cutting replacement rates or imposing stricter eligibility criteria for future retirees. Second, in many countries, young people's job insecurity may make it harder to pay pension contributions and establish a contributory record that meets the (new) requirements for a full old-age pension. From a comparative perspective, we anticipate considerable cross-national variation, with the strongest tensions in the United Kingdom and perhaps Denmark (where poverty has risen fastest among the young). Also in Slovenia and Germany rapid ageing may lead to concerns about financing pensions among the young.

2. *Elderly care and healthcare*: the demands on the state to provide (or finance) health and elderly care will increase in the future, but we expect interests to be shared *across* generations. While the elderly, on average, consume more healthcare services than other age groups, all age groups have an interest in being covered by a health insurance or a national healthcare system (Naumann 2014, p. 277). Without elderly care, more responsibility falls on family members, and especially female family members whose opportunities to take paid employment are reduced. Here we expect the distinction between defamilialising and familialising welfare states to be relevant, in which the former offer more formal care (see Chap. 6). Defamilialised welfare states are generally characterised by markedly higher labour market participation than those that leave care as a private responsibility. Therefore, the importance of affordable formal care is likely to be stressed more strongly in countries where such services are not so well developed and care responsibilities still fall on the family (such as Germany, Slovenia and the United Kingdom).
3. *Services and transfers to children*: The most obvious supporters of public services and benefits to young children and youth are working-age parents. Moreover, access to high-quality education is fundamental to enhance children's prospects as adults. A more complex argument would be that even elderly people might reason that they have an (indirect) interest in investment in education. Children and youth are future workers and public investments in education help ensure that children grow to become productive citizens (as discussed by the social investment approach, see Chaps. 2 and 8), which, in turn, may be part of the solution to the financial pressures caused by population ageing (Lister 2003; Jenson and Saint-Martin 2006).

Citizens' Views on the Future of Age-Related State Welfare

We analyse our empirical data below. It consists of transcripts of the national Democratic Forums. Our analytical strategy is to (1) identify the most salient intergenerational issues discussed in each country; (2) assess the degree of consensus or conflict between the young and the old in relation to these issues; and (3) discuss the extent to which the argument pointed to future intergenerational solidarity—and if so, in a private (family) or collective (societal) form. Using the software package Nvivo, the respective national research teams assigned all statements to broad thematic categories. The coding also identified the person behind each statement (see Appendix at the end of this volume for participant characteristics). Each national team wrote a report to summarise the main topics and arguments in their country. Our analysis relies on a review of the statements coded in the category 'intergenerational issues' as well as the theme 'old-age pensions'.

Denmark

The view that individuals should as far as possible take responsibility for their own lives, including saving for an adequate old-age pension, dominated the Danish discussions. At the same time, state welfare should be available for those who need it—'the weak, the fragile, the sick, the poor and the elderly' (see Table 5.2, DK-1). This view emerged also in the final plenary session. There was almost unanimous support in favour of the proposal to *preserve* the basic old-age pension provision and means-test supplementary services, which would be regulated according to the recipient's income.

Following the logic of social investment, there was much emphasis on and support for investments in services and education for young people. It is interesting to note that the supporters of this view included some of the more senior Democratic Forum participants. In other words, it was not only the young participants with children who were interested in services for young people. A statement by a 64-year old self-employed woman illustrates the point:

> Child services and youth services should be kept at the same level in the future. I'm still working despite the fact that I'm a golden oldie and I pay quite a lot of tax. So some of the golden oldies contribute to shouldering the burden of an aging population (DK-76)

In fact, in the final plenary session, one of the proposals, which received unanimous support, was to invest in education as in the other countries. At least for some of the participants, the rationale behind investments in young people in general and education in particular was to boost productivity. As a corollary it was important not to 'over-invest in the elderly' and prioritise those 'we can see a future for' (see Table 5.2, DK-5). Arguably, one may interpret such statements as being hostile towards the elderly, implying a lack of solidarity and perhaps an emerging conflict. However, several elderly participants shared this view. It was not a discourse driven by younger age-groups who wanted more for themselves. Hence, the Danish debate illustrates how old people display solidarity with the young.

The young showed considerable understanding when it came to the prospects of less generous old-age pensions compared to current old-age pensioners (see Table 5.2, DK-6). They seemed quite prepared to retire later and save for their own retirement, seeing old-age pensions mainly as a safeguard for those who did not have the means to save individually or in an occupational plan. While not explicitly suggesting that the current retired population should lose their pensions, they framed public spending on the old and the young as something of a trade-off. They were not very optimistic about the generosity of the pension they would get. Some believed they would not even get a pension when they reached old age, yet the young participants did not complain about this. Instead they advocated investment in education for young citizens as the main instrument. In addition, the welfare state should help finance some of the costs of having children. In the final plenary discussion, about two-thirds of the participants supported a proposal to make it financially more attractive to have children (see Table 5.2, DK-6). In response to the question of how to make it more attractive to have children, a 51-year old male participant suggested to increase childcare benefits or to lower childcare costs.

The issue of public versus private responsibility in caring for dependents also came up. On the one hand, there was support for stronger intergenerational ties, but within the family rather than at the societal level. Denmark should move towards a more familialised model (see Table 5.2, DK-2), although some participants disagreed. For instance, two older participants highlighted that one of the most important achievements of the welfare state is precisely that it takes care of elderly people who need help, no matter whether relatives are present or not (see Table 5.2, DK-3 for full quotations):

> It's the welfare society's job to care for you if you're not able to do it yourself. It's difficult to make that the duty of relatives. (DK-59)
>
> …if we remove the old-age pension and everything to do with domestic assistance and the whole shebang, then we might just as well go home because then there is no welfare state. … I would personally not be able to go to work if there wasn't anyone to look after my 92-year-old mother. (DK-80)

The two statements promote the welfare state as an intergenerational contract. DK-59's statement represents a powerful expression of solidarity with the younger generations on the part of the old, rather than a commitment to self-interest. Here the reasoning is based on an understanding of generation with reference to kinship. There is a desire to reduce the burden on younger family members. By contrast, DK-80's statement may appear selfish. In the absence of the societal intergenerational contract, she would have had to forego her personal income from paid employment. However, implicitly DK-80 may also be saying that without the collective or shared responsibility for child and elderly care, she would not be able to pay taxes and make a contribution to the country's economy in the way she does now.

In addition to the contrasting positions presented above, some opinions fell somewhere in the middle, between giving the state full responsibility and leaving care responsibilities to the family. Here the emphasis was on letting people choose whether to assume such responsibilities, considering that not everyone is able to reduce or forego paid work (see Table 5.2, DK-4). In the final plenary session, a large majority favoured increased opportunities for self-care with the possibility of compensation, arguing that if a person chooses to stay at home to care for their sick mother they may be entitled to financial compensation.

This result may be interpreted as a strong willingness to care for relatives if made affordable financially. One reading of this finding is that solidarity between generations remains strong, but that it may be exercised increasingly at the family rather than societal level in the future. At the societal level, there will still be an intergenerational contract but it might gradually move from a universal to a more residual format.

Norway

Despite Norway's privileged economic position, population ageing is a key topic in the Norwegian discussions as much as in the other countries. The participants recognised that this shift represented a great financial burden on society, leaving fewer resources available for other tasks. But there was no evidence of explicit tensions between old and working-age people. We found expressions of common interests and solidarity in both directions—support for the young expressed by the elderly and the other way around. It was not the case that those who highlighted that the rising costs of old-age pensions will come at the expense of resources spent on other purposes were mainly young participants (see Table 5.2, NO-1).

There was considerable pessimism regarding old-age pensions for current and future workers, even more so than in Denmark. Yet, no one suggested that current retirees should receive less to save money for the future (see Table 5.2, NO-2). The suggestion that the retirement age should rise to deal with the rising pension costs due to the increasing old-age dependency came up repeatedly. This proposal received widespread acceptance (see Table 5.2, NO-3). However, some participants asked whether increasing the proportion of older workers reduces opportunities for the young and contributes to youth unemployment (see Table 5.2, NO-6). The issue was presented as a potential dilemma rather than as an absolute truth. This perceived drawback of a higher retirement age might be a partial explanation why the participants were split down the middle (with exactly half the group in favour and the other half against) in the final plenary vote over a proposal to increase the retirement age.

Notably, the breakout group with the youngest participants came up with the most severe proposals to cut back on future pension entitlements by suggesting a high minimum retirement age (70 years). The justification was to reduce future pension costs and increase tax revenue.

Their second proposal was to reduce the generosity of public old-age pensions and impose increased savings through the mandatory occupational pension. This should reduce public pension costs and maintain or increase spending on other social spending categories. If we think of the young as an age group that will themselves reach old age eventually, these proposals may seem surprising. Rather than favouring the maintenance of current generosity, they suggested reducing benefits for future pensioners like themselves, while current old-age pensioners would be unaffected by these proposals since they have already retired. The result may appear paradoxical. The young were being strict on themselves while protecting those who were old today.

If we, instead, consider the young as a generation that also have to pay for the current pensioners, these policy proposals are based on a coherent logic that shows some solidarity with current pensioners but includes an element of self-interest. Young people today are highly aware of the financial challenges facing the welfare state. Weighed against the prospect of losing other public provisions, which they could benefit from in the immediate future, they accepted the postponement of retirement and less generous public pensions than their parents. They did not open an explicit conflict line across generations or question the obligation to pay for the benefits of today's pensioners. But in both Denmark and Norway they believed that, given current structural conditions, the only alternative was to choose between less generous future pensions or cuts in other areas of state welfare. At the same time, the current old generation seemed to be more strongly protected by the young in Norway than in Denmark. A possible explanation for this (subtle) difference is that, relatively speaking, the Norwegian economy and labour market suffered less than most other economies during the Great Recession. Thus, the young could afford to be more generous towards the elderly.

With regard to state welfare targeted at youth, there was some attention to young people's mental well-being, which in one instance was brought up under the topic of intergenerational relations (see Table 5.2, NO-8). Asked to explain how youth's mental well-being and investments in mental healthcare relate to intergenerational questions, an older participant replied that

It solves it so that the youth get well and can provide for the elders. (NO-33)

Arguably, this represents a somewhat unexpected expression of common interest across generations. In simple terms, if the young do well, the elderly will also benefit. This logic resembles that of the social investment approach (see Chaps. 2 and 8), even if the latter puts a particularly strong emphasis on childhood education.

Education was a prominent topic in discussions on both days. It was not framed explicitly as an intergenerational issue as it was in Denmark. Nonetheless, there was broad agreement in favour of investments in public education and children and youth in general (see Table 5.2, NO-7). Here the participants generally seemed to prefer public over private solutions. It was seen as important to ensure that nobody was left behind and that young people avoided unemployment. Education improves the labour market prospects of young people and enhances the productivity of future workers. The statements that pointed to the importance of the state investing in young people and children came from younger participants as well as more senior ones. Thus, again we do not see signs of an emerging 'age conflict'. However, the breakout group with the oldest participants paid less attention to education policy than the other breakout groups.

Also with regard to care, we found expressions of solidarity with the elderly on the part of the younger participants in Norway. But, as in Denmark, there were suggestions that family responsibility should be reinforced (see Table 5.2, NO-4). One participant suggested that family and friends are 'more caring'. This is interesting as it expresses an implicit mistrust of the state's ability to meet desired care standards. Hence, we are talking about a private form of solidarity—between generations within the family or among close friends, perhaps suggesting a weakened belief in the public intergenerational contract. There was considerable (though not unanimous) support for this view. Another participant expressed a similar view but with a slightly different rationale. While the former highlighted the quality of care, the latter saw family care as a response to increasing financial pressures on the state. The pressure on elderly care services in the future makes informal care provided by relatives more likely. The calls for more informal care in Norway (and to some extent in Denmark) deviated from our initial expectation of increased demand for publicly organised elderly care and that this would be favoured over familial care. However, the results confirm that the quality of care is something people find important.

Germany

Retirement and old-age pensions were prominent topics under the heading of intergenerational issues throughout the forums and were discussed from several angles. One of the main concerns was old-age pensions for young people now entering the labour market. As in the Danish and Norwegian cases, the pensions of those who will retire in the more distant future were not only a concern of the young. Several of the older participants explicitly compared future pensions with their own old-age pension entitlements and demonstrated awareness of their 'lucky' position compared with young people.

Considerable attention was paid to the issue that younger generations will receive a lower old-age pension, and it was, perhaps surprisingly, articulated most strongly by the older participants. One elderly participant argued that the situation is unjust towards young people, who pay contributions but will get less in return. Furthermore, it is worth noting that these statements, underlining the disadvantaged position of the young, were made independently of each other and in all three breakout groups during day one when the discussions were less guided than on day two (see Table 5.2, DE-1). While it was a common perception among the participants that the role of public pensions would continue to decrease and there was some interest in flexible retirement, nobody explicitly proposed to introduce a higher statutory retirement age. Instead, there were calls for more support to help the current generation of workers save for retirement (see Table 5.2, DE-4).

Several German participants referred to poverty in old age as a serious problem. Some of them identified some form of basic pension, basic social security or social pension as a potential policy solution. The basic pension would protect those who are old today as well as the current younger generation who will be tomorrow's pensioners. This kind of basic old-age benefit should be generous enough and set up in a way that prevents old-age poverty today and in the future. It would protect young people who have problems entering the labour market today and who, therefore, do not manage to start paying into the pension system. It would also be less bureaucratic and stigmatising than having to apply for a mean-tested benefit. Old-age poverty or the need for a basic retirement income was undoubtedly a topic that was commented on more (but not exclusively) by the oldest participants, perhaps because they were potentially more directly affected and, thus, had a more immediate interest in the issue (see Table 5.2, DE-2). However, the DF discussions did not point in the direction of age-based conflict here. A 41-year old participant first suggested that the idea of a basic social security went in the direction of protecting the old but changed his mind after hearing a counter-argument. While there was considerable attention to the prevention of old-age poverty, several participants—predominantly younger ones—argued that retirees ought to be compensated for work efforts (see Table 5.2, DE-3).

Elderly care in relation to population ageing and as an intergenerational issue did not receive much attention in the German forums—especially compared with the other countries. However, a 46-year old female participant pointed out that generational fairness had to do with access to care regardless of your age. If you need to be cared for, you should get help no matter whether you are old or young (see Table 5.2, DE-5).

While elderly care was not such a prominent issue in Germany, the participants were much more concerned about maximising the opportunities of children and young people. Seeing children as the future, they identified multiple advantages of investing in children, particularly through the education system. A good level of education enables you to work and enhances the likelihood of finding a good job. There was a mix of old and young participants who voiced opinions in this direction. Thus, one may speak of intergenerational solidarity around this topic (see Table 5.2, DE-6), something which we can also say about the issue of fertility in connection with population ageing. The need for more children emerged as an issue connected to population ageing to maintain the principle of each generation paying for the next, the intergenerational contract. Thus, it is necessary to make it more attractive to have children. Currently there is too little support (see Table 5.2, DE-7).

Slovenia

There was a rich discussion of issues that are linked to age and intergenerational relationships in Slovenia. Participants highlighted elderly poverty and the problem of inadequate pensions more strongly than in the other countries (as illustrated by quotes in Table 5.2, SI-1 and SI-2). This fits with the picture given in Fig. 5.2. Even if the risk of poverty or social exclusion among elderly people in Slovenia decreased between 2007 and 2015, they are still slightly more at risk than the rest of the population. There was great awareness that the population is ageing. The participants explicitly connected the issues of elderly poverty, poor health and an increasing need for elderly care. The government response should be to finance formal care in order not to burden the young.

More specifically, several participants—old as well as young—argued that low pensions force old people to postpone retirement or to take another job after they have retired. Sometimes they are also tempted to take undeclared jobs to earn enough to make ends meet. Beyond the economic situation of the elderly, the participants also made a connection between the extended labour market participation of senior workers and labour market opportunities for young people. It was suggested that when old people stay longer in the labour market, they take jobs from younger people (see Table 5.2, SI-1).

When asked to elaborate why poverty among the elderly was a problem, the Slovenian participants also pointed out that pensions were low, which in turn led to poverty, poor health and associated care needs. The elderly deserved to be better treated. One person also argued that poor elderly in need of care cannot afford a place in a nursing home and, thus raised the question of who is going to take care of the elderly (see Table 5.2, SI-3). The question led to a discussion of the potential role of children or young people as carers for their elderly parents and close relatives. It was pointed out that the working-age generation also have their own struggles. They have to work and are not always paid very high wages. As a consequence, it is often difficult for adult children to provide care for their elderly parents (see Table 5.2, SI-5). Moreover, population ageing leads to more elderly people, who tend to be poorer and more ill, and thus a growing demand for elderly care (see Table 5.2, SI-2).

With regard to policy solutions, a 52-year-old retired participant called for state involvement to cover the cost of nursing homes for those in need of care. His justification was the importance of ensuring that the burden of caring for parents does not fall on their children (see Table 5.2, SI-5). The argument can be read as supportive of strengthening the welfare state as an intergenerational contract based on collective responsibility for dependent elderly people. Since many young people struggle financially, they cannot be expected to care for their parents too. In this regard, a particularly striking counterargument came from a 45-year-old man, who advocated a private, intra-family form of solidarity with the elderly, illustrating that the participants were not in full agreement on whether responsibility for elderly care should be primarily a matter for the family or assumed by the welfare state:

> You said, I apologize, that you wouldn't have the children burdened, but I also think a bit differently, that also the children should start paying back to the elderly and their parents, today that's already written down in the law. (SI-83)

What the argument fails to recognise in its criticism of state responsibility for the elderly is that in the latter case, the young also make a considerable contribution, but they do so by paying income tax according to economic ability. In this way, needy elderly people are not dependent on the capacity of their children to provide or pay for care. Another interesting observation with regard to the individual characteristics of who said what in this discussion is that the elderly participants did not express an expectation that their children would take care of them. Instead, there was a general concern about the currently difficult labour market situation of young workers similar to the way the participants expressed frustrations about low pensions and the treatment of elderly in general. The notion of 'decent' pensions came up again and again, and a common view was that the state should act as a guarantor (see Table 5.2, SI-3). Analogous to the concern for the challenging situation of young workers, some of the older participants, in particular, pointed to the problem of poverty in families with children. There are too many such families (see Table 5.2, SI-4). In addition, young people today—the pensioners of tomorrow—have poorer prospects of getting a proper pension (see Table 5.2, SI-8). Overall, we can say that the two age groups—the old and the young—did not demand resources explicitly at the expense of each other and that they demonstrated reciprocal consideration of each other's situation.

The need for higher pensions and the importance of facilitating formal elderly care were also raised in the final plenary session. This time the issues were explicitly linked to opportunities for the young. Reporting from one of the breakout groups, one of the participants pointed out that new services for the elderly mean new jobs for the younger, active population:

> Well, raising the pensions and insight into the pension fund, we thought that was very important as well ... because the money is flowing from private funds back to nursing homes again ... if the pensions were raised, that would mean that more elderly would have the option of staying at nursing homes. Having more elderly at nursing homes would open new jobs for the young. (SI-72)

The above quotation sums up several of the core issues that the Slovenian participants were concerned about. Moreover, the line of reasoning confirms the impression that, overall, solidarity between old and young is quite strong.

United Kingdom

The UK was the only of our five cases in which we observed some (weak) signs of cleavages between the young and the old. As in the other countries, there was a strong awareness of population ageing. The participants questioned the future of the State Pension, and not everyone was convinced that it would still exist in 2040 (see Table 5.2, UK-1). To compensate for a low or non-existent future State Pension, an expansion of private pensions was proposed. The issue was not accepted without reservations as some raised concerns about low-income earners who could not afford to save privately, but disagreements did not seem to run along intergenerational lines (see Table 5.2, UK-2). Another measure to alleviate the pressure on the public pension system would be to further increase the retirement age (see Table 5.2, UK-8). Again, the issue was controversial and, for instance, one of the older female participants expressed a clear unwillingness to accept a retirement age beyond 67. By contrast, the most vocal advocate of a retirement age between 70 and 75 was a young participant in the age group 25–34. There are too few statements on the topic to conclude that there is an age cleavage, but the observations are nonetheless interesting.

However, as in the Slovenian discussion, several UK participants argued that low pensions and a rising retirement age take labour market opportunities away from young people (see Table 5.2, UK-3). One of the youngest participants highlighted two related concerns. First, she was worried about her parents and whether they could afford to retire, exemplifying intergenerational solidarity between family generations. The specific case illustrates how some elderly are forced to postpone retirement because their pension would otherwise be too low. Others will, due to the gradually increasing State Pension age, be prevented from retiring at the same age as current retirees.[2] Second, the young participant pointed out that it is difficult for young people who are not able to get jobs when old people can work as long as they like. She frames the labour market opportunities of the young and the old as a trade-off. Also an elderly female participant presents the same view. Overall, these statements are examples of intergenerational solidarity at the level of attitudes going both ways—from the old to the young and young to the old.

The younger generation also received criticism (see Table 5.2, UK-4). Two middle-aged male participants argued that adults with children rely too much on their own parents. Old people have contributed enough when they retire and it is wrong of young people to rely on their parents for help when they have children. They should have a better plan, so that old people, when they retire, are allowed to have a 'quality life for themselves'. What these arguments neglect is the fact that grandparents may benefit from and find pleasure in spending time with their grandchildren and help their adult children (for example Di Gessa et al. 2016).

At the same time, in another breakout group there was a call for more incentives to provide informal care for older people by family members (see Table 5.2, UK-5). Suggested measures included special leave of absence from a paid job and tax breaks. It was mainly younger participants who voiced their opinions on this issue. One of the youngest women opposed the idea of rewarding informal carers since she claimed that in many cases the person in need of assistance would be entitled to a carer anyway.[3] Thus, she thought it was better to let that person keep the care job. She also suggested that it was problematic from an employer's perspective if people are entitled to leave to do informal care asking how that is 'fair on the employer' (see Table 5.2, UK-5 for full quotation). In response, it was pointed out that sometimes people have a desire to care for close relatives themselves—especially if the relatives are at the end of their lives.

We also observed a belief that population ageing will bring new jobs as demand increases in the area of elderly care (see Table 5.2, UK-6). The reasoning was the same as in the Slovenian case. More elderly people means a growing number of people who will need assistance. These considerations arguably go in the direction of solidarity with the young. Notably two of the relevant statements came from two retired women, demonstrating consideration for the labour market opportunities of future generations despite not being themselves directly affected.

If we compare the forums in the five countries, the most striking discussion hinting at a potential conflict between the elderly and the young took place in the UK. Among some participants there seemed to be a sense that the elderly get more resources than the young (Table 5.2, UK-7) and are a higher priority for the welfare state. This perceived outcome was attributed to the fact that the elderly tend to vote more often than young people do. One of the youngest participants (under 24 years) adopted a long-term perspective in his reasoning. He feared that gap between what today's elderly get compared with what the current younger generation will get when they reach old age will grow even bigger as long as so many young people keep away from the ballot boxes.

The Future(s) of the Intergenerational Contract: New Boundaries Between Collective and Private Solidarity

In light of the above evidence, what can we say about the likely future of the welfare state as an intergenerational contract? Table 5.1 provides a comparative overview and summary of our findings. As expected we observed extensive cross-country variation, confirming the idea that perceptions of the intergenerational contract and solidarity are influenced by differences in the socio-economic context in each country as well as by existing institutional configurations. At the same time, there were interesting similarities. Across countries the participants raised similar even if not identical intergenerational themes; most topics were related to population ageing as the main driver of contemporary policy challenges.

In all countries the conversations in the Democratic Forums revealed that, in general, young people care about the needs of the elderly, who are by and large considered a deserving group. Particularly when it comes to income in old age, there was a general consensus across countries that it is important to combat old-age poverty and that the state should provide at least a basic safety net for the elderly. Nonetheless, except in Slovenia, we observed an expectation of weakened of state responsibility. The turn was towards more individual responsibility in the case of retirement income and (especially in Denmark, Norway and partially the UK) more familial responsibility in elderly care. The Slovenian participants demanded the most from the state, particularly in the area of elderly care.

The simple hypotheses set out in the first part of the chapter were confirmed only to some degree. Our findings fit with hypothesis one in that many young people stated that they could not expect to get the same public pensions as current retirees. However, they were generally surprisingly tolerant of the financial burden they face. Perhaps most evident in the Norwegian case, younger people appeared to accept stricter eligibility criteria and lower generosity for themselves, while continuing to pay for today's pensioners. Arguably, it was to be expected that we would find the

Table 5.1 Attitudes to the welfare state and to intergenerational issues

	Denmark	Norway	Germany	Slovenia	United Kingdom
Welfare regime	Social-democratic	Social-democratic	Conservative	Post-Socialist	Liberal
Demographic ageing	Moderate	Limited	Strong	Strong	Moderate
Poverty and social exclusion across age	Working-age most vulnerable	Working-age most vulnerable	Working-age most vulnerable	Elderly most vulnerable	Young people most vulnerable
Intergenerational themes in focus	Elderly care, old-age pensions and retirement, young people (esp. education)	Elderly care, old-age pensions and retirement, education, labour market opportunities of young people, elderly care	Old-age pensions and retirement, opportunities of young people	Elderly care, old-age pensions and retirement, Social status of elderly, labour market opportunities of young people	Old-age pensions, elderly care, distribution of resources between old and young
Policy problems/challenges	Provision of elderly care, financing pensions	State welfare needs adjustments, stronger care needs in the future, public finances under pressure	Young people's future retirement income, current and future old-age poverty	Growing demand for care. Old-age poverty with consequences for health, adverse labour market conditions/low wages, child poverty	Low public pension now and even more so in the future. Lack of jobs for young people. Old prioritised over young

(continued)

Table 5.1 (continued)

	Denmark	Norway	Germany	Slovenia	United Kingdom
Perceived causes of problems/ challenges	Population ageing, fewer young people, low fertility	Population ageing, more old people in relation to workers	Population ageing, low fertility	Population ageing, low pensions, adverse labour market	Population ageing, old people take jobs from the young. Old people vote, young do not
Policy solutions	Family care (controversial), but financial compensation for informal carers. Higher retirement age. Individual responsibility for old-age pensions and services. Social investment. Child benefits	Higher retirement age, more private retirement saving, more familial care. Social investment	Decent basic pension. Maintain pensions adjusted to years of work. Support individual retirement saving. Social investment. Make it attractive to have children	More public care, esp. nursing homes. State should guarantee a decent retirement income for all elderly. Incentives for private retirement saving	Higher retirement age, compulsory private pension (but challenge for low income earners), incentives for informal care

Overall intergenerational solidarity or conflict	Solidarity both ways, but more solidarity with the young. Elderly prepared to contribute	Strong solidarity both ways. Strengthening of family solidarity	Solidarity expressed both ways, but especially towards children and workers (also as future pensioners)	Quite strong solidarity both ways	Solidarity with elderly through the family. Some signs of conflict
Expected (or desired) future of intergenerational contract	Less collective responsibility for elderly. Individualisation beyond social safety net/basic needs. Stronger at the family level. State funding for the young	Old age: Some individualisation. Children/youth: State welfare	Retirement income: Individualisation beyond basic social security. Children/young people: Collective, state responsibility. Care: Basic needs for everyone	Care: Strengthening of state responsibility (also to alleviate burden on active population). Retirement income: Decent public pensions and possibility of private saving	Weaker. Future of state pension questioned. More individualisation in retirement income

least frictions in Norway, which faces the mildest ageing pressures and has a low level of unemployment. In line with this logic, even if the predicted age-based conflicts over pensions were also absent in the other countries, the concerns about the level of retirement income for future generations were strong among participants of all ages in Germany, Slovenia and the United Kingdom. In the latter country, we might anticipate an emerging conflict between generations due to opposite voting patterns and a sense among young people that the elderly are prioritised.

With regard to elderly care and the second hypothesis, the picture is mixed. It was surprising that the Norwegian and Danish participants framed informal care in such positive terms. Given the high female labour market participation and the norm of dual-earner households, we expected to find more arguments in favour of formal, state-supported care, which is often considered a precondition for labour market participation of women in particular. A partial explanation for the Norwegian finding may be that the quality of formal elderly care is often criticised in the media. Thus, some people might get the impression that formal care is of poor quality. If you do it yourself, at least you know what you get. In Denmark, arguments went in both directions. Some statements (by some older participants) were in line with hypothesis two. In the absence of formal care, some people will be cut off from labour market participation. Conversely, there was a call for more family care resting on the (moral) duty to take responsibility for close relatives. In the end, the Danish participants supported a compromise which involved giving people the opportunity (but not obligation) to take on care responsibilities with compensation for income loss. The participants also discussed more informal care in the UK, motivated by affection for family members. The Slovenian case was closest to the second hypothesis. Here we recorded a strong interest in strengthened state responsibility for elderly care. This was as expected since such services are less developed than in the Scandinavian countries.

Turning to the third hypothesis, it is perhaps unsurprising that the social investment discourse emerges clearly in Denmark and Norway. In terms of public social spending, they are the least age biased of our cases (see Fig. 5.1). We note that investment in children and young people, especially through education, is emphasised also in Germany. The partici-

Table 5.2 Quotations used in the text

DK-1	**Individual responsibility in old age but protection of the weak DK-50** (female, age 65, retired): [...] responsibility for your own life. [...] But at the same time, society should still take responsibility for the weak, the fragile, the sick, the poor, the sick elderly. I am old, but I'm not sick so there is no need to take responsibility for me.
DK-2	**Towards a more familialised model: Families should be responsible for dependent relatives. DK-66** (female, age 33): Maybe it's the same as with gender and going part-time. Maybe we should work less and look after our own children and elderly people more. We have a responsibility toward each other, there should be a change in attitude....
DK-3	**The welfare state should take care of the elderly. DK-59** (female, age 69, retired): I was around back when people looked after their elderly. I think it's exceptional that the welfare society has taken that on. It's the welfare society's job to care for you if you're not able to do it yourself. It's difficult to make that the duty of relatives. **DK-80** (female, age 63, efterløn (early retirement)): I'm going back a little here because that's what I made a note of, the thing about old-age pension. I think that if we remove the old-age pension and everything to do with domestic assistance and the whole shebang, then we might just as well go home because then there is no welfare state. It's all about how we, instead of looking after our elderly people and children ourselves, have agreed, as a society, to pay more tax to allow the state to care for our old and our young. It seems like a great idea. I would personally not be able to go to work if there wasn't anyone to look after my 92-year-old mother.
DK-4	**Give people a choice whether to care for relatives themselves. DK-55** (male, age 51): You could set it up as an option, like everyone's right/duty to take parental leave. Maybe as an option but not an obligation. **DK-85** (female, age 25): [...] it's a good idea for people to have the option to do it.
DK-5	**Investments in young people. DK-74** (male, age 33): [W]e should preserve and enhance productivity in society, and that's why I don't believe in over-investing in the elderly who aren't productive. ... we shouldn't take money that's being invested in people who are assets and put it into people who are not assets. I'm a big supporter of the golden oldies and staying longer on the labour market, but I fundamentally disagree with people getting money. **DK-78** (female, age 61, unemployed): [...] the system should take responsibility for the young and not use so many resources, job centres, for example, [...] on oldies like me in the job centre, almost month after month. [...] Here I also think there is a question of priorities and that Denmark and our society have a responsibility to do something more for those that we can see a future for. **DK-65** (Day 2, plenary session) We agreed on a proposal to continue to invest in education and the future. We don't want to see any further cuts in the area of education in the future. **MODERATOR** (Day 2, plenary session): Looking at it from a generational perspective like that applied in this discussion we don't want the elderly to be given money at the expense of education.

(continued)

Table 5.2 (continued)

	Necessary to increase the retirement age, spend more on the young and make it more attractive to have children. **DK-57** (male age 30): I can understand why the retirement age has been pushed back. And I don't think there are many in my generation who believe they'll get an old-age pension when the time comes. **DK-62** (male, age 32): But the idea that there won't be an old-age pension for our generation is nonsense, because there will and the funds are being set aside quietly bit by bit. […] I'm more interested in finding out how we're going to decide whether to put our efforts into older or younger citizens. I mean, increasing benefits for elderly people and removing money from education, research and state education support. Think again. Who's going to finance it in the future? **DK-57** (male, age 30): [DK62] may well be right. We might get some pension. I just think that the money could be used better, for example on education. If we knew that we had to save for our pensions then we'd do it, right? **DK-60** (male age 35, student): There have been reforms which have put the retirement age up. It's been necessary. […] Perhaps we should turn it around a bit and look at the younger generations. […] We need to provide better incentives for having children early on in life. […] I know people get child benefit but I think we need to do more financially to make it attractive.
NO-1	**Population ageing is costly and leaves less money for other tasks. NO-20** (female, age 52, employed FT): The elder boom forces us to prioritize money for elder care, and then there is maybe even less left.
NO-2	**Uncertain future of old-age pensions. NO-14** (female, age 44, employed FT): I think I belong to the generation that doesn't get the pension I am entitled to. **Moderator (blue breakout group)**: Are you worried about earning enough to get by in life? **NO-13** (female, 25–34): I assume we have to work longer. […] I suppose we have to rise the pensionable age. **NO-11** (male, age 31): The national insurance as we know it today was launched in the sixties. It is actually pretty new. But now we expect it to be a publicly accepted welfare good to keep, but it might not be like that in the future.

NO-3	**Necessary with higher retirement age (and/or lower pensions) to meet other costs. NO-14** (female, age 44, employed FT): Raising the pension age is also a way of financing and getting more resources for healthcare services. **NO-11** (male, age 31): I believe that one has to reduce the pensions even more than today, long-term. Then one will need to spend one's own money to buy welfare services. The alternative is to leave the pension unchanged, but lower other services.
	Discussion in red breakout group (with the youngest participants)
	NO-8 (male, age 25): We keep getting older and older, so it has to go up at some point. **NO-1** (female, age 19): Should have the opportunity to retire early if you age early. **NO-11**: We have tried that early retirement model and everything now, and to retire whenever you want to after you reach 62. People have worked hard. They are tired. But it doesn't really work so well with what we are trying to achieve now. Average pension age is very low. People retire very early. I talk about people who have acquired rights after the old pension model, which was a lot better than the one we have today. **NO-2** (female, age 25): But can raising the pension age be a bullet point? **NO-11**: Can write forced pension age. **NO-2**: Does everyone agree? [Yes. *Several people agree*]. **Moderator:** Do we dear say how old they should be? **NO-11**: Before we got the early retirement it was 67. [...] Now it is also from 62. Then it should be at least 72 if you ask me. **NO-10** (male, age 27): I believe a few years can make a big difference. 3–4 years. You suggested 72? That could be rather high. **NO-11**: Depends how far ahead we think. **NO-8**: I mean, if it is 2040, that is 25 years from now. 72-year-olds are probably quite fit in 25 years. **NO-11**: Maybe we don't have to be that specific. Could we say like … **NO-2**: Over 70. **NO-11**: 70 plus, then. Several people agree. When you say forced pension age, that meant that you [...] aren't allowed to retire before you are 70.
NO-4	**Families should take more responsibility for dependent relatives. NO-24** (male, age 34, FT work): [...] here in Norway, we aren't that extended family which you find in other cultures. We have sort of made the responsibility of caring for the elder's public, and the government will never be as caring as the family and friends. It is really sad, but it is a reality. If we push care over on the government, the government will answer 'This is the care you get for your money' and they would rather lead it over to health and prioritizing and such. The public can never give as good care as we can do as family and friends. It's just the reality. **NO-15** (female, age 44): I have thought about something, bit of a touchy topic: How long before the next of kin have to care for their old relatives? In many countries, there is of course … when you don't have the same public systems the family has to be there, but if the country actually gets a more squeezed economy ahead, one has to demand more of the next of kin perhaps. Then again, you have the ones who don't have children and the ones with children living far away. A difficult topic, but I think it is relevant to discuss it at least.

(continued)

Table 5.2 (continued)

NO-5	**Towards more individual responsibility for retirement income and old age but public pensions needed as a safety net. NO-21** (male, age 54): In respect of generation and pension: The pension is there to ensure social security for everyone. **NO-14** (female, age 44): You cannot put all of the responsibility on the state and say that we don't believe people are capable of saving for themselves, so we will save for them. **NO-21**: But that is what we do today. Then we should have removed the pension system from the state all together. **NO-14**: No, I'm not saying that either, but it was to push it to extremes, though. They do pamper us. **NO-21**: I agree, but then we need a minimum pension and an individual earmarked pension on top of that. **NO-22** (male, age 56): I wrote more individual responsibility and means-tested benefits, but it is a little risky because then you punish the one who is hard-working and award the one who is not. Has to find the right way of doing it without motivating in an unintentional way. That is a challenge. I fear that we are moving towards means-testing, that we get a smaller minimum pension and the rest is up to you. [...] More individual responsibility, I believe that will come. **NO-22** (male, age 56): If I were young today, I would have started doing that foundation-saving a bit earlier than what I did. **NO-14** (female, age 44): I have. Luckily. **NO-22**: Yes, there lies a big responsibility on the individual, because you cannot trust the government to the same degree. I believe the insecurity will be greater ahead than what it has been. **NO-14**: It is very positive to make the individual accountable to a bigger degree. We have been pampered for many years. **NO-5** (female, age 39): It is of course the individual's responsibility. One should plan. **NO-9** (male, age 26): I believe, to a certain degree, that the individual's responsibility should increase a little. **NO-1** (female, age 19): But not everyone has the means to save up, right. To save up for your own pension, to the same degree. We have households struggling to make ends meet even though they aren't poor. My mother is a single provider and a teacher. She doesn't have much to set aside for pension savings and still live decently.

NO-6	**Later retirement might squeeze out the young. NO-23** (male, age 34): In relation to what was said, some politicians who want old people to work longer. I think we have to look beyond Norway: How do they do it in Sweden for example? They do it like if you want to work longer you have the possibility. But it has its consequences. The youth aren't let in. How many unemployed young people in Sweden? Pretty many. That's why we have them here in Norway. The young. They won't let them have a chance. They want the old people with experience, so the young people don't get the chance because they lack the experience. **NO-33** (male, age 66): It is a dilemma here too, in respect of working long or not. About pension and pension age very high. The pension reform, the way it was implemented, and also the way it seems to be carried on now, those who are 45 today will have to work until at least 75 to get full pension? Should they quit at 62 and get a lot less in pension to give the young people a chance? There is no fixed answer, but it is a dilemma. **NO-15** (female, age 44): Will it lead to fewer young people getting a chance, as possible, that is positive, but what about the youth? People in the establishing phase don't get jobs, because suppose we only have a given number of jobs available? People in the establishing phase don't get jobs, because grandma and grandpa insist on keeping their jobs even if they could afford to retire.
NO-7	**Invest in children and young people. Important that nobody is left behind and is given the opportunity to enter the labour market. NO-15** female, age 44): Prevent people from being left out. Important with early focus on children and youth. **NO-23** (male, age 34): Firstly to get jobs for the youth, because it costs the state almost a million a year if an 18–19-year-old doesn't attend school and is unemployed. If they do a good job and makes sure that youth gets a job they have saved a million a year. If they employ a thousand people we have saved a billion. We have to take the problem seriously now before we are there in 2040. **NO-29** (female, age 53, day 1 plenary session) We were on to the youth who have to get a chance [...]. **Moderator** (day 2, green breakout group): The main argument for financing of studies and making the young people work? **NO-30** (female, age 70): Future employees. **NO-11** (day 2 plenary session, reporting from red group): We had many discussions, but what we all agreed on was that education is the cornerstone for future [...] so we wanted to go in for a mandatory year in nursery school before school, and it should be free of charge, also to better the language and vocabulary, both for Norwegian children and for immigrants.

(continued)

Table 5.2 (continued)

NO-8	**Concerns for young people's mental health.** *NO-23 (male, age 34): [...] Some talk about the youth today. We have never had better youths. These boys do their homework, spend time with the family, almost never go out, never get high. They are as good as can be. But they are the ones to struggle psychologically more than ever [...].*
DE-1	**Younger generation will receive lower pensions than current retirees.** *Moderator (Day 1 green breakout group): Family, generations and retirement. What comes to mind there, what is important?* **DE-27** *(male, age > 65): That families don't have a chance to put anything aside for retirement.* **DE-28** *(male, age > 65): The topic that comes up again and again is that the younger generation will never be able to get the level of retirement fund support that those who are now retiring are able to get.* **DE-10** *(female, age 63): We were talking about retirement, and I can't complain, I receive a good pension, but when I think of the younger generation, like my son who is in his late 40's, and he's received information about what his pension would be if her were to retire, and now it's about 800 euros, and I think to myself that something isn't right. Because if you don't work at all, you get a basic benefit of 800 or so, so something is wrong there.* **DE-34** *(male, age 46) Injustice, because the younger people pay in, but they'll only get a small percentage of what we're getting in pension payouts.* **DE-28** *(male, age > 65): Well, but retirement is also a subject that we can discuss with regard to retirement in the future. People retiring now are pretty much OK, but what about people who will retire in 10 years' time? Or much later?*

DE-2	**Basic social security to prevent old-age poverty. DE-12** (female, age 33): Elder-poverty. **DE-06** (female, age 43) The prevention of elder-poverty. You might have a person who did their training when they were 17 and has worked all their life, but then ... **DE-32** (male, age 69) If they have basic social security, then they won't fall into poverty. That the basic security income has to be set up in such a way that these problems of elder-poverty don't arise. **DE-21** (male, age 41): This is moving more in the direction of protecting the elderly here, with the older part of the population receiving the advantage, and there's nothing wrong with that, but on the other hand, fairness refers to the younger people too and how they have to pay more and more pension fees that they will likely not get back later on. **DE-32** (male, age 69) We're not just protecting the old, we're protecting the workers. **DE-21**: Yes, the younger people will also be old at some point, so it affects everyone. **DE-23** (male, age 70): Well, we know it's a problem for the pension fund that not enough younger people are paying in, and if they're not working, then they can't provide for their own private retirement insurance either. That won't work. We have to figure out how everyone at the end of their lives can have a kind of basic retirement income. Where that's going to come from, I can't say, but somehow we can't just go around in circles where we have fewer people working, and the rest don't get anything either. **DE-10** (female, age 63) It's not right that after I've worked, then I have to go and apply to the state for welfare money. **DE-23** (male, age 70): And you should then avoid this situation of having to go there on bended knee and fill out a thousand forms, and then all this bureaucracy itself costs a lot of money, all the management and administration of this to fill all this out and file it, plus it's embarrassing for those people on top of it all. **Moderator 4**: So what measure should I write down then? **DE-23** (male, age 70): I'm not really sure. Solidarity pension or social pension or something like that. It's just that everyone should get something so that they can get by.

(continued)

Table 5.2 (continued)

DE-3	**Retirees should be compensated for work effort or contributions paid. DE-32** (male, age > 65): Then to make it dependent on the time you spent working, the years that you were working. Those who've worked for decades and paid into the system should expect more than those who didn't pay in at all. [...] it's to do with generational equality and fairness. Not with basic security. That's a separate point for me. **Moderator 3**: What is the goal to be called? **DE-32**: I don't know, pension alignment. To their work history. The pension I get is dependent on what my work history was, how long I worked. It should be reflected in the pension amount. **DE-09** (female, age 29): And work should play a role. [...] You have to have a pension that is relative to the pay-in time period. Someone who worked for 40 years must be appreciated for their work, maybe a subordinate pension that is added to the basic pension, a kind of bonus for every year to reflect the pay-in period. **DE-14** (female, age 30): Right.
DE-4	**Support for active population to help them save for retirement—privately or through a reformed public system. DE-27** (male, age > 65): [...] at the moment it's completely impossible for the current generation to pay for the costs of this 1–2 ratio while at the same time trying to save something for themselves so that they have something to live off of when they're retired. This has to be supported. **Researcher**: Adequate opportunity for private retirement insurance. **DE-27** (male, age > 65): That's right. **DE-14** (female, age 30): It's better if I get more money now and invest for myself, because in 45 years, I don't even know if Germany will still exist, let alone whether or not I'm guaranteed a pension payment. So I'd rather save for myself.
DE-5	**Generational fairness means access to care when in need—independent of age. DE-07** (female, age 46): I would say in my opinion generational equality/fairness is that if someone gets sick, the steps taken should be independent of whether they're old or young. Sometimes when older people get sick, we say they're going to die soon anyway, so we don't need to do so much—to put it bluntly. Healthcare equality for young and old.

DE-6	**Multiple advantages of investing in children, particularly through education but also in other areas. DE-17** (female, age 66): The children are the future, and the more education we invest in them, the more taxation support they will provide. **DE-22** (male, age 24): Education is our future. I am passionately of this opinion, and therefore I would invest as much as possible in the area of education, and that starts early in preschool. **DE-18** (male, age 52): I'm talking about when you start at the roots, when the children are little, you start young. When they get really good education, health(care) and so forth, then they don't end up being a burden for the society, when you're healthy, you are not a burden, or when you have better education, then you can work, get better jobs. The one thing leads to the next.
DE-7	**More children needed to address population ageing, but incentives are poor. DE-14** (female, age 30): The working population needs to bring more children into the world and be supported. **DE-18** (male, age 52): You have to make it more attractive for Germans to have children. **DE-21** (male, age 35–44) But the problem is that you need to animate people to want to have more children so that there are more people paying into the system. Those that pay will have damn high contributions to the retirement pension fund, and that is increasing. I'm sure you've seen that. It's not just that older people get less in pension or lower buying power because of lack of pension increase, but also that the younger people are paying more and more into the system. **DE-18** (male, age 52): If the current generation saves for the next as it is now, then we're back to this idea that people have to have more children. We always come back to the same point. More children mean that they work more and pay into the fund for the next generation. **DE-02** (female, age 41): But they do so little to support having children here in this country, so that I would never do it again, honestly. It is almost a punishment here in this country, really.

(continued)

Table 5.2 (continued)

SI-1	**Low pensions force old people to work and squeeze out young people. SI-83** (male, age 45): [...] look, we're making people work at 67 years of age. At 67 years of age, I can't imagine that a worker at an assembly line is as productive and successful as a young person. A young person would do 10 times as much—I'm exaggerating—or twice as much as this old person and it would be better if we enabled this old person to retire, you'll have additional benefits on account of your health, because you're old and have back problems, while the younger person will be more productive. But in this country, the young sit at home while the elderly work. **SI-86** (female, age 25): [...] No, increase the pensions on such a level that they don't need to work. A person that is—I don't know—60 years old, they should retire and that's it. **SI-81** (female, age 59): That's right, and an appropriate pension, as it should be. **SI-86**: And not that you're old and retire and need to work. **SI-81**: You need to work because your pension is too low, that's right. **SI-86**: And because it's more profitable for the state to extend it for a couple of years while the young sit at home, naturally. And here's the circle, a domino effect, the system, something, needs to be changed. **SI-81**: You see, pensions have actually been lowered so much from 2000, from the beginning of January 1, onwards, that the elderly are forced to work, actually, because they cannot survive ... [...] And let me tell you that ... and forces the elderly to go and—either get a job, or do undeclared work, or additional occasional work, that is limited to how much—60 hours, that's very little, how much money do you get out of that. [...] And they take the work away from younger people. **SI-57** (female, age 36): And another thing, when it comes to the age: it seems like we will be forced to work until we have crutches and wear hearing aids, while the young will be unemployed. This leads nowhere. And what are they trying to achieve? That one works so long there is no longer any need to put them in retirement and receive pension money. **SI-50** (male, age 35): Many of them [elderly persons] are forced to [work], in order to make the ends meet.
SI-2	**Population ageing means more frail and poor elderly in the future. Moderator:** Taking care of the elderly. Why will that be an important topic in 20, 25 years? **SI-88:** (female age 43, FT work): There'll be more and more of us. **SI-77** (female, age 38, PT work): And they're more and more ill. **SI-81**: (female, age 59, retired): And more and more poor.

SI-3	**Low pensions lead to poverty in old age and a range of other problems. The state should act as a guarantor. SI-57** (female, age 36): Small pensions, the elderly cannot make the ends meet, most of them. **SI-81** (female, age 59, retired): Low pensions. **SI-88** (female age 43, FT work): And illness goes hand in hand with poverty, I suppose. **SI-87** (male, age 52 retired): And the question is, who'll be able to take care of them, their children are not obliged to. **SI-86** (female, age 25, FT work): This is also why we're discussing this problem—taking care of the elderly. Because they can't do it on their own—they can't all of a sudden afford nursing homes [...]. **SI-58** (female, age 49): Yes, and how come we have slipped so low when it comes to values, how can we allow that pensioners, who worked their whole lives, cannot afford food here in Slovenia. **SI-82** (day 1 plenary): We talked about the poverty that's developing because pensions have been too low for the last ten years, pensions have dropped drastically and more and more problems are linked to that. People can't pay for the care home. They can't even pay the bills. They can't afford the basic things. So essentially there should be a guaranteed minimum pension, right now the pension can be lower than social benefits and that's not OK. **SI-62** (Day 1 plenary): We see the role of the state as, the state should give some kind of guarantee for a decent pension.
SI-4	**Problem of poverty in families with children. SI-53** (female, age 55): And many children too [cannot afford food in Slovenia], lots of parents don't have a job. **SI-56** (male, age 68): That as well. **SI-53** (female, age 55): And there are so many of them. **SI-56** (male, age 68): It happens that both parents don't have jobs. **SI-53** female, age 55): Again, there are many families where both parents are unemployed.

(continued)

Table 5.2 (continued)

SI-5	Difficult for young people to take care of elderly, more state responsibility.
	SI-70 (female, age 34): Yes, of course, it's difficult with the job and, I don't know, everything, to take care for them. **SI-80** (male, age 67, retired): The children can't even take care of themselves. **SI-88** (female age 43, FT work): Well, you can't, if you're at work the whole day and working for minimum wage, how can you take care of the parents as well. You can't even take care of yourself. **SI-87** (male, age 52, retired): It needs to be made sure that the children will not be burdened by their age and if they can't take care of themselves, that they'll be able to go to a nursing home and that'll be financed by the state. **SI-78**: If they can't do it themselves, the state has to. **SI-88**: Also to pay the difference. **SI-82**: Change the limitation of this payment difference, to just pay as much as it needs to be paid, if a person's pension is EUR 400 and the fees for taking care of someone who's bedridden are EUR 1200, the state should contribute these EUR 600. **SI-50** (male, age 35): Let's look at the role of the state in this area, care for the elderly, the state should take over the role of the guarantor, I mean in a way that it should guarantee each elderly person a decent pension. Because many pensioners—ok, some have extremely low pensions and need to work. Many pensioners have been through a lot and once they retire at the age of 65, or 67, or, why not, even younger, should still be able to afford a luxury they were unable to afford before, to do something they did not have the chance to before. But once they are retired they cannot afford this because they can hardly make ends meet with the pension.

SI-6	**Elderly deserve better treatment. SI-58** (female, age 49): The elderly should not be pushed into the corner, to the margins, they should still be actively involved, [...] an older person with rich professional experience has immense knowledge and can contribute. **SI-51** (male, age 27): Well, we should be thinking in the direction, one day we too will be older and ask the question, what is going to happen to us, in 2040. So, if we squeeze the elderly into the corner today, we should ask ourselves, what is going to happen to us, where do we end up, if this is how we treat them today. **SI-60** (female, age 40): I think that is what we should be changing, our attitude towards the elderly. Because in our culture, we have a very, I will say, poor attitude towards the elderly. [...] these people gave us something, we are their descendants and we will once be in their shoes. [...] Eastern cultures: they appreciate their elderly, respect them, because they contributed to the society. [...] While in Slovenia they get pushed aside. You have seen the commercials; they are all showing young people, right? Of course the young are important, but we should not be forgetting about the elderly, because one day we'll be there too one day. And let's take the opportunity while they are still with us to learn as much as we can from them. But most of all make sure they have a roof above their head, that really is fundamental, it is so sad that everyone is just waiting for them to die. And we call ourselves a social state, yeah, right. **SI-56** (male, age 68): And the state is trying to save at pensions, social transfers, health care, everywhere. **SI-51** (male, age 27): And we are doing nothing about it. At least the young aren't. And experiences vanish. **SI-57** (female, age 37): We are all ageing; let's take care of them the same way we would like to be taken care of ... **SI-61** (female, age 47): That we will be taken care of.
SI-8	**Poor pension outlook for young people. SI-51:** If I take a look at us, young ones in 2040, well, one won't even get a chance to find a job before they are 30—how am I going to be actively employed for 40 years [needed to get a full pension], if I am to start working at 30? **SI-50** (male, age 35): And not the way things are today, when everyone tells you to save up, well how, if there is nothing to save. If labour taxes were lower, then net pay checks would go up, and one could actually have some money extra to save for the old age. **SI-60** (female, age 40): I think the government and all of us are turning a blind eye. There aren't many representatives of really young people here, those just entering the labour market. They're really forced into precarious work. We all know, everyone here will have a pension, I hope, but the young people still don't have a single day of full-time employment. Where do you think they'll get their pensions from if they have to work in self-employment? [...]. I really know a lot of young people who are forced into these forms of work, they don't have maternity leave or sick leave, they can't get a loan.

(continued)

Table 5.2 (continued)

UK-1	**The State Pension will disappear in the future. UK-45** (female, age > 65): I don't think there will be a state pension in 2040. **UK-44** (female, age 35–44): the state pension probably won't exist. I think we are all in agreement on that.
UK-2	**Private pensions to compensate for lack of State Pension:** **UK-86** (male, age 25–34): And making compulsory private pensions. **Unknown** (Day 1, plenary session): 40–42 year olds now will be, will have to think about it, have they got a private pension in place now? Because in 25 years' time, they're going to be 67 and if the retirement age doesn't go over any higher than that, they're going to be having what is going to be a pretty, you know, just barely adequate State pension. A private pension has got to be the way forward. **UK-44** (female, age 35–44): That's why I encourage my two children to get their own private pension and just build it up. **UK-45** (female, age > 65): We said they are, most of them, sort of, from our generation [inaudible 0:01:52] have saved for their retirement. So, yes, you've got your old age pension, but most people, that I know certainly, have got private pensions as well, and have invested their money. So they're quite comfortable, and they have got money to spend, the older people. **UK-67** (male, age 25–34): It could be more mandatory, some sort of policy for private pensions, to take the pressure off the Government, so there's more businesses have to provide private pensions. **UK-45** (female, age > 65): The only thing I'll say is that, I'm one of the ones that never saved, so I've had nothing in private pension. So if didn't have my old age pension, I would be struggling. **Unknown** (female): But you're not one of the naughty ones, 'cause a lot of people don't save now. They don't pay into pensions, because pensions got hit through recession and everything, a lot of people went bust. **Unknown** (female): I'm for [mandatory private pension contributions) but then what about people on low income. **Unknown** (female): I don't disagree with that, but what I was thinking was that actually some people just can't afford to put the mandatory amount in. Being forced in to doing it if you haven't got it, to be forced into it, then you're in a sticky situation.

UK-3	**Demanding senior workers to retire later, squeezes out younger people. UK-81** (female, age < 24): People getting older. I think with people working longer and not receiving necessarily as much pension as they need to live properly, people are having to work a lot longer and therefore the younger generation are suffering because they can't get into the jobs that the older generation are in. Which is, you know, older generation can work as long as they like, but it should be that the Government see that they've worked all their lives and they should be helping them to retire. I'm worried about my mum and dad being able to afford to retire, so I'm having to think what can I do to help them, that's sell their home, they'll have to downsize and that was what they wanted to be as our money when we were older, so it's a shame that that's come into force with the pensions. **UK-80** (female, age 45–54): Yes I think it's more to the people that's sitting at home, support people to retire at 65 or 60 and then get them people out into work. **UK-86** (male, age 25–34): In a sense you're saying that because people can't retire that they're still working and taking jobs that you younger people could be in. **UK-80** (female, age 45–54): I'm not allowed to retire now until I get to 67 [unclear] got to work until I'm 67. **UK-81** (female, age < 24): Whereas if you could retire at 60, that's 7 years that [unclear] younger person could get that role and then get into and then they can retire at 60. It just has a knock-on effect on the rest of us. **UK-47** (female, age > 65): The thing is they are putting the pension age up so people are having to work longer and they are struggling and younger people leaving school and college, university, there's no jobs for them at the other end of the scale and they are making the older people who have worked all their lives and they are not giving the younger ones a chance.
UK-4	**Younger generation relies too much on their parents. UK-84** (male, age 45–54): The amount of grandparents now that you see picking kids up from school or dropping kids off is phenomenal. There's something going on there [unclear] if you've grandparents and stuff like that to help you sometimes, then maybe [unclear] ... **UK-89** (male, 45–54): I think a lot of people too much in our society rely too much on the older people. They have contributed, they have lived, they have laid the foundation for us and too much the grandparents are being [unclear] of their kids, you need have a more robust plan. It's your life, your parents brought you up, [unclear], they're shouting, they'll go they'll put you in your room and then you've got to give them the opposite like start having children, the granny can pick up, the granddad can pick up, I think that's so wrong, I think older people, when they retire, need a quality of life for themselves, now there's [unclear] retired.

(continued)

Table 5.2 (continued)

UK-5	**Incentivising informal care by family members. UK-46** (male, age 35–44): For the people who look after relatives to be able to keep the aging population in their own homes to be cared for by younger relatives and maybe giving the younger relatives are great contacts or anything that they have to go out and earn their money so they can perhaps cut down their hours at work to care for that aging relative. **UK-40** (female, age 25–34): Its employment, so with the aging population, so for example, so instead of like, we are talking like it's going to cost more, our money that's for research and so forth, but like what you mentioned though if we could be given like special leave or you know so that we can perhaps look after elderly parents and relatives and just take some time off work and I think okay if they want to save some money in that sense then give us that extra benefit there from work. **UK-44** (female, age 35–44): Yes, tax breaks for relatives. **UK-40**: Yes tax breaks for relatives and [unclear] time off work for family and friends to pay to my mom. **UK-45** (female, age > 65): No because you are relative you can claim Carers Allowance. **UK-51** (female, age < 24): [Unclear], but not to take a paid rate from your job to be a career. I think that's wrong. Why should you be paid to leave work to go and look after your family members when they are most likely going to be entitled to have a carer anyway? So why not give another person the job instead of you leaving your job to go and do another job temporarily and be paid the same time. You are saying it needs to be fair that everyone's, how is that fair for the employer? How is it fair that they … **UK-40**: It's not always the case just turning to a carer to look after their mom, it's you personally you want to spend the last couple of months or weeks with your mom. It's not always the case just turning to a carer to look after their mom, it's you personally you want to spend the last couple of months or weeks with your mom.

UK-6	**Demand for elderly care creates jobs. UK-40** (female, age 35–44): And I think that with the aging population also comes jobs in a way because then there's lots of people to look after them I think. **UK-45** (female, age > 65): There will be, there will be help for the unemployed because obviously more carers are going to be required. From 2040. **UK-47** (female, age > 65): More jobs. **UK-44** (female, 35–44): create jobs, people are getting older, there will be more carers needed.
UK-7	**The elderly get more since they vote while a lot of young people do not. Moderator** (Day 1, green breakout group): And we have spoke about one point to think about, we mentioned the cost of getting old. We talked about there's more people with long term illnesses, but do we think that's an issue with costs? **UK-44** (female, age 35–44): It's a strain on the NHS. **UK-45** (female, age > 65): Well it is for the NHS, but I have never been to the doctors so much since I have [unclear]. Getting older. **UK-44** (female, age 35–44): There is more time to think about the fact that you might have something wrong, because when you are at work all the time you just get on with it don't you and plough on. […] They ignore the under 24's because we vote the least and then the kind of over sixty fives come out the most and vote, so then that's who they prioritise because that is one of the [unclear]. **UK-43** (male, age < 24): I think it's all down to, because the generation that aren't voting now in 2040 will be the older generation, so if we are still not voting then there might be a more even spread, but I think at the moment they prioritise them a lot more because they are [unclear]. **UK-44** (female, age 35–44): I think it's only, it's because they are older and wiser that's all. As you get older you become wiser and you think more about it, then you have your family and you have to think about it. Yes, but they vote don't they?
UK-8	**Contested increases in retirement age. UK-88** (male, age 25–34): I just think the retirement age needs to be between 70 and 75. **UK-87** (female, age > 65): it's unfair. I put money in my pension pot for me to be entitled to live an extra 30 years and retire at 67, why should I be [inaudible 00:05:44] for somebody that's … **UK-80** (female, age 45–54): it's a work person, the older person who's broken down automatically because their body physically doesn't let them go to work, I would rather that person goes at 60 and have somebody at the age of 20 who's going to do double the amount of work.

pants who advocated social investment included some older as well as younger people. Part of the explanation may be that elderly people wish young people well, but in our review of the forum material, we also recognise the logic presented in the third hypothesis.

The conversations suggest that intergenerational solidarity is generally quite strong, with some indications of tension, mainly in the UK. Yet, the intergenerational state welfare contract is going through a process of change. It is not likely to disappear completely but may weaken especially with respect to old-age pensions. In some countries, we observed arguments that suggest a possible return to greater intergenerational solidarity within families (Table 5.2).

Notes

1. AROPE refers to the share of the population that fits in one or more of the following categories: at risk of poverty after social transfers (set at 60% of national median equivalised disposable household income), severely materially deprived and living in a household with very low work intensity. The AROPE rate is one of the headline indicators of the EU 2020 strategy (see Eurostat 2017).
2. The State Pension age for men is currently (August 2017) 65 years. For women, it will reach 65 years in November 2018. After that the equalised State Pension Age for both women and men will increase to 66 by October 2020, to 67 by 2028 and to 68 by 2037.
3. It is important to note that in reality this argument is inaccurate since care is means-tested and very few cases are poor enough to get free care.

References

Andersen, J., Schøyen, M., & Hvinden, B. (2017). Changing Scandinavian welfare states—Which way forward? In P. Taylor-Gooby, B. Leruth, & H. Chung (Eds.), *After austerity: Welfare state transformation in Europe after the great recession*. Oxford: Oxford University Press.

Di Gessa, G., Glaser, K., & Tinker, A. (2016). The impact of caring for grandchildren on the health of grandparents in Europe: A lifecourse approach. *Social Science & Medicine, 152*, 166–175.

Ebbinghaus, B. (2011). *The varieties of pension governance. Pension privatization in Europe*. Oxford: Oxford University Press.
Esping-Andersen, G., & Sarasa, S. (2002). The generational conflict reconsidered. *Journal of European Social Policy, 12*(1), 5–21.
Eurostat. (2017). People at risk of poverty or social exclusion. Statistics explained. Retrieved May 28, 2017, from http://ec.europa.eu/eurostat/statistics-explained/pdfscache/22124.pdf.
Immergut, E. M., Anderson, K. M., & Schulze, I. (2007). *The handbook of west European pension politics*. Oxford: Oxford University Press.
Jenson, J., & Saint-Martin, D. (2006). Building blocks for a new social architecture: The LEGO™ paradigm of an active society. *Policy & Politics, 34*(3), 429–451.
Kohli, M. (1987). Retirement and the moral economy: An historical interpretation of the German case. *Journal of Aging Studies, 1*(2), 125–144.
Kohli, M. (2005). Generational changes and generational equity. In M. L. Johnson (Ed.), *Cambridge handbook of age and ageing*. Cambridge: Cambridge University Press.
Kohli, M. (2006). Aging and justice. In R. H. Binstock & L. K. George (Eds.), *Handbook of aging and the social sciences*. San Diego, CA: Academic Press.
Kohli, M. (2008). Generational equity: Concepts and attitudes. In C. Arza & M. Kohli (Eds.), *Pension reform in Europe: Politics, policies and outcomes*. London: Routledge.
Lindh, T., Malmberg, B., & Palme, J. (2005). Generations at war or sustainable social policy in aging societies? *The Journal of Political Philosophy, 13*(4), 470–489.
Lister, R. (2003). Investing in citizen-workers of the future: Transformations in citizenship and the state under new labour. *Social Policy & Administration, 37*(5), 427–443.
Lynch, J. (2006). *Age in the welfare state: The origins of social spending on pensioners, workers, and children*. Cambridge: Cambridge University Press.
Naumann, E. (2014). Increasing conflict in times of retrenchment? Attitudes towards healthcare provision in Europe between 1996 and 2002. *International Journal of Social Welfare, 23*(3), 276–286.
Pampel, F. C. (1998). *Aging, social inequality and public policy*. Thousand Oaks: Pine Forge Press.
Svallfors, S. (2008). The generational contract in Sweden: Age-specific attitudes to age-related policies. *Policy & Politics, 36*(3), 381–396.

6

The Provision of Care: Whose Responsibility and Why?

Heejung Chung, Maša Filipovič Hrast, and Tatjana Rakar

Introduction

Care has become one of the important focal points of the restructuring of state welfare during the first wave of the new risk policies that enable increased participation of women in the labour market, and also in response to the challenges resulting from the ageing population. These new risk policies have developed relatively recently, and in several countries are still developing. Care systems have developed quite differently in European countries, incorporating different arrangements which give the various actors very different roles within the welfare mix. The new demographic and economic conditions pose new challenges for the sustainability of the welfare state and raise questions about the (new) division of

---

H. Chung (✉)
University of Kent, Canterbury, UK
e-mail: h.chung@kent.ac.uk

M. F. Hrast • T. Rakar
University of Ljubljana, Ljubljana, Slovenia

© The Author(s) 2018
P. Taylor-Gooby, B. Leruth (eds.), *Attitudes, Aspirations and Welfare*,
https://doi.org/10.1007/978-3-319-75783-4_6

responsibilities among the family, the state, third sector or the market (Bettio and Plantenga 2004; Saraceno and Keck 2010).

These factors can affect support for the state provision of care policies. In general, there is strong public support for provision in these areas across the population (Chung and Meuleman 2017). Beyond this, knowledge is limited. Using Democratic Forum data from the United Kingdom (UK), Germany, Norway and Slovenia, representing four distinct welfare and care regimes and degrees of familialism and defamilialism, we examine citizen's support for both childcare and elderly care. Here we focus on two aspects—namely, who should be responsible for care and why. In relation to the reasoning that frames people's support for state provision of care, we distinguish economic from social justifications: whether entitlement to care provision is based on the right to take part in the labour market for the carer, or whether care is provided as part of the social rights of the recipient as a citizen.

The structure of the chapter is as follows. Firstly, we provide an overview of the current division of responsibility between state, market and family in provision of care and describe the distinctive care regimes that have developed in the four countries observed. We then present attitudinal data that sets the context and shows relatively high support in all countries regarding state provision of childcare and policies for the elderly. This is followed by the analysis of the forum data. Finally we discuss the relationship between the current care regime of the observed countries and the role ascribed to the actors in the future. We find that in some of the countries these correspond while in others they seem to diverge, and that current practice, policy settings, and both economic and social framings influence people's ideas.

The Division of Responsibility in the Provision of Care

Traditionally, care has been provided largely by informal social networks, such as parents in the case of childcare, or children and spouses in the case of elderly care alongside extended family members (Daly 2002). However, with the introduction of the welfare state, in many countries care provision have been taken up by different bodies. Esping-Andersen (1990, 1999) distinguishes between three different sources of care: the state, family and market. In addition to this triad, the third sector—that is, non-governmental organisations, unions or employers—take an increasingly active role in providing different types of welfare to individuals (Evers 2005; Seeleib-Kaiser and Fleckenstein 2009). In terms of care, Esping-Andersen theorises 'familialism', where the obligation is assigned to the household, defamilialism through the market where individuals rely on market sources for care, and defamilialism through the state, where the state takes the responsibility to provide care (Esping-Andersen 1996).

Market provision refers to simply buying care directly either through an agency which provides a range of care services, residential provision for older people or contracting with individual providers. Government involvement in the provision of care can entail a range of issues (Daly 2002). First and foremost, governments can provide care services directly through public childcare provision, and government elderly care provision. They can also regulate to guarantee various types of leave for informal carers to allow families/parents to provide care directly. Secondly, rather than providing and administering care, the government can play a role in finance, by subsidy or funding for care providers, and by providing sufficient funds to make sure that family members can purchase care through the market. Finally, the role of government also includes providing regulation/guidance for care providers, such as third sector organisations but also employers, in the provision of care.

Individual responsibility is defined as an individual caring for children or family members directly, or using informal social networks to provide the care. Especially in elderly care this remains the largest area of care provision. With declining state involvement in care, individuals are left to find alternatives and the importance of market and other actors increases. A large body of literature has addressed the different welfare mixes that have developed in answer to the care needs of the population and have consequently developed into different care regimes (see Daly and Lewis 2000; Esping-Andersen 1996; Ferragina and Seeleib-Kaiser 2015; Leitner 2003; Rummery and Fine 2012; Saraceno and Keck 2010).

Care Regimes and Defamilialism

Different welfare models have incorporated care differently (Daly and Lewis 2000), and there are significant differences in the development of childcare and elderly care across Europe, forming different care regimes and support for defamilialism (Bettio and Plantenga 2004; Borsenberger et al. 2016; Ganjour and Widmer 2016; Haberkern and Szydlik 2010; Kalmijn and Saraceno 2008; Saraceno and Keck 2010; Leitner 2003; Österle 2010; Pavolini and Ranci 2008; Rummery and Fine 2012; Daly 2002). One approach distinguishes liberal, conservative and social democratic care regimes corresponding to Esping-Andersen's (1990) typology of welfare states. Differences in the care regime types are shown in expenditure on child and elderly care, with Norway the highest on both and the UK lowest on childcare and Slovenia on elderly care (see Figs. 6.1 and 6.2) with corresponding differences in the level of inclusion. These differences also correspond to differences in the extent to which the state or market is concerned with defamilialism or to which the family provides support.

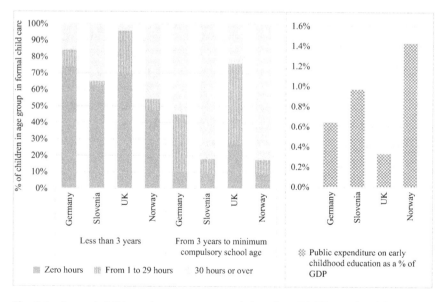

Fig. 6.1 Formal childcare by age group and duration (2015); total public expenditure on early childhood education (% GDP, 2013). Source: Eurostat

The Provision of Care: Whose Responsibility and Why? 187

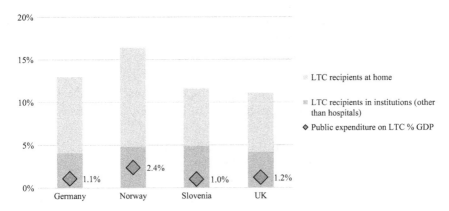

Fig. 6.2 Long-term care recipients and expenditure on long-term care (% GDP, 2014). Source: OECD. *For UK LTC recipients no recent data available, estimated value for 2004

However, when developing childcare services and services for the elderly, countries have introduced various mixes of providers that require different levels of familialism, and policies can vary substantially between child and elderly care. The typologies of care regimes and the placement of the countries in the various regimes differ according to which indicators are taken into account. For this reason we use typologies based on the degree of familialism and defamilialism (Leitner 2003; Saraceno and Keck 2010) in our analysis and have chosen our countries to represent different positions. We have modified the de/familialism typology slightly, since our focus is predominantly on the welfare mix in the provision of care services. This typology distinguishes between supported familialism, familialism by default and defamilialism. In regard to degree of familialism and the similarity of care arrangements between childcare and elderly care the Scandinavian countries usually emerge in cluster analysis as a distinct group with high levels of defamilialism for both childcare and elderly care, as the welfare state is the main provider of care, and therefore familialism is optional (see e.g. Saraceno and Keck 2010; Leitner 2003). Scandinavian countries support dual-earner dual-carer systems where there is generous support for childcare services for under three-year-olds and paid parental leave, including individual entitlements for fathers (see Thévenon and Luci 2012; Korpi et al. 2013). Similarly, in terms of elderly care the Scandinavian countries have the highest levels of both residential and homecare services coverage (Saraceno and Keck 2010) and are characterised as service-based care systems (Haberkern and Szydlik 2010).

Germany in general can be placed in the category of supported familialism or explicit familialism, in which the welfare state provides benefits to support families (more extensively in childcare than elderly care), which are still the main providers of care. Regarding childcare this is done through long (partly low-paid) leave entitlements mostly for mothers, or generous child benefits and only moderate levels of childcare provision. However, it should be noted that in recent years Germany has not only increased public provision of childcare but also extended leave rights for parents. In terms of elderly care, the German care system is characterised as family based. There is a strong obligation to provide intergenerational care alongside the established social insurance system for long-term care. State elderly care provision has a lower priority and is meagre (see Haberkern and Szydlik 2010).

Our third type is familialism by default, or implicit familialism, in which the support provided by the welfare state is minimal, and families are the main providers of care (for example, CEE and southern European countries). Slovenia is an example of countries characterised by substantial differences in regard to arrangements for child and elderly care. The childcare regime is defamilialised (Kanjuo Mrčela and Černigoj Sadar 2011), while elderly care can be characterised as familialism by default (Hlebec et al. 2016). Slovenia has a well-developed policy of parental leaves including fathers' leave and a comprehensive network of childcare provision similar to that in Scandinavian countries, while elderly care is poorly developed, especially in regard to home care services.

The UK care regime according to Saraceno and Keck (2010) is close to familialism by default for all care obligations, but with higher degrees of defamilialism, although this is based on market provision. Thévenon and Luci (2012) and Korpi et al. (2013) described this group as a market-oriented regime, made up of countries who generally provide limited assistance in terms of public childcare provision, short leave or low-income replacement for leave, and few specific entitlements for fathers. Elderly care has comparatively high homecare coverage provided through the market.

According to the different levels of familialism in the countries under consideration, we suggest that the different current roles of the actors will affect the debates regarding the future provision of care, either supporting the existing welfare mix or indicating a preference for changes in the roles of specific actors within it. The relationship between the state, the market and the family is further affected by the impact of the recession and the consequent austerity measures, and by rising demand for care due to population ageing (Eichler and Pfau-Effinger 2009; Pavolini and Ranci 2008). While childcare policies have generally expanded in most European welfare states (Ferragina and Seeleib-Kaiser 2015), we can observe an opposite trend toward refamilialism in elderly care as a strategy by which governments as well as households cope with the impact of the recession. This has reinforced family care and foregrounded traditional care values and the concept that family provides the best quality of care (Deusdad et al. 2016; Eichler and Pfau-Effinger 2009).

Support for Public Care Provision

The research in general indicates high support for welfare policies for the elderly, as well as for children. Despite the wide range of welfare state cuts implemented across the sector, one area that has expanded recently is the provision of childcare and other programmes to support working families (Ferragina and Seeleib-Kaiser 2015; Taylor-Gooby et al. 2017a). Support for and state intervention in childcare is relatively high in all European countries, although there is variation between countries and individuals. Using the European Social Survey of 2008/2009, Chung and Meuleman (2014, 2017) examine citizens' support for government-funded childcare among the general public and parents. There is a high level of support for government involvement in childcare for working parents among both groups, with an average of eight on a scale from zero to ten. Germany and Slovenia rank slightly above the European average, with Slovenian showing more support. Norway is not included in the data, but its neighbouring country Denmark displays even higher support for public childcare, although Sweden ranks slightly lower. The level of support was lower in the UK, yet still strong at seven on average.

The same is true of policies for the elderly. When considering the deservingness of different social groups, the elderly are usually considered as the most deserving (van Oorschot 2000; Svallfors 2008). In general, in all countries more than 90 per cent of respondents believe that public authorities should provide appropriate home care and institutional care for elderly people (Eurobarometer 2007, 66). According to Svallfors (2008, 389) support for older people is endorsed by society as a whole. In examining peoples' attitudes toward preferable options for care of elderly parents, Eurobarometer (2010) data shows that only 37 per cent of Slovenians preferred family care, while in the UK and Germany 60 per cent and 55 per cent answered that the best option for care of an elderly parent who lives alone and needs regular help, would be care provided by children. Also acceptability of institutional care is much higher among Slovenians (57 per cent—well above the EU27 average of 32 per cent), while in Germany only 37 per cent of respondents agree and even fewer in the UK—27 per cent. This most likely reflects the limited care options in Slovenia. Unfortunately, we do not have data for Norway, but in the Scandinavian countries, for example in Denmark, a relatively low share (31 per cent) answered that one of the children should regularly visit the home of elderly parents in need of care. In addition a very high share of respondents (74 per cent) believe that the best option would be moving elders to a nursing home/sheltered housing; this was similar to Slovenia. The welfare mix loosely corresponds to the expressed preference for care.

The literature regarding the reasons behind the support for the public provision of care services is relatively sparse. Previous analyses (Chung and Meuleman 2014, 2017; Goerres and Tepe 2012) of support for government's involvement in care provision distinguished three approaches. Self-interest theory entails that those who are currently or are most likely to benefit from the public policy will be most supportive of it (Blekesaune and Quadagno 2003; Kangas 1997; Svallfors 1997; Knijn and Van Oorschot 2008). Ideological stance has also been shown to be an important predictor of attitudes (Edlund 2006; Gevers et al. 2000; Blekesaune 2013). This is based on the idea that 'attitudes towards the welfare state are rooted in more general value systems regarding the proper relationship between the individual, the state and other institutions' (Blekesaune and Quadagno 2003, 416). Further, the principle of equality has been shown to be of relevance to many welfare attitudes, including that towards childcare (Van Oorschot et al. 2012; Chung and Meuleman 2017). Finally, one crucial element explaining support for public intervention is the standard of current provision, both in terms of quality and quantity (Chung and Meuleman 2017; Ellingsæter and Gulbrandsen 2007).

Based on the data from the 2001 International Social Survey project Ganjour and Widmer (2016) distinguish four different country clusters in relation to norms of support in this field. The first pattern is normative family support, characterised by a strong belief that adult children should take care of their elderly parents. The second pattern is normative state support: the belief that it is predominantly the role of the state to take care of children and the elderly. The third pattern is normative mixed support, stressing the obligation of adult children to provide support for elderly parents as well as the responsibility of the state to provide childcare and elderly care. The fourth pattern, self-reliance, is based on a comparatively low level of both normative family and state support. Their analysis showed that Germany is characterised by patterns of normative state support and self-reliance, correlated with the corporatist regime, while in the UK, following the liberal regime, respondents stressed the pattern of normative family solidarity with a strong emphasis on self-reliance, but also normative state support. The latter is characteristic of all the Scandinavian countries; an exception is Norway where the pattern of normative mixed support between family and state is relatively strong. Slovenia was not part of this study, but according to the available data Slovenia could potentially be placed in the pattern of normative state support.

Most of the literature on support for care has examined individuals' beliefs on what the role of government should be, but careful consideration of the different modes of care has not been undertaken. We know very little about how citizens feel regarding the different degrees of responsibility that each of the different bodies should take, and we do not know why people believe these responsibilities should be divided as such. The existing studies have yet to examine the reasoning respondents use to justify their preferences. Based on the previous studies of the justifications and rationales for conditionality of welfare provision (Paz-Fuchs 2008, 76; Dwyer 2002) we can distinguish economic from social justifications in the reasoning that frames support for state provision of care. Economic

Table 6.1 Division of responsibility in the provision of care

Country	UK	SLO	DE	NO
Childcare				
Existing care regime	Defamilialism by the market	Defamilialism	Supported familialism	Defamilialism/optional familialism
WHO				
Family	Provider of informal care/bonding	Education in values Freedom of choice policies	Main provider of childcare in early years	Provider of childcare in early years
State	Provider and financer of childcare	Dominant provider and financer of childcare	Dominant financer of childcare, subsidiary provider of care	Dominant financer and provider of childcare
Employers	Complementary provider and financer of childcare Provider of flexible working policies	Complementary provider and financer of childcare	Complementary provider and financer of childcare Provider of flexible working policies	Complementary provider and financer of childcare
WHY				
Social arguments	Gender equality Early education of state Bonding with grandparents	Education role (family and state) Benefit to the children: quality childcare (state) More time spend with family	Gender equality Integration of migrants/ early education Bonding with parents/ investing in children Acknowledging women's unpaid labour Increased fertility rate	Gender equality Bonding with parents

Economic arguments	Women's labour market participation More tax gained/contribution to society Skills maintenance for firms Education as investment for future	Women's labour market participation Dual earner model as a precondition for the survival of families	Women's labour market participation		Women's labour market participation
Elderly care Existing care regime WHO	Familialism by default	Familialism by default	Supported familialism	Defamilialism	
Individual	Predominant; use of assets (housing) Healthy lifestyle Choice not to receive care	Not often mentioned (difficult due to lack of means)	Supplementary private care insurance	More individual responsibility	
Family	Paid family care; cutting hours at work Freedom of choice (between family and formal care)	Limitations to family care (burden) (Normative) duty and legal obligations for family care Family financing of formal care services	Important in provision of care Help in financing care Absence of family care as a negative trend Multigenerational households as a solution	Provide better quality of care Multigenerational households as a solution	

(continued)

Table 6.1 (continued)

Country	UK	SLO	DE	NO
State	Supporting family care Formal care provision Encouraging healthy lifestyle	Ensuring high pensions to pay for elderly care Provider of services (home care) Subsidising services (institutional) Ensuring quality of care (standards) and quality of life—social inclusion of elderly	Financing care Ensuring nursing care Continuation of supported familialism	Limits of state responsibility
WHY				
Social arguments	Ageing as universal need Reciprocity argument Emotional closeness argument (for family care)	Ageing as universal need Reciprocity argument Elderly preferences for family care Normative expectations in community for family care	Better quality of care if provided by family Family—multigenerational solidarity	Better quality of care if provided by family Family—multigenerational solidarity
Economic arguments	Care as business Care to enable work-life balance Obstacles to care—capacity issues, financial sustainability issues	Care opening up job opportunities Work-life balance (state responsibility) Targeted care only for the vulnerable (state responsibility)	Affordability of care—help of family in provision and financing of care Work-life balance	Reducing economic burden (with individual responsibility and increased family care)

justifications base entitlement to care on utilitarian or fiscal rationales framed in terms of financial exigencies and labour market functioning and the right to take part in the labour market for the carer. Social arguments refer to the notion of social citizenship or whether care is provided as part of the social rights of the recipient as a citizen, as well as notions of morality and contract based on the reciprocity of human relations. These are arguments that relate to the normative rights of people, their well-being, deservingness, reciprocity and solidarity. We apply this distinction in the analysis of Democratic Forum discussions in order to grasp the differences and similarities in the rationales behind the participants' justifications for the roles of different actors in care within the comparative perspective of the countries we examine.

The Democratic Forum Research

The data used here comes from Democratic Forums carried out in the four countries (UK, Norway, Germany and Slovenia) in 2015 (for more detail see Chap. 1). The analysis of attitudes toward care (for elderly and children) focused on the responsibility of different actors and on the arguments put forward by the participants. The latter are classified into social arguments relating to the normative rights of people, their well-being, perceptions of reciprocity and intergenerational solidarity, quality of care, social goals and benefits and citizenship rights; and economic arguments relating to financial reasons, labour market functioning, work-life balance, employment opportunities and investment purposes. In some cases it was difficult to disentangle the justifications of a particular participant because they were intertwined or concerned provision in general without indicating whether family, state, market or the third sector should be responsible. The analytical scheme is presented in Table 6.1.

Who Should Be Responsible for Childcare?

First and foremost, the issue of childcare was not equally important in all countries. Childcare was one of the most prominent issues raised in the UK forum, followed by Germany and Slovenia, but there were barely any discussions of childcare in the Norwegian case. This may be due to the fact that in Norway, and to some extent Slovenia, public provision of childcare as well as generous parental leaves are well established and of good quality, making it a non-issue in these countries. On the other hand, public childcare provisions have only developed recently in the UK and Germany, lagging behind in both quantity and accessibility, and this makes it a core issue for many.

We expected the differences between our four countries in existing care provision would be a major factor in explaining the differences across Democratic Forums in their attitudes towards the question of who should be responsible for childcare. For example, in Norway the discussion centred on the flexible and equal division of parental leaves for parents, while in Germany much of the discussion concerned the recognition of reproductive labour, and in the UK on workfare and the economic benefits of childcare. Similarly, in Slovenia leave policies and childcare services were recognised as vital to integrate women in the labour market, while their role in equalising children's opportunity was not emphasised.

In Norway the equal division of leave was seen as a key issue that needed to be addressed, especially to achieve gender equality. Such equal division of leave was also mentioned in the UK and Slovenia but only briefly, but there were debates in all four countries on how this could be achieved. Some argued that the equal division of leaves between men and women cannot be enforced by the government and needed to be managed by the couple/parents themselves.

In all four countries, there was a general consensus that childcare provision was a crucial element of the welfare state and that the government should have some responsibility for the provision of public childcare, but there were differences between them in who should receive state care, except in Slovenia where it was accepted as universal. In the UK for example, many participants voiced their concerns about providing free childcare for parents who did not work.

> I think offer childcare to people who are working, the free childcare for people who are working, and should take it away from people…. (UK-80)

...just take away from people who don't work.... (UK-88)

However, there were also general concerns about the current provision of childcare. The most important factors across all four countries were the lack of places and of flexibility in opening hours, including the need for longer opening hours for parents working different shifts. A concern about the quality and payment of staff emerged in Germany, while in the UK one crucial element mentioned frequently was the cost of childcare. The UK has one of the most expensive childcare systems in the OECD costing up to two-thirds of the second earner's income (OECD 2011), prohibiting women's employment chances and pushing people onto benefits rather than paid employment. This was picked up several times by the respondents.

(Cost of childcare) limits women's opportunities because actually to pay for two kids to be in childcare at £1,600 a month, say, it's actually more beneficial for them to stay at home and look after them and get the benefits than to pay that £1,600 because to get £1,600 a month you'd have to earn £25,000 a year. (UK-69)

One of the main solutions to these issues in all four countries was the provision of company daycare facilities. For example, a German participant said:

I think the idea of being able to bring my child to work just great. If I start work at eight o'clock and can bring my child there to the firm or next door or something, and they're looked after so that I can visit my child at midday break and then drive home with my child at the end of the day. (DE-28)

Similar points were made in Slovenia, additionally emphasising the benefits to the children of spending more time with parents.

Participants mentioned the responsibilities of employers in providing flexible working arrangements—a common policy being used in companies across Europe (see also, Chung 2018). Many believed that flexible working allowed for a better work-life balance. This was particularly the case in Germany where the use of flexitime, flexible scheduling and working from home was mentioned repeatedly.

> I think the idea of flexible work times is also good, because maybe you have to work a certain number of hours per week, but if they need to leave early to pick up the children, then maybe the next day they can come in early or stay late to make up for the lost time. (DE-26)

In Norway, providing flexibility was seen as a relatively easy move for companies to address the pressing need for childcare.

> I don't think most workplaces will suffer from allowing more flexitime for those with children. (NO-9)

Yet participants in other countries were more concerned about the feasibility of these policies for small and medium-sized companies. In the UK the possibility of cooperative daycare for these companies were discussed. In Slovenia the fear of the employer's abuse of company daycare was present:

> On the one hand it's good, on the other it is a double sided blade, because the child is in care and looked after and you can stay at work very late, until six, if you have to. Or seven, or eight. (SI-57)

Concerns about longer working hours were part of a more general discussion in which, despite advocating more flexible and longer opening hours for childcare facilities, participants emphasised that there should be state-regulated limits to overtime. In all four countries, there were also discussions of the extent to which government could enforce such childcare-related policies on companies, but in general the consensus was on government supporting companies in providing these policies through tax breaks and similar devices rather than a strict regulatory approach:

> The state can do things to make it easier or more attractive to take such steps, but they should keep out of it for the most part, because those are

contractual conditions that the employer and employee decide with one another. (DE-22)

Informal care responsibilities were another source of provision mentioned in the forums. Participants in the UK mentioned the use of informal care networks, such as grandparents, due to lack of availability and the high cost of childcare. Some participants argued for the payment of informal carers in the same way as formal care providers. In Germany participants talked positively about the informal care provided by extended families in the past, but this was not seen as a solution for the future.

Finally there were references to parents taking the main responsibility for childcare. As mentioned earlier, the Norwegian discussions centred mainly on the use of leave policies in the early years of the child's life and how both mothers and fathers should take leave, especially to advance gender equality. Another solution mentioned in Norway was the use of part-time work or reduction of hours for parents to address childcare needs.

> We often hear that we are so productive and efficient in Norway. That we are beyond what is expected. A lot is to be achieved. Maybe we should arrange for the possibility to only achieve 60 to 80 per cent at work, to have a variable. Maybe allow for families with children to reduce the work hours when the children are young. (NO-24)

This reduction of hours during the early years of the child's life was mentioned particularly in the German forum, which may reflect the wide use of this arrangement in Germany. Many people mentioned the benefit of having parents (mothers) take care of children during the early years.

> I agree, half-day work and the rest is paid, because you could choose this. For me this has the advantage that raising children at home is better than them being raised at a day care. (DE-23)

In Slovenia some participants emphasised freedom of choice policies, but there was no general agreement.

> We don't enable the women to decide whether they are going to stay at home or go to work. Because they must work in order to have enough to live. (SI-55)

A unique element of the German forum data was the importance of recognising women's unpaid care labour, especially in relation to pension contributions. Many participants raised the problem of pension rights for women who have not fully taken part in paid employment during child rearing, and that part-time working should be recognised and subsidised by the state.

> The problem is that childrearing is not recognized or appreciated as a job. That is the problem. It's not valued. (DE-2)

Economic Versus Social Arguments for Childcare

The predominant social argument for childcare provision was gender equality, which was mentioned by participants across all four countries. Childcare was addressed during the breakout session discussing gender issues, and many participants looked at changes to childcare provision as a major way to level the playing field for men and women.

> It can make it more interesting to hire women if you know that the men also have to take days of leave. (NO-11)

> The benefit is that employers will be less discriminatory when hiring people, because people can decide freely on who is to take the leave.… (SI-75)

A social argument that was used to justify informal care—by parents and extended families—was the idea of bonding between families and children. Slovenian participants emphasised the role of parental childcare in relation to learning social values.

Another social argument for formal childcare concerned the educational rights of children. This was especially the case in the UK. Talking about the role of free childcare hours, a UK female participant said:

[Childcare is] to benefit the children, not the parents. It's to get children into education sooner. (UK-n.i.)

For many participants, this also related to concerns about a lack of parenting skills among certain groups in the population, and the need for reforms in education and training systems in the UK (See Chap. 4).

For German participants, childcare was also a way to integrate children from migrant families into German society through interactions with 'native' children from an early age.

it's important that the students be spread out, so that children with a different migration background have the chance to grow up with German children, so that they can speak better German as opposed to them all being together and just speaking their own language maybe. (DE-16)

The most prominent economic argument for providing childcare was to bring more women back into paid work (see also, Chung and Van der Horst 2018). This theme was mentioned in all countries alongside the idea of gender equality. Especially in the UK, where the cost of childcare was seen as a key barrier to women's employment, many people mentioned women's increasing labour market participation as a key benefit. Companies were also seen to benefit from the skill-maintenance aspect of retaining mothers in the labour market.

Just to maintain skills. You spend 15 years training somebody up and they're in charge of a team, and it's successful, then you don't want them to leave, do you? Who's going to benefit from it? So, the employer [should provide]. (UK-n.i.)

Participants argued that unemployed people who get free childcare should do voluntary work since this will benefit society. The UK participants also noted how more childcare—whether provided by the state or by employers—would provide more jobs. The economic argument that greater participation by women will increase tax and contribution revenues was not emphasised in the other three countries. Educating children could also be understood as a social investment strategy for the development of the economy. This was most prominent in the UK as the material quoted earlier shows.

Finally, an interesting social argument about whether child benefits should be reduced or increased had to do with fertility rates. Participants in Norway and more so the UK feared that generous child benefits encouraged migrants (in Norway) and the unemployed (in the UK) to have more children:

> today we have a three-year rule about transitional money when you have children. Then a mother can stay home for three years with full payment in those three years. But they have no limitations as to how many years in a three-year period a mother can take. That is why we have some immigrant women in Norway who keep getting children, but they aren't very noticeable. (NO-30)

> these benefits that people who are on benefits, apparently the more children that they seem to have the more benefits they're going to get so therefore more children are being born and the population is growing again so we're going to have overcrowding. (UK-83)

On the other hand, in Germany where childcare policies have been in part developed to tackle the low fertility rate in the past decade, increasing the birth rate was seen as a reason to introduce more generous childcare policies. In Slovenia, despite having a lower fertility rate than the UK and Norway but slightly above Germany (Eurostat 2017), the encouragement of birth rates through investment in family policy was only briefly mentioned, and the issue of immigration was not part of the discussion.

Who Should Be Responsible for Elderly Care?

In all four countries the state was seen as responsible for ensuring care for the elderly, but to different degrees. Slovenia stands out as advocating an all-encompassing role for the state. The state is seen as responsible for providing pensions sufficient to finance care and also providing care services (such as domiciliary care), and ensuring the social inclusion of elderly people, for example:

> That's why the state needs to visit them (the elderly) and check up on them every five years. (SI-83)

This emphasis on the role of the state indicates dissatisfaction with the current position of familialism by default.

In other countries the state's role was seen as more limited, and more emphasis was placed on the role of the family or individual responsibility. In the UK care was seen mainly as an individual responsibility, ensured through private savings and liquidation of assets, for example:

> And of course they have to sell their houses to pay for their own care. (UK-44)

However, this was often seen as unfair; the existing pattern of individual responsibility is accepted but also questioned. This is in line with the regretful tolerance of a perceived inevitable shift towards greater individual responsibility across social provision that Taylor-Gooby et al. (Chap. 2 and 2018) have labelled 'reluctant individualism'.

The role of the family was emphasised in all four countries, but especially in Germany and Norway. Care by the family was normatively expected, and in the case of Slovenia the existing legal obligation to care was also mentioned.

> The children, if they, the children, are wealthy, let's say that a person has three children and they're wealthy, it's their responsibility to take care of their parents, but no one says this aloud in Slovenian society, but it is according to the law.... We can't transfer everything to the society. (SI-83)

However, in this familialistic system participants acknowledged the excessive burdening of family carers and argued for a bigger role for the state.

On the other hand, in Germany and Norway the increased role of the family was emphasised as a solution to sustainability issues and to provide better care. Surprisingly, in Norway, overall, much of the discussion was centred on how the government should take less responsibility than is currently the case:

> We have sort of made the responsibility of caring for the elderly public, and the government will never be as caring as the family and friends. It is really sad, but it is a reality. (NO-24)

The responsibility of the family in Norway was recognised as a preferred role in providing higher-quality care, but also as a more realistic solution or necessity due to economic pessimism about welfare state sustainability, showing similarities with discussions in Germany. However, one should consider the care regime in both countries in interpreting the data, as the trend to defamilialism was very strong in Norway, and the attitudes expressed show that the trend might have reached its limit. On the other hand, in Germany, support for familalisation follows the expressed view and should in the opinion of the participants be continued.

In addition, in Norway the market was seen as one of the solutions in regard to future care issues, contrary to Slovenia and Germany, but as a complement to the state rather than replacing it. One possible reason for this divergence is the focus on individual responsibility. This was closer to the UK discussions, but in the UK paying for care in the market was perceived as the primary solution.

> Now we get private offers that can take you out for fresh air. It costs you 1000kr and you get 30 minutes five times a week. So, the elders become more like a product. (NO-25)

In the UK we do not find a discrepancy between people's attitudes and the actual provision of care. Defamilialism and individualism seems to be strongly integrated into people's attitudes as a norm, and discussions went on to mention more radical individualistic solutions such as the right not to receive care. However, this should be interpreted in line with the notion of 'reluctant individualism'.

Between Economic and Social Arguments

Social justifications regarding the general provision of care for the elderly were strongly based on assumptions about the deservingness of the elderly, mainly on their need which is universal (everybody gets old), and consequently also partly on self-interest (since discussion focused on the future and the participants said they were basically talking about themselves):

> That's right, accessible for all. God forbid that this is to happen to me. (SI-61)

Furthermore, the arguments for care seem to be based on protecting basic human rights and dignity:

> One can keep his or her dignity. (SI-58)

> I do believe it should be the public's responsibility to make good solutions for when you are old and weak even if you have no money. There shouldn't be a great class distinction on what one can and cannot do. (NO-31)

In general, social justifications for elderly care based on deservingness mainly followed the reciprocity argument. The understanding of reciprocity was twofold. Firstly, the past: older people worked all their lives and therefore deserved something in return:

> So they can enjoy their hard-earned retirement. (SI-65)

Secondly, future reciprocity: if older people are supported now they will be able to help their children and grandchildren.

> The thing is the older generation bolster the younger generation, so if you don't give the older generation a bit of help when they need it ... how are they then going to help their children who are then bringing up their grandchildren? (UK-44)

The social justification of the greater involvement of the family in care for older people in Germany and Norway was based on intergenerational solidarity as providing better quality of care. Participants criticised the absence of family, seeing it as a negative trend in society. Social arguments based on the underlying normative value of the family saw state interventions as creating a vicious circle by undermining the family as a support network.

> We have sort of made the responsibility of caring for the elderly public, and the government will never be as caring as the family and friends. It is really sad, but it is a reality…. (NO-24 – see above)

> I think it's a problem that people don't need children anymore…. It used to be that family was your old-age security, and that has been taken away by this social welfare system. It's no longer necessary…. (DE-9)

From the point of view of economic argumentation, discussions in all four countries on future care for the elderly were linked to the sustainability and financing of the welfare state. This was more pronounced in the UK, and also to some extent in Norway and Germany, while less explicit in Slovenia. Economic reasoning in the UK was marked by the notion of 'reluctant individualism' (Taylor-Gooby et al. 2018), meaning that people are disciplined not to expect too much from the state and therefore rely predominantly on themselves. In Slovenia, on the other hand, the ability of the state to finance increased care needs in the future was taken for granted.

Economic arguments actually relate to the existing familialism by default and to families' lacking the resources to provide good services. The expected and legally binding reliance on intergenerational solidarity in the provision of care was seen as a salient issue, especially in a time of economic crisis which meant that more families were unable to provide for the elderly both in financing and in relation to work-life balance pressures. Surprisingly, the Norwegians incorporated to a considerable extent a market-oriented reasoning similar to that in the UK that underscored the cost of social welfare and the fact that someone has to pay for it. It was assumed that everybody should be responsible for their own life, not the state. In the discussions, the belief that the welfare state simply cannot bear the economic cost was offered as the main reason why the state should take less responsibility:

I don't believe society will be able to meet the requirements we are facing. (NO-30)

However, besides the sustainability issues that were mostly linked to economic arguments for limiting state care and expanding the role of other actors, more positive economic arguments in relation to elderly care seemed to be much rarer and mostly pertained to the debates about how the growth of care needs opened up job opportunities (for example in SLO and UK).

And I think that with the aging population also comes jobs in a way because then there's lots of people to look after them I think. (UK-29)

A social investment perspective linking the provision of elderly care to labour market participation, for example the need for leave from work to take care of sick or frail older family members, was advanced everywhere except Norway. This could be linked to the high levels of defamilialisation and gender equality characteristic of the Scandinavian countries. In the UK this was somewhat contested by the needs of employers and work-life balance issues.

Why should you be paid to leave work to go and look after your family members when they are most likely going to be entitled to have a carer anyway? So why not give another person the job instead of you leaving your job to go and do another job temporarily and be paid the same time. You are saying it needs to be fair that everyone's, how is that fair for the employer? (UK-51)

In UK another economic argument put forward was the issue of choosing not to receive care, which was also seen as a solution to sustainability issues and as a way to prevent a poor quality of life in one's later years. A similar theme was present in Norway, however, more in relation to prioritising healthcare.

I would like to have the right to die when I want to die. And that will affect a lot of people, 'cause it would save a lot money on care…. (UK-41)

Discussion and Conclusion

The care issues received significant attention among the participants in the Democratic Forums and the need to provide care was uncontested. The discussions on the role of different actors seem to be firmly embedded in the current provision and care regime typology (see Table 6.1).

Regarding the welfare mix, all four countries were largely similar in that all three welfare providers—that is, the state, family and employers—were found to be important in the provision of childcare. There were differences across countries in the extent to which the parent's right to care was thought of as something to protect, as in the cases of supported familialism in Germany and optional familialism in Norway, whereas in the UK more support was given for a defamilialism, although this was largely driven by market objectives. Such changes in the positioning of the countries could again be partly understood in terms of recent policy developments. In the UK recent policy changes entitle working parents up to 30 hours' free childcare per week for children three years of age or older. Such policy changes seem to have shifted the attitudes of parents towards support for state childcare provision (Chung and Meuleman 2017). Interestingly, in Slovenia it seemed that state responsibility in childcare is somehow taken for granted due to the long-standing tradition, and the discussion went more in the direction of proposing alternatives such as childcare organised by employers. In line with previous studies on work-life balance policies (Seeleib-Kaiser and Fleckenstein 2009), we found that in all four countries there was an increasing belief that companies should also take an active role in facilitating workers' work-family balance. Many believed it to be something companies should be doing for their own economic benefit for skill maintenance, without much state involvement apart from tax relief and other supportive mechanisms.

In the case of elderly care the embeddedness of participants' attitudes within the current system in Germany and the UK led to similar solutions that followed current provision, while in the two other countries analysed, Norway and Slovenia, it seemed to lead to novel solutions. In the UK the future of the provision of care seems to be recognised as a familial and individual responsibility, although sometimes reluctantly, and this is often based on economic arguments. In Germany, the role of the family was also advanced, and that of the state was often seen as supporting family care, which corresponds to existing patterns of supported familalism. The arguments were strongly social (the normative value of family care) as well as economic (sustainability). They both follow the pattern of strong self-reliance (based on individual and family) (Ganjour and Widmer (2016). Normative family solidarity was not as strongly evident as one might expect in the UK, while it was surprisingly very pronounced in Germany. In both countries the state was also recognised as an important actor, but with several limitations in capacity and in the quality of such care.

On the other hand, in Norway and Slovenia some dissatisfaction with the limitations of the current care regimes was evident. In Slovenia, participants recognised the limits of familialism and increasingly favoured the role of state, and this was also based on social as well as economic arguments (the inadequacies of families in financing care). These findings seem to be in line with what Ganjour and Widmer (2016) described as normative state support, showing a disparity between the current provision of care and societal preferences. They confirm the thesis that in 'familialistic welfare states', where there are strong obligations between relatives and care is mainly provided by family, the outcome is a demand for the state to take on more responsibility (see Haberkern and Szydlik 2010).

Furthermore, in Norway participants discussed the limits of defamilialism and called for an increasing role for the family, based again on economic sustainability as well as social arguments—the quality of family care, solidarity. The discussions in Norway seem to follow a normative mixed support model between family and the state. This reflects what Daly (2002) perceives as one of the ironies of contemporary welfare states, since 'welfare states are now required to call forth a form of solidarity which their own practice has helped to diminish' (Daly 2002, 260).

Our analysis supports two overall conclusions: first, preferences for future care arrangements are firmly embedded in current care provision as well as ongoing debates, but also indicate dissatisfaction with and limits to the current care regimes, and how attitudes shift in accordance to policy changes. In the case of childcare, the discussions in the forums were framed largely by ongoing debates in each country. Equal division of parental leaves dominates the Norwegian discussion, while in Germany many participants focus on the recognition of women's unpaid work in relation to pension entitlement, and in the UK largely on workfare and policies to encourage women (back) to work. In Slovenia, where the dual-earner model prevails, women's labour market participation was justified on economic grounds as essential to the survival of families.

Second, the balance between social and economic framings varies in each country. In the UK and Slovenia support for the implementation of childcare policies was based largely on the economic benefits, either through increasing women's labour market participation or through investment in children's early childhood education. Economic arguments were also emphasised in regard to elderly care, with participants in the UK emphasising the limits to state funding, while those in Slovenia stressed the limits to individual and family budgets. On the other hand, although such economic framings also emerged in Germany and Norway, social arguments took precedence in childcare as well as elderly care. These mainly concerned gender equality, acknowledging women's unpaid labour/contribution to society and providing better quality care for children and the elderly, with an emphasis on emotional bonds through intergenerational solidarity.

This chapter provides a unique insight into citizen's attitudes towards the provision of care, an under-examined area in the current welfare attitude literature, and shows how Democratic Forums can contribute to understanding such attitudes. We find that the preferred welfare mix in the provision of care and its social and economic framing is more complex than many previous studies have suggested. We also find that country and regime distinctions still remain relevant in understanding the pattern of attitudes and justifications in that much of the discussion mirrored the political legacies and the specific debates taking place within the countries.

References

Bettio, F., & Plantenga, J. (2004). Comparing care regimes in Europe. *Feminist Economics, 10*(1), 85–113.
Blekesaune, M. (2013). Economic strain and public support for redistribution: A comparative analysis of 28 European countries. *Journal of Social Policy, 42*(1), 57–72.
Blekesaune, M., & Quadagno, J. (2003). Public attitudes toward welfare state policies. *European Sociological Review, 19*(5), 415–427.
Borsenberger, M., Fleury, C., & Dickes, P. (2016). Welfare regimes and social cohesion regimes: Do they express the same values? *European Societies, 18*(3), 221–244.
Chung, H. (2018). Dualization and the access to occupational family-friendly working time arrangements across Europe. *Social Policy & Administration, 52*(2), 491–507.
Chung, H., & Meuleman, B. (2014). Support for government intervention in child care across European countries. In M. León (Ed.), *The transformation of care in European societies* (pp. 104–133). Hampshire: Palgrave Macmillan.
Chung, H., & Meuleman, B. (2017). European parents' attitudes towards public childcare provision: The role of current provisions, interests and ideologies. *European Societies, 19*(1), 49–68.
Chung, H., & van der Horst, M. (2018). Women's employment patterns after childbirth and the perceived access to and use of flexitime and teleworking. *Human Relations, 71*(1), 47–72.
Daly, M. (2002). Care as a good for social policy. *Journal of Social Policy, 31*(2), 251–270.
Daly, M., & Lewis, J. (2000). The concept of social care and the analysis of contemporary welfare states. *The British Journal of Sociology, 51*(2), 281–298.
Deusdad, B., Pace, C., & Anttonen, A. (2016). Facing the challenges in the development of long-term care for older people in Europe in the context of an economic crisis. *Journal of Social Service Research, 42*(2), 144–150.
Dwyer, P. (2002). Making sense of social citizenship: Some user views on welfare rights and responsibilities. *Critical Social Policy, 22*(2), 273–299.
Edlund, J. (2006). Trust in the capability of the welfare state and general welfare state support: Sweden 1997–2002. *Acta Sociologica, 49*(4), 395–417.
Eichler, M., & Pfau-Effinger, B. (2009). The 'consumer principle' in the care of elderly people: Free choice and actual choice in the German welfare state. *Social Policy & Administration, 43*(6), 617–633.

Ellingsæter, A., & Gulbrandsen, L. (2007). Closing the childcare gap: The interaction of childcare provision and mothers' agency in Norway. *Journal of Social Policy, 36*(4), 649–669.
Esping-Andersen, G. (1990). *The three worlds of welfare capitalism*. Princeton: Princeton University Press.
Esping-Andersen, G. (1996). Welfare states without work: The impasse of labour-shedding and familialism in continental welfare states. In G. Esping-Andersen (Ed.), *Welfare states in transition*. London: Sage.
Esping-Andersen, G. (1999). *Social foundations of post-industrial economies*. New York: Oxford University Press.
Eurobarometer. (2007). *Special Eurobarometer 283/Wave 67.3—TNS Opinion & Social*. Health and long-term care in the European Union report, TNS Opinion & Social, Brussels.
Eurobarometer. (2010). *Special Eurobarometer 355/Wave 74.1—TNS Opinion & Social*. Poverty and social exclusion report, TNS Opinion & Social, Brussels.
Eurostat. (2017). Eurostat database. Retrieved from http://ec.europa.eu/eurostat/data/database.
Evers, A. (2005). Mixed welfare systems and hybrid organizations: Changes in the governance and provision of social services. *International Journal of Public Administration, 28*(9–10), 737–748.
Ferragina, E., & Seeleib-Kaiser, M. (2015). Determinants of a silent (r)evolution: Understanding the expansion of family policy in rich OECD countries. *Social Politics: International Studies in Gender, State & Society, 22*(1), 1–37.
Ganjour, E., & Widmer, E. D. (2016). Patterns of family salience and welfare state regimes: Sociability practices and support norms in a comparative perspective. *European Societies, 18*(3), 201–220.
Gevers, J., Gelissen, W. A., et al. (2000). Public health care in the balance: Exploring popular support for health care systems in the European Union. *International Journal of Social Welfare, 9*(4), 301–321.
Goerres, A., & Tepe, M. (2012). Doing it for the kids? The determinants of attitudes towards public childcare in unified Germany. *Journal of Social Policy, 41*(2), 349–372.
Haberkern, K., & Szydlik, M. (2010). State care provision, societal opinion and children's care of older parents in 11 European countries. *Ageing and Society, 30*(2), 299–323.

Hlebec, V., Srakar, A., & Majcen, B. (2016). Care for the elderly in Slovenia: A combination of informal and formal care. *Revija za socijalnu politiku, 23*(2), 159–179.
Kalmijn, M., & Saraceno, C. (2008). A comparative perspective on intergenerational support. *European Societies, 10*(3), 479–508.
Kangas, O. (1997). Self-interest and the common good: The impact of norms, selfishness and context in social policy opinions. *Journal of Socio-Economics, 26*(5), 475–494.
Kanjuo Mrčela, A., & Černigoj Sadar, N. (2011). Social policies related to parenthood and capabilities of Slovenian parents. *Social Politics, 18*(2), 199–231.
Knijn, T., & Van Oorschot, W. (2008). The need for and the societal legitimacy of social investments in children and their families. *Journal of Family Issues, 29*(11), 1520–1542.
Korpi, W., Ferrarini, T., & Englund, S. (2013). Women's opportunities under different family policy constellations: Gender, class, and inequality tradeoffs in western countries re-examined. *Social Politics: International Studies in Gender, State & Society, 20*(1), 1–40.
Leitner, S. (2003). Varieties of familialism. *European Societies, 5*, 353–375.
OECD. (2011). Doing better for families. Retrieved from www.oecd.org/social/family/doingbetter.
Österle, A. (2010). Long-term care in Central and South-Eastern Europe: Challenges and perspectives in addressing a 'new' social risk. *Social Policy & Administration, 44*(4), 461–480.
Pavolini, E., & Ranci, C. (2008). Restructuring the welfare state: Reforms in long-term care in western European countries. *Journal of European Social Policy, 18*(3), 246–259.
Paz-Fuchs, A. (2008). *Welfare to work. Conditional rights in social policy.* Oxford: Oxford University Press.
Rummery, K., & Fine, M. (2012). Care: A critical review of theory, policy and practice. *Social Policy & Administration, 46*(3), 321–343.
Saraceno, C., & Keck, W. (2010). Can we identify intergenerational policy regimes in Europe? *European Societies, 12*(5), 675–696.
Seeleib-Kaiser, M., & Fleckenstein, T. (2009). The political economy of occupational family policies: Comparing workplaces in Britain and Germany. *British Journal of Industrial Relations, 47*(4), 741–764.
Svallfors, S. (1997). Worlds of welfare and attitudes to redistribution: A comparison of eight western nations. *European Sociological Review, 13*(3), 283–304.

Svallfors, S. (2008). The generational contract in Sweden: Age-specific attitudes to age-related policies. *Policy & Politics, 36*(3), 381–396.

Taylor-Gooby, P., Leruth, B., & Chung, H. (2017a). *After austerity: Welfare state transformation in Europe after the great recession.* Oxford: Oxford University Press.

Taylor-Gooby, P., Leruth, B., & Chung, H. (2018) Identifying attitudes to welfare through deliberate forums: the emergence of reluctant individualism. Policy & Politics online first. DOI: https://doi.org/10.1332/030557318X15155868234361.

Thévenon, O., & Luci, A. (2012). Reconciling work, family and child outcomes: What implications for family support policies? *Population Research and Policy Review, 31*(6), 855–882.

Van Oorschot, W. (2000). Who should get what, and why? On deservingness criteria and the conditionality of solidarity among the Dutch public. *Policy & Politics, 28*(1), 33–48.

Van Oorschot, W., Reeskens, T., & Meuleman, B. (2012). Popular perceptions of welfare state consequences. A multi-level, cross-national analysis of 25 European countries. *Journal of European Social Policy, 22*(2), 181–197.

7

Healthcare Futures: Visions of Solidarity and the Sustainability of European Healthcare Systems

Maša Filipovič Hrast, Ellen M. Immergut,
Tatjana Rakar, Urban Boljka, Diana Burlacu,
and Andra Roescu

Introduction

The literature on solidarity and deservingness has often focused on distinctions between different types of social risks, and on the impact of welfare state regimes on ideas about solidarity and deservingness (Arts and Gelissen 2001; Mau 2004; Petersen et al. 2011; van Oorschot 2000;

M. F. Hrast (✉) • T. Rakar • U. Boljka
University of Ljubljana, Ljubljana, Slovenia
e-mail: masa.filipovic@fdv.uni-lj.si

E. M. Immergut
European University Institute (EUI), Fiesole, Italy

Humboldt University of Berlin, Berlin, Germany

D. Burlacu
Humboldt University of Berlin, Berlin, Germany

A. Roescu
University of Southampton, Southampton, UK

© The Author(s) 2018
P. Taylor-Gooby, B. Leruth (eds.), *Attitudes, Aspirations and Welfare*,
https://doi.org/10.1007/978-3-319-75783-4_7

van Oorschot and Komter 1998). When it comes to health, Europeans display higher levels of solidarity with the sick than do respondents in other continents, and in almost all studies of deservingness the sick are singled out as being highly deserving of medical treatment (Abela 2004). The only exceptions and causes of variation are with regard to self-inflicted illnesses and persons that are viewed as not belonging to the political community. Scholars have found substantial empirical support for the propositions of these theories of solidarity and deservingness.

From our Democratic Forums, however, a more nuanced view emerges. The participants expressed very different understandings of the risk community and the basis for its rights and duties. This chapter analyses attitude patterns on healthcare solidarity and perceived levels of sustainability in four countries: the United Kingdom (UK), Norway, Germany and Slovenia. In the UK, solidarity is *exclusive*, with high support for government's responsibility for the sick, but with high barriers to outsiders. In Norway, solidarity is *universal*. Participants supported provision for everyone regardless of citizenship, but are critical of special privileges and disregards for particular groups because this would undermine the idea of an equal common service. In Germany, solidarity can be categorised as *contributory*. Participants are concerned that all contribute fairly, and about the financial stability of the health insurance system in the face of large numbers of non-contributors. Finally, in Slovenia, health solidarity may be seen as *egalitarian*. It is based on a socialist ideal of identical treatment of all, despite the reality of corruption, which has become enmeshed with the capitalist profit motive.

To some extent, there are historical and institutional bases for these patterns. Norwegian universalism and Germany contributory solidarity can be traced to their social democratic and conservative roots, respectively. As can be seen in Fig. 7.1, Norwegian healthcare is largely tax financed, and residents receive health services directly in public institutions. There is however a significant level of social insurance, as well as a very small proportion of private insurance financing. In Germany, by contrast, healthcare is largely paid for by social insurance carried by statutory sickness funds, with wage-earner contributions covering spouses and dependent children. Higher-income workers, public servants and the self-employed generally opt out and are covered by private insurance.

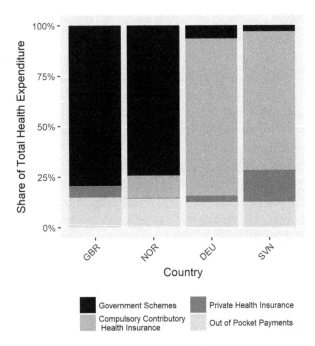

Fig. 7.1 Healthcare financing. Source: OECD Health Statistics 2017. Note: We wish to acknowledge Alexandru Moise for his help in providing R coding for this figure

Thus health insurance coverage is based on civil and occupational status, in line with the traditional conservative model. In a similar vein, attitudes in the UK and Slovenia can be related to their liberal and socialist roots, but here the picture becomes quite a bit more complicated. Although the UK is considered to be a liberal welfare state, its health system has the highest proportion of public financing in our sample, and the third largest in Europe, after Denmark and Sweden.

This is a general problem in the analysis of welfare state regimes. The institutional logic of healthcare systems often departs quite markedly from the supposed type of welfare regime (Bambra 2005). Perhaps nowhere is the discrepancy more glaring than in liberal welfare states. Although they do indeed share the common feature that the balance between state and market is decidedly tipped in the direction of the market, the justification and meaning of these liberal restrictions is very different, and the public healthcare programs cover the entire range of variation in the public-private mix in health. Canada has a full single-payer system with strong prohibitions on private medicine. The UK as well is largely single payer but includes a significant amount of private insurance funding. New Zealand follows the UK/Canadian model, but Australia is far more privatised. The United States (US) is a great outlier with largely occupationally based healthcare in combination with special programs for retirees (Medicare), the poor (Medicaid), and a comparatively large uninsured population (Béland and Gran 2008).

The exact public-private mix and its historical development are relevant to understanding the impact of institutions on healthcare attitudes. Slovenia today has the least amount of government funding for health in Europe. But only a few decades ago—before its independence in 1991— it was entirely publicly funded with no private healthcare. Not surprisingly, Slovenians complain about out-of-pocket payments and the unfairness of the social insurance contribution rules. At the same time however, and somewhat paradoxically, the level of unmet needs and the barriers to health services (as measured in public opinion surveys) are the lowest among the four countries analysed in this chapter. The country currently follows the financing pattern of a conservative welfare state, but was socialist in the recent past, and the attitudes expressed in our forums fit this legacy.

Nevertheless, in all countries examined in this chapter, we see particular interpretations of solidarity (which we term 'framings') that do not flow directly from these institutional and historical patterns. In each country, participants in the Democratic Forums expressed opinions about who is to be included in the health safety net, who is to be excluded, threats to their system and possible solutions. Indeed, the participants expressed significant criticisms of their health systems and raised fundamental questions about their social and political legitimacy. The next section offers a brief literature review and summary of the current empirical evidence from quantitative surveys. We then elaborate on these framings of solidarity and our evidence in the remaining sections of this chapter. We conclude with some speculation on the sources of these different framings and their implication for the optimism and enthusiasm with which the participants are willing to adapt healthcare for the future.

Healthcare Solidarity and Deservingness

Deservingness theory aims to explain public attitudes regarding who is deserving of social solidarity. Empirical research has shown that five conditions are related to the degree of support for public aid to recipients: need, control, reciprocity, attitude and identity (Petersen et al. 2011; van Oorschot 2000). Support for social benefits is higher for those who are seen as needy, and whose vulnerable situation is viewed as the result of external forces beyond their control. 'Reciprocity' refers to what is expected of recipients in return for aid, and 'attitude' to behavioural expectations of recipients, for example being grateful for aid. 'Identity' refers to the perception that recipients belong to one's own community. When it comes to healthcare solidarity, research thus far has focused mainly on whether health disparities are attributed to individual behaviours or to biological or systemic factors (Gollust and Lynch 2011; Murphy-Berman et al. 1998; Rigby et al. 2009). When illness is caused by individual behaviour (for example smoking, drinking, extreme sports) more people think that the individual should bear responsibility for healthcare costs, and demand for government provision is lower than when biological factors or events outside individual control, such as accidents, are involved.

Cultural attitudes about deservingness may be influenced by institutional settings, however. As Larsen (2008) points out, different welfare state institutions may frame solidarity in terms of one or more of the deservingness criteria. Selective policies frame solidarity in terms of need and control by restricting social benefits to those in need and without control over their well-being. Consequently, such programs create a social cleavage between beneficiaries and contributors. Universalistic and more inclusive policies, by contrast, obviate the need to classify beneficiaries in terms of need and control, and thus foster a community of risk-sharers. As such, the level of solidarity is expected to be higher, and the cleavages less relevant. In a similar vein, Mau (2004) has developed the concept of reciprocity into a theory of the moral economy of welfare states. Here, he distinguishes amongst four distinct types of reciprocity, which in his view are the basis for social solidarity. These types are defined in terms of the extensiveness of provision—comprehensive or residual—and the extent of conditionality of benefits—weak or strong.

Historically, most European health systems included charitable (residual/strongly conditional) provision of healthcare through religious orders and the charitable practices of doctors and hospitals. As mentioned above, the US also maintains a means-tested health insurance program (Medicaid, comprehensive/strongly conditional), for which recipients must liquidate nearly all assets to qualify. But with the development of universal health coverage, nearly all European health systems provide comprehensive healthcare benefits with few entry barriers. However, one could say that in a national health service system, such as in the UK and Norway, conditionality and reciprocity are more generalised than under social health insurance, which has traditionally organised the insured into occupational or status groupings, such as the long-term German distinctions between civil servants, salaried employees and industrial workers (Immergut 1986, 1992). Moreover, the extent of private health insurance, either as an opt-out of replacement for social health insurance or in order to cover supplementary services, may divide different pools of beneficiaries and contributors in healthcare systems. The effect is to foster contributory solidarity within specific risk communities rather than the generalised solidarity of the national health services. Further, to the extent that private insurance and private out-of-pocket payments increase, we might expect both generalised and contributory solidarity to be threatened (Gevers et al. 2000; Jordan 2010, 2013; Maarse 2006; Maarse and Paulus 2003). Hence, the literature on deservingness and solidarity indicates that while solidarity for the sick may be generally very high, there may be important variations based on the specific institutional arrangements in place in a given country.

Large-scale cross-national surveys show results much in line with the theoretical literature. Healthcare solidarity is high in all four countries. In answer to a question in the 2008–2009 European Social Survey (ESS) about whether governments should be responsible for healthcare for the sick, all four countries scored above eight on a ten-point scale (UK—8.7, Germany—8.3, Norway—8.9, Slovenia—8.6). The 2011 International Social Survey Program (ISSP) shows strong opposition (more than 70 per cent in each country) to the idea of limiting public provision but interestingly is much more divided on rationing by age.

We do however observe higher discrepancies between countries when it comes to analysing socio-economic differences in health access, health-

Healthcare Futures: Visions of Solidarity and the Sustainability... 221

care rights for migrants and whether healthcare entitlement should depend on behaviour. Nearly 30 per cent of UK respondents believe it as fair that high-income people should have better access with less than half that in any of the other three countries.

There are large variations in willingness to include immigrants in healthcare, with large majorities in favour in Slovenia and Germany, nearly half in Norway and less than one-fifth in the UK (Fig. 7.2). Following other studies and in line with deservingness theory, fewer respondents support public healthcare provision for individuals that engage in high-risk behaviour, but more than half think such people should receive publicly funded care in Slovenia and Norway, with rather lower levels in Germany and the UK. Thus, we observe important differences in our country respondents, but they are not immediately traceable to healthcare institutions. German and Slovene respondents are most open to providing healthcare to non-citizens, while Norwegians and Slovenes are most tolerant of health-damaging behaviour and those in the UK are most accepting of better healthcare treatment for the well-off.

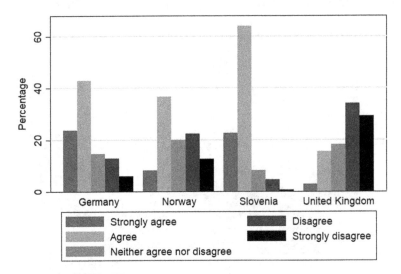

Fig. 7.2 Willingness to include immigrants in publicly-funded healthcare (2011, ISSP). Source: ISSP 2011 – Health and Health Care. Survey Question: How much do you agree or disagree with the following statement: People should have access to publicly funded health care even if they do not hold citizenship of [country]

Turning finally to respondents' evaluations of their national health systems, we note that respondents in all four countries were largely satisfied (with averages above three on a four-point scale). There was considerable variation in willingness to pay higher taxes to improve the system: two-fifths in the UK compared to a third in Norway and a fifth in Slovenia. Somewhat surprisingly, respondents in Slovenia reported the lowest financial barriers to treatment, and respondents in Germany and the UK the highest financial barriers, whereas respondents in Norway reported the most severe waiting list barriers (Fig. 7.3). The relatively low perceived barriers to treatment from waiting times in Slovenia—on a par with those in Germany—are somewhat surprising. Long waiting lists for several specialised treatments are one of the key problems of the healthcare system and receive much media attention. However, access to general practitioners is very good and this might explain the response.

Thus, despite high levels of support for government provision of healthcare in all four countries, there is considerable variation in the conditionality of support and in the groups included. Respondents in Slovenia and Germany are most supportive of the provision of public

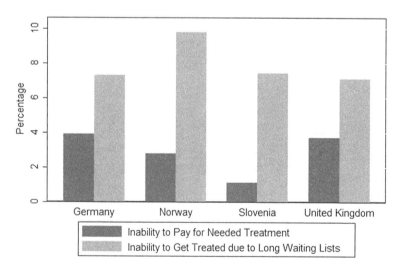

Fig. 7.3 Access to treatment (2001, ISSP). Source: ISSP 2011 – Health and Health Care. Survey Question: During the past 12 months did it ever happen that you did not get the medical treatment you needed because: a) you could not pay for it? b) the waiting list was too long?

healthcare to non-citizens, whilst respondents in Germany and the UK are most critical of those with damaging health behaviour. Surprisingly, respondents in such a rich country as Norway report difficulties in obtaining medical treatment because of long waiting lists, while in Slovenia, the poorest country, respondents report the least difficulties in obtaining treatment, either because of financing issues or waiting lists. In terms of private payment for superior treatment, respondents in the UK are most accepting, while those in Germany and Slovenia are most opposed.

While these large-N surveys can provide a point of departure for understanding welfare state attitudes, they do not offer clear explanations for why respondents in these countries express the attitudes that they do. In order to explore the rationales and justifications that underlie these opinions and attitudes more deeply, we now turn to our Democratic Forum results.

Empirical Analysis of the Democratic Forum Material

In this section we present the analysis of the Democratic Forums in relation to the issues of solidarity within the healthcare system as they were expressed by the participants in the four countries (the UK, Germany, Norway and Slovenia). We focus our research on

- the inclusiveness and conditionality of the solidarity expressed by participants; and
- how participants relate their perceptions of problems and proposed solutions to these issues.

We identify the groups with whom solidarity is acknowledged and those that are excluded or seen as abusing solidarity. We analyse the ways in which deservingness criteria are applied, the consequences in terms of who is viewed as deserving and responsible, and the kinds of arguments on which it is based. We also link the discussion of solidarity with the problems of the healthcare systems people identify and the solutions they propose. In addition, we briefly present the data from the before and after survey to illustrate the general attitudes of participants and (potential) attitudinal changes. The coding of the forum data we used is given in Table 7.1.

Table 7.1 Coding list

Issue	Coding	Examples
Solidarity with whom	Included	Listing the deserving such as nationals, hardworking people…
	Excluded	Those that abuse the system, health tourist, those going private, migrants, the irresponsible…
Arguments used	Behaviour	Irresponsible health behaviour, abuse, etc.
	Identity	The argument was based on the specific identity (nationals or migrants status)
	Reciprocity	The argument was based on past contributions (for example through social insurance)
	Other	Other arguments used (e.g. health needs)
Perceived issues relating to healthcare	Problems	How the problem is understood: sustainability, quality or something else
	Solutions	Solutions given, such as changing the insurance principles, privatisation

As expected from the attitude surveys, participants in all countries express relatively high levels of solidarity. However, there are different national versions of solidarity corresponding to the differences in the level of inclusiveness and understanding of the basis for solidarity.

United Kingdom

In the UK, we observe what we describe as exclusive solidarity. This type of solidarity defines the relationship between the community and individual, and in particular the rights and responsibilities of individuals, with an emphasis on the latter, as well as the limits to solidarity. The emphasis of the discussions on the healthcare system was on restricting the criteria for inclusion and therefore solidarity to certain groups in the population. The key criterion was nationality, which corresponds to the 'identity' criterion for deservingness (van Oorschot 2000). While this was the most important criterion in the discussions, socially responsible behaviour, the 'reciprocity' criterion, played a significant but secondary role. In this regard, the deserving are the social groups who are characterised by working hard, paying taxes and financing the National Health Service (NHS)—or being old and having special and pressing needs. They are seen as having contributed to financing the system and are therefore entitled to healthcare. Here the reciprocity and need criteria are applied.

On the other side we have the undeserving that are excluded from solidarity. In this regard, the NHS is perceived as a system which needs to be protected and shielded from outsiders. Linked to the predominant identity criterion for deservingness, the social groups to which the solidarity principle does not extend are especially foreigners, such as immigrants, health tourists and EU nationals living in the UK, who, in the eyes of the forum participants, threaten the sustainability of the health system. Here solidarity reaches its limits:

> Well some people just come for the Health Service, they come over here for twelve months because they know there's a problem and they'll get seen to straight away whereas in the US you know or whatever you have to pay. (UK-88)

> The NHS is one area that we are saying that we spend a lot of money on, so I mean in this case with non EU nationals, you know, it's fair enough that they don't have access to the NHS. (UK-40)

In addition to 'the outsiders', there are those 'from within' who are also seen as exploiting the system. One such group identified by participants are the unemployed:

> There is more time to think about the fact that you might have something wrong, because when you are at work all the time you just get on with it don't you and plough on? (UK-44)

Another group which seems to be set outside the solidarity principle are the ones who are irresponsible in regard to their health. Here the criteria of personal responsibility or control for deservingness can be observed. Irresponsible health-related behaviour such as overeating and lack of exercise qualifies an individual to be placed outside the solidarity principle.

> I think keeping people healthy, or making them, again, more self-conscious on their own wellbeing [is a priority]. (UK-64)

On the other hand, there are some social groups who are perceived also as non-deserving simply because of the fact that they have enough money to afford private healthcare. Some participants felt that solidarity should be reserved for people who cannot afford private healthcare and not for those who can afford private services, putting forward the criteria of need and means testing. Solidarity within the NHS is therefore viewed as solidarity with those who are in need of care, if they, of course, fulfil the above criteria of deservingness.

> I think it's more for the people that aren't like ourselves that can afford to pay for it. (UK-81)

The UK seems to stand out in this regard as the majority of the debates have been dominated by the notion of (un)deservingness. These topics have been present in debates in other countries but have nevertheless not been as strong or emotionally charged as in the UK. The criterion for defining undeserving others has often been identity (for example, immigrants vs. natives, EU vs. non-EU nationals). This can also be seen in the identification of the problems faced by the healthcare system. In the UK, immigration is perceived as a major threat to the sustainability of the healthcare system on the grounds that it leads to the overcrowding of the NHS, and thus threatens the access of the deserving. Here, we see the greatest difference in the perception of threats to sustainability: only in the UK is there a widespread wish to keep outsiders from entering the healthcare system.

> Yes, it was very, very similar. We were saying we anticipate that in 2040 we'll still have the same issues that we personally do now but it will probably be tenfold. Overcrowding which will lead to housing issues, not enough social housing, strain on the NHS, strain on education and who is going to pay for it? … So stricter border controls, making the right people come to the country, not just anyone and everyone and the prevention for people coming here to get healthcare really. They're coming here on a trip knowing perhaps that they're unwell or need help and then going to the doctors while they're here. (UK-n.i.)

The solution is tighter eligibility controls and stricter monitoring. In this regard the first policy proposed is to prevent extensive immigration to ensure the sustainability of the healthcare system.

> Prevent people coming in just to get healthcare or you know, things like that. They can't just come in to get benefits, I know that but you know if they needed to see a doctor, then they can see a doctor, and, you know. Money that we do have should be spent here, rather than sending it abroad. (UK-44)

What can appear as somewhat surprising are the pragmatic attitudes towards privatisation. One would perhaps expect a more emotionally driven response especially following the positive as well as protective attitudes towards the NHS. Privatisation is however considered almost as a given and a suitable response to sustainability problems, criticism of NHS financing and over-bureaucratisation, and seems in line with reluctant individualism (see Chap. 2 and Taylor-Gooby et al. 2017). It is not that the participants all agree on systemic policy measures, but they do feel something has to be done in order to assure the functioning of the NHS in the future.

> I think—not that I want to, because I think I pay enough tax—but I think we probably do need to. The only way you are going to increase the amount of money we have got is to increase taxes. But as part of that, what if, say, the NHS was optional. So I can choose not to get free healthcare, but then that would come … I would get like a tax subsidy for that. I wouldn't pay as much tax. (UK-86)

All of these discussions were also reflected by results of the before and after surveys carried out amongst the participants of the forums. The proportion seeing healthcare for the sick as a government responsibility dropped after the forum, and the UK fell from having the highest support for government responsibility for the sick amongst the four countries in the before survey to having the lowest ratings amongst the four, while the share perceiving the public healthcare system as unaffordable in the future was the highest.

Germany

The corresponding debates in the German forums focused on the concept of solidarity in and of itself. Indeed, we see here a debate on the core principles of the conservative welfare state regime, which divides beneficiaries according to occupational status. These divisions and privileges were openly questioned on grounds of fairness and sustainability. Furthermore, the increased opportunities for leaving the public insurance system seem to have exacerbated the public-private health insurance divide in Germany. There were also discussions on deservingness, but there is no vested emotional interest in the debate as in the UK, but instead a more pragmatic approach. This approach is not concerned with identifying the social groups who take advantage of the system, but more with systemic reflection on long-term sustainability. The German debate in regard to solidarity thus seems to be much more pragmatic and more inclusive and can be categorised as contributory solidarity. The emphasis was often on the desire to expand the community of contributors in order to make the system fairer and more sustainable, rather than to prevent outsiders from entering the system or to exclude the irresponsible.

This perhaps explains why the private-public split dominates in questions of solidarity. Participants express mixed attitudes toward increasing the share of private health insurance in Germany. The more powerful voices in the debate saw the private provision of services as the biggest threat to solidarity in the German healthcare system and a sign of inevitable changes.

> The biggest problem is health insurance where 15.5% are in private schemes. That's a scandal. (DE-27)

The outrage some of the participants of the forums express has to do with perceived development of the German healthcare system into a two-class system, with privileged groups enjoying better treatment than those with compulsory public health insurance.

> But we don't have a real solidarity system or shared risk pool. Self-employed people are excluded from this, public officials are excluded … if it were a real shared risk pool system, then it would probably work better. The architects

have their own system, pharmacist have their own, doctors have their own insurance ... if they would all pay in with these good incomes, the state healthcare system would be a lot better off overall and work better. (DE-11)

Some participants are resigned to contributory equity, with different outcomes in relation to different levels of contribution:

But if that's the way it is, those who pay more should get more out of it, more services. (DE-10)

But others are not:

Because it's unequal treatment of patients. One may not believe it, but when state-insured people go to the doctor and they get a diagnosis from their doctor and need a specialised treatment, like an MRT scan, then you have waiting times of three to six months in the best case, whereas a private patient gets the diagnosis, and then the doctor just makes a call and can send the patient right over to another practice for the test without waiting time. (DE-29)

Despite some extremely critical views on private insurance in Germany, it was still also proposed as a solution to the problem of sustainability of healthcare system, indicating mixed attitudes. Some of the participants see it as a solution and as assuring the fairness of the system.

I intentionally got private, because there are benefits there that I want and have paid for, which I would otherwise not have. And then with the question of retirement pension, I don't want to be dependent on a system where I have to watch and see whether there are enough young people coming up who can then pay for my bills. Instead, I'll build up my own retirement savings. I think that is more just and fair. (DE-34)

Thus, the concern is both with the sum of resources available to the public system and with differences in treatment of public versus private patients. Support for providing universal healthcare access remains strong, however:

Adequate medical care for each and every person, those who've paid and have not paid, homeless people, whoever. (DE-5)

As in the case of the UK, participants in Germany also discussed undeserving 'insiders' who do not exercise individual responsibility when it comes to choices they make in regard to their lifestyles and health behaviour. Similarly, participants criticised those who visit doctors too frequently (again showing irresponsible use of the system).

> It's about people. At my age, I know people who go to the doctor too often. When I go to the practice, I see some young people, and if you're sick you're sick, but I sometimes get the feeling, particularly with my generation, that going to the doctor really becomes a hobby. (DE-11)

Nevertheless, the discourse of the debate is less harsh towards them than in the UK, and therefore the responsibility/control criteria were relevant but not the main argument for determining the level of solidarity. The limits to personal responsibility were recognised and also the need to educate people about healthier lifestyles.

> Here with personal responsibility, the state has the smallest role to play, but you can achieve quite a lot with relatively little effort through education and these stoplight labels showing how much sugar, fat and so forth are in things. (DE-24)

The threat to solidarity is also detected from outside. In this context the refugee crisis is briefly mentioned. Here the contributory basis of the system is questioned as refugees are perceived by participants as a sustainability issue. They do not pay into the system, and their high needs could sink it:

> The problem is not getting better. We're supposed to be talking about the future, and this is getting worse, isn't it? I'm thinking about millions of refugees who don't pay into the system, but are still covered, and there I see a catastrophe coming in the future if I'm honest. (DE-18)

The criterion for deservingness is not so much based on identity as in the case of the UK, and views on refugees seem to be more pragmatic and less emotionally charged. Meeting the needs of refugees is perceived as a sustainability threat that affects a contributory as opposed to a tax-based system. It is thus a financial issue not a deservingness issue.

Norway

Interestingly, in Norway the solidarity issue hardly appears in the context of deserving and undeserving social groups. It seems that solidarity with different social groups is assumed due to strong support for the universal features of the system. Thus we can talk about universal solidarity. This type of solidarity presupposes protecting a common good that should be universally accessible. An additional issue is the quality of the services. While there is strong support for universal access to high-quality services, however, there is marked concern both about the limits to growth of such a system and the moral basis of any effort to prioritise or ration.

On the one hand, participants are aware of the fact that prioritising is inevitable due to sustainability issues, so that it can be seen as a possible solution to excess demand:

> There has to be a limit for what to treat. Many elders would actually rather die a natural death, but if the heart stops a little when in a nursing home or a retirement home, they are bloody sent away in an ambulance to receive CPR. ... That is wrong prioritizing. (NO-30)

However, some also disapprove of the concept of prioritising, which is viewed by the participants of Norwegian Democratic Forums as a threat to universally accessible medical services and eventually a threat to solidarity, and therefore identified as a problem of the healthcare system. Even more importantly, they are aware of the ethical and moral dilemmas it brings to the forefront and to the logic of the healthcare system in general. The criterion of need is therefore important and the greater the need, the more solidarity with the person. However, there also seems to be a limit to this criterion, and very high healthcare needs must be balanced by other issues (including reciprocity) when priorities are set.

> I feel that just this thing with prioritizing is a very difficult philosophical and ethical question, because there are many ways to do it. The doctors have made a promise—to save lives no matter the cost. We can use the throw-dice model which is fair or unfair depending on how you see it, and one can use a type of business-case argumentation; what are the chances that this person will contribute to the gross national product or to tax income and so on? (NO-29)

In spite of undeniable expressions of support for universality, there seems to be what we can describe as the notion of choice becoming a growing element in the concept of social justice, which also affects the solidarity features and consequently the support for certain health policies. This is also linked to privatisation as a problem and a solution for the future of the healthcare system. The participants emphasise the need for equality to play the lead role. However, even here, solidarity with more vulnerable members of society is taken into consideration and the health services as a universally accessible common good is respected.

> I feel that if you have worked and earned that capital, you should have the right to spend the money to buy that service, so long as you don't steal somebody else's place in line, somebody who doesn't have the money. (NO-9)

The public/private debate in Norway is not as polarising as in the case of Germany. Participants believe that the two sectors can co-exist and not erode the principle of solidarity and equality. Those taking up private insurance and unburdening the public healthcare system could therefore also be seen as exhibiting solidarity by taking more (individual) responsibility for their healthcare as they are making the health system financially more stable.

> I hope and think we have a public health service on the level it is today and that we have a private health service in addition to that. (NO-21)

Even when it comes to immigrants, the participants do not take a radical view but express solidarity with them, and the identity criterion of us vs. them is not applied. They are seen as a special vulnerable group from the perspective of health services provision. It almost seems as if the forum wants to make them part of their community as soon as possible.

> I think about integration. I haven't defined immigration/immigrants. Not only thinking about refugees, but important to integrate everyone regardless. For example, through language teaching, working life, Norwegian culture. They who suffer from trauma get treatment for that. (NO-2)

There are however certain groups to which the deservingness principle does apply, but more weakly. This can be shown by the stress laid on individual responsibility for one's own health, therefore applying the control criterion of deservingness.

> But I think that one also has to take responsibility for one's own health. If you choose to eat McDonald's three times a week, not to work out, and lose everything because of drink, that is your choice. But then I don't necessarily think that you should get the same health service as the one who takes care of himself. (NO-14)

In Norway the weakening of the solidarity principle is linked to individually and socially irresponsible health related behaviour, over-usage of medical services and abuse of the rules which apply to the concept of prioritising.

> Regarding objectivity, we think we have a very logical healthcare service, but I don't think so. As a health system worker, if I need an appointment, I will get it within the next 14 days, even if the wait is 6 months, because I know the system. If you are a journalist or politician, you get the same treatment. Not because they are the elite, but because they will make a hell of a fuss and hospitals aren't too keen on fuss. … But today we have a kind of elitist discrimination, because one takes the one who makes the most noise, they are treated first, because then things go so much smoother, but it's not right that way. (NO-24)

It is therefore the actions of individuals which set the weakening of solidarity in motion, the actions that threaten the common good, and not certain social and cultural features of groups of individuals. This is in stark contrast to the notion of exclusive solidarity in the UK.

Slovenia

Slovenia seems to resemble Norway in regard to solidarity. Participants from both the Norwegian and Slovene Democratic Forums express support for universalism as the main principle in policy design of their respective healthcare systems, although egalitarianism along with distrust of private healthcare provision was much more pronounced in Slovenia. Hence, the type of solidarity attached to such characteristics can be identified as egalitarian solidarity. As solidarity is based on belief in a common public good, universal coverage is essential and private insurance is seen as a threat to the continuity of public healthcare, with extremely negative consequences for public health in general.

> I see it this way, if there isn't any money for public healthcare, this will become a problem. You will have to pay for every service and think twice before signing your child up for a procedure, or yourself actually on some tests that will cost a couple of thousand euro, that you perhaps won't have on an account somewhere, and that will … increase the mortality. That the people will not be prepared to finance that, if we allow everything to fall apart or if there won't be enough funds for that. (SI-77)

It seems that exclusion criteria do not exist in Slovenia as almost no groups were discussed as potentially excluded, and the belief in universal coverage of the healthcare system is unchallenged. Healthcare, as is the case in Norway, is perceived as a public good. This could be the reason why the level of trust in the proper functioning of the system and its ability to ensure fairness and equal treatment for all is even more important. Inequality and equality of access have been the main topics when it comes to discussing solidarity within the system. Due to the egalitarian views of the participants in the Slovene forums, the perceived inequalities, which have in their opinion become inherent in the system, are unacceptable. Consequently, one of the solutions proposed was increasing the egalitarian principles so that supplementary payments in the system should be based on income (as is already the case with obligatory health insurance), which participants perceived as fairer than the current lump sum payment.

It is not fair that we are all required to pay the same insurance, regardless of our income; whether we earn 5,000 EUR, 1,000 or only 500 EUR a month. (SI-58)

The private co-payments for health insurance are therefore highly distrusted and seen as an unacceptable method of differentiating people and also as eroding risk sharing. This attitude is strong among the general population and is reflected in recent proposals for reform which include abolishing existing individual co-payments through private health insurance schemes.

When the level of trust in the system's ability to ensure equality is low, as is increasingly the case in Slovenia, solidarity with different social groups does not diminish. However, the groups who take advantage of the system seem to be sliding out from under the solidarity umbrella. This is particularly evident in queue-jumping, which creates a division in the otherwise uniformly accessible provision of health services. It divides the population between those who can afford private medical services, plus those with the connections to 'jump the queue' in the public system and those who cannot do either. Social and economic capital enable a part of population to afford better health services and to become 'the other from within'.

Let's say that, if you need to see a doctor and the waiting list is too long, but if you go to a private practice, you get seen much sooner, that's not fair. It's not a given that you have the money for the private practice. (SI-87)

Waiting lines are therefore a symbol of deeply rooted systemic problems. In this regard, private healthcare is perceived as eroding universalism.

There are already long waiting lists to see doctors as it is, while the medical professionals are under a lot of strain, which only contributes to longer waiting lists. ... The long waiting lists will backfire and not far in the future, in 25 years, but much sooner than that. (SI-50)

In Slovenia the discussions of solutions to financial sustainability and demographic change that were the main identified problems of the system, as in Norway, remain firmly based on universalism. However, in contrast to Norway, there is virtually no positive aspect to be found in the Slovene debate in regard to privatisation as a solution to problems of sustainability. Privatisation is linked to differences in service quality and accessibility. People who can afford to use private practitioners are entitled to a higher level of service, and this reinforces the belief that the universalism of the system is being eroded. This debate further supports the Slovene value system and attitude to solidarity. Privatisation is generally perceived as a threat to universal and uniform service provision.

> So, someone who can afford to go to private practice, will receive a higher quality of service than someone who can't afford that. And I see this here as quite a problem. (SI-86)

> I think I am in favour of cancelling private healthcare. Because what it really is, is: we all like to say that health is worth more than wealth, yet those who are not able to afford specialist check-ups because of financial difficulties, are what, simply supposed to die? So the specialists are only working for the privileged ones. I support the fact that doctors should be well-paid, even paid double the money, if they work double the time, because they are able to work such long hours; however, those who work in public institutions in the morning and in private practices in the afternoon, that means, have a full-time job and run their own practice, I cannot be in favour of that. They should only work in public healthcare, in their regular working hours and be paid well for it, so that everybody can have equal access to healthcare. (SI-57)

This distrust of private provision in either form, through private health insurance or private practices (that can be paid out of pocket), distinguishes Slovenia from other countries, where positive views or partial acceptance of the private sector, especially in the light of sustainability problems, are mixed with some mistrust. It seems to reflect the disillusion or inherent mistrust of the populace in what the capitalist society with private market provision within the welfare mix can bring to improve the quality of life for all. This is linked also to the common issues of corruption and high earnings or double earnings in the private healthcare sector of doctors working in public as well as private practice. It is also reflected in high support for government as responsible for healthcare for the sick, which increased in the post-forum survey, so that support was higher in Slovenia than any other of the four countries. The surveys also reflect the lack of concern for the sustainability of public healthcare, as the highest proportion of respondents answered that public healthcare spending will be able to increase in next 25 years (19 per cent compared to seven per cent or less in other three countries).

Discussion and Conclusion

The four framings of healthcare solidarity that emerged from our Democratic Forums show that the principles of solidarity remain strong but that they vary significantly between our countries, and have different consequences for the future outlook of healthcare systems. In the UK, the NHS is perceived by Democratic Forum participants as 'a thing of beauty' (as one participant put it) that must be defended from outsiders. Indeed, even though there were some concerns about those who abuse or overuse the healthcare system from within, it was not the main focus of the UK's exclusive solidarity. This is defined as against the 'other', whether these are 'health tourists', EU nationals or other groups. Returning to our survey data, exclusive solidarity is a vision that makes sense of the perception that increased taxation is necessary to pay for adequate services, that financial barriers to access are too high and that allowing unequal health access in order to unburden the public system may even be necessary. Even though participants value the NHS highly and are generally satisfied with it, they feel a need to defend it against illegitimate use by outsiders, and may be disappointed that the government does not defend it adequately.

In Germany, the equivalence principle of contributory equity was the subject of debate in our forums, and indeed, in public debate. The privileges at the heart of the conservative model were questioned, and the ability of some to purchase better treatment was criticised. Nevertheless the focus was not on defending the system against outsiders but on how to universalise contributions so as to meet future needs. The prominence of contributory reciprocity makes sense of the survey findings that individual responsibility for health is important to German respondents, and

Table 7.2 Healthcare solidarity in the Democratic Forums

Solidarity type	Exclusive solidarity	Contributory solidarity	Universal solidarity	Equalitarian solidarity
Country	UK	Germany	Norway	Slovenia
Included	Hard-working Poor Old British	Solidarity with all coupled with concern that all then indeed contribute	Solidarity with all	Solidarity with all
Excluded	Immigrants Abusers Over-users Health tourists EU nationals	Abusers Over-users Irresponsible (Refugees/immigrants)	Irresponsible Over-users Abusers	Abusers
Description	A beautiful island to be defended against invaders	High solidarity with worries about two class approach	Protecting the (good) commons	Solidarity based on egalitarianism; distrust of capitalism
Problems perceived	Immigration Ageing of population Risk behaviours Financial sustainability	Financial sustainability Private health insurance Ageing population Refugees/immigrants Two-class medicine	Ageing population Prioritizing Financial sustainability	Ageing population Privatization Corruption
Solutions proposed	Increased control and reduced eligibility (for migrants) Increased personal responsibility Possible privatization Choice (not to receive care)	More universal system with universal contributions Less unequal treatment Increased personal responsibility Privatization as addition to public system	Privatization as addition to public system Increased personal responsibility Prioritization Choice (not to receive care)	Increased control and regulation Increased personal responsibility Pronounced egalitarianism (e.g. income-related payments)

the discussion of migrants and refugees in terms of resources not rights may explain why Germans appear to be relatively accepting of public provision of health services for non-citizens. There was some support for allowing private resources to improve the financing of the system, but certainly a strong opposition to better treatment for higher-income groups, the privately insured and for the privileges of public servants.

In Norway, there was strong support for generalised solidarity, but also high awareness of the limits of the commons, and the need to manage resources for a sustainable future. Although foreigners were not singled out in the Democratic Forums, the need to protect the commons (also a topic of Norwegian public discourse) may explain the relatively high resistance to providing healthcare to non-citizens and the negative comments in the Forums about privileged access by journalists and celebrities. Despite the country's wealth, survey respondents report not being able to access health services because of long waiting lists, yet the Democratic Forums make it clear that they accept the need to set priorities in order to be in shape for the tremendous demographic shifts of the decades to come, at the same time that they question the ability of government to establish ethical criteria for rationing.

Finally, in Slovenia, we observe support for universal healthcare and dissatisfaction with parts of the existing contributory system, as well as unease with what has been lost from the past with capitalism and the entry of the profit motive into the healthcare system. While survey results show a lack of barriers to healthcare access in Slovenia, the Democratic Forums demonstrate that private healthcare lacks public legitimacy. There is a tension between the objective improvement of health services in Slovenia since the double transition to capitalism and democracy and the resentment of private for-profit medicine that conflicts with egalitarianism. The public-private mix in health in Slovenia contains the lowest proportion of public tax financing and highest proportion of private health insurance expenditure among the four countries. The transition has been indeed radical.

In sum, the Democratic Forums reveal important sources of concern and dissatisfaction that are not apparent from public opinion surveys, but that may affect public discourse and even election results. Some elements of our national patterns may be traced to the structure of the health system, such as the relatively higher concern with capacity and rationing in our two mainly tax-financed national health services (UK and Norway). But others, such as concerns over private health insurance, bear little relationship to the size of this sector. The causal relationship between these framings of solidarity within media debates would make an interesting question for future research. From this four country comparison, despite the high levels of support for public provision of medical care and the strong perception that the sick are a highly deserving group, we observe significant problems of legitimacy in each country: abuse from outsiders in the UK, privileged occupational groups and the privately insured in Germany, lack of consideration for limited resources and unfair access by elites in Norway and unfair health insurance contributions, private access and private profits earned in public institutions in Slovenia. Further research is required to determine whether these issues originate in the financial problems of those systems or in a need for better communication of the rationales and justifications for health policies by political leaders. What we do know, however, is that the future of these healthcare systems will depend upon making significant adjustments and justifying them in ways that are compatible and acceptable within the normative frameworks of these visions of solidarity.

References

Abela, A. (2004). Solidarity and religion in the European Union: A comparative sociological perspective. In P. G. Xuereb (Ed.), *The value(s) of a constitution for Europe*. Valetta: European Documentation and Research Center, University of Malta.

Arts, W., & Gelissen, J. (2001). Welfare states, solidarity and justice principles: Does the type really matter? *Acta Sociologica, 44*(4), 283–299.

Bambra, C. (2005). Cash versus services: 'worlds of welfare' and the decommodification of cash benefits and health care services. *Journal of Social Policy, 34*(2), 195–213.

Béland, D., & Gran, B. (2008). *Public and private social policy. Health and pension policies in a new era*. Basingstoke: Palgrave Macmillan.

ESS Round 4: European Social Survey Round 4 Data. (2008). Data file edition 4.4. NSD – Norwegian Centre for Research Data, Norway – Data Archive and distributor of ESS data for ESS ERIC.

Gevers, J., Gelissen, J., Arts, W., & Muffels, R. (2000). Public health care in the balance: Exploring popular support for health care systems in the European Union. *International Journal of Social Welfare, 9*(4), 301–321.

Gollust, S., & Lynch, J. (2011). Who deserves health care? The effects of causal attributions and group cues on public attitudes about responsibility for health care costs. *Journal of Health Politics, Policy and Law, 36*(6), 1061–1095.

Immergut, E. M. (1986). Between state and market: Sickness benefits and social control. In M. Rein & L. Rainwater (Eds.), *Public/private interplay in social protection: A comparative study*. Armank, NY: Sharpe.

Immergut, E. M. (1992). *Health politics: Interests and institutions in Western Europe*. Cambridge: Cambridge University Press.

ISSP Research Group. (2015). International Social Survey Programme: Health and Health Care – ISSP 2011. GESIS Data Archive, Cologne. ZA5800 Data file Version 3.0.0. Retrieved from https://doi.org/10.4232/1.12252.

Jordan, J. (2010). Institutional feedback and support for the welfare state: The case of national health care. *Comparative Political Studies, 43*(7), 862–885.

Jordan, J. (2013). Policy feedback and support for the welfare state. *Journal of European Social Policy, 23*(2), 134–148.

Larsen, C. A. (2008). The institutional logic of welfare attitudes: How welfare regimes influence public support. *Comparative Political Studies, 41*(2), 145–168.

Maarse, H. (2006). The privatization of health care in Europe: An eight-country analysis. *Journal of Health Politics, Policy and Law, 31*(5), 981–1014.

Maarse, H., & Paulus, A. (2003). Has solidarity survived? A comparative analysis of the effect of social health insurance reform in four European countries. *Journal of Health Politics Policy and Law, 28*(4), 585–614.

Mau, S. (2004). Welfare regimes and the norms of social exchange. *Current Sociology, 52*(1), 53–74.

Murphy-Berman, V. A., Berman, J. J., & Campbell, E. (1998). Factors affecting health-care allocation decisions: A case of aversive racism? *Journal of Applied Social Psychology, 28*(24), 2239–2253.

OECD. (2017). *OECD health statistics 2017*. Paris: OECD Publishing. Retrieved September 15, 2017, from https://doi.org/10.1787/health-data-en.

Petersen, M. B., Slothuus, R., Stubager, R., & Togeby, L. (2011). Deservingness versus values in public opinion on welfare: The automaticity of the deservingness heuristic. *European Journal of Political Research, 50*(1), 24–52.

Rigby, E., Soss, J., Booske, B. C., Rohan, A. M., & Robert, S. A. (2009). Public responses to health disparities: How group cues influence support for government intervention. *Social Science Quarterly, 90*(5), 1321–1340.

Taylor Gooby, P., Leruth, B., & Chung, H. (2017). *After austerity: Welfare state transformation in Europe after the great recession.* Oxford: Oxford University Press.

van Oorschot, W. (2000). Who should get what, and why? On deservingness criteria and the conditionality of solidarity among the public. *Policy & Politics, 28*(1), 33–48.

van Oorschot, W., & Komter, A. (1998). What is it that ties…? Theoretical perspectives on social bonds. *Sociale Wetenschappen, 41*(3), 4–24.

8

Labour Market Challenges and the Role of Social Investment

Katharina Zimmermann, Heejung Chung, and Jan-Ocko Heuer

Introduction

During the last few decades, most welfare states across Europe experienced crucial changes in the work-welfare nexus. After the Second World War, many European countries had established relatively generous welfare systems, which achieved, to different degrees and across different dimensions, a de-commodification of labour in the sense that they made the social well-being of individuals less dependent upon the labour market (Esping-Andersen 1990). However, post-war welfare states soon came under financial pressure, and since the 1970s we can observe clear welfare state retrenchment and re-commodification (Offe 1984; Pierson 2001). Against the backdrop of developments such as technological advancements, globalisation, European integration, demographic changes or

---

K. Zimmermann (✉) • J.-O. Heuer
Humboldt University of Berlin, Berlin, Germany
e-mail: katharina.zimmermann@hu-berlin.de

H. Chung
University of Kent, Canterbury, UK

© The Author(s) 2018
P. Taylor-Gooby, B. Leruth (eds.), *Attitudes, Aspirations and Welfare*,
https://doi.org/10.1007/978-3-319-75783-4_8

changing family patterns, the relationship between work and welfare was refined in various ways, and labour markets, forms of employment, collective bargaining structures, vocational training schemes, unemployment protection and labour market policies underwent significant changes (Taylor-Gooby et al. 2017).

These social, economic and political dynamics had a crucial impact on the individual risks European citizens face during their lifetime: for instance, demographic changes altered dependency ratios and put pressure on pensions, and technological changes increased the demand for high-skilled workers and hence fostered the social exclusion of poorly educated people. As a consequence of these so-called new social risks (Bonoli 2010; Pierson 2001; Taylor-Gooby 2004), (long-term) unemployment and (in-work) poverty increased in many European countries (Heidenreich 2016). Furthermore, we can observe an increasing privatisation of social security, changes in social rights (Ferrera 2005), marketisation, flexibilisation and the rise of labour market insecurity (Chung and Mau 2014). Most European welfare states reacted to these new social risks, fiscal and economic pressures, and the changed conditions of labour markets by introducing various alterations in social and employment policies. As we will elaborate below, active labour market policies, which had been introduced from the 1970s onwards as a complement to passive benefits, have become embedded in strong supply-side oriented activation measures since the 1990s. More recently this was linked to so-called 'social investment' strategies, which emphasise the role of investments in education and human capital in increasing employability, cater to the needs of a dynamic labour market and thus contribute to decreasing welfare budgets and a more productive economy (Morel et al. 2012).

Welfare state retrenchment, re-commodification, activation and also, to some extent, social investment strategies have been broadly studied by social policy scholars. However, notwithstanding our relatively solid knowledge on policy strategies, policy implications and the organisational dimension of the changing work-welfare nexus, so far we have limited knowledge about people's attitudes, aspirations and expectations in relation to the legitimacy of these developments. Most studies still focus on people's preferences in relation to passive and/or active labour market policies, or on the role of governments in job or unemployment protection (for example Andreß and Heien 2001; Svalund et al. 2016), while perceptions of activation or social investment as possible tools are rarely touched upon (for noteworthy exceptions see Aurich 2011; Busemeyer 2017). This is not least due to crucial limitations in the availability of suitable data.

Although more recent scholarly activities seek to overcome these shortcomings by introducing the new paradigms in cross-national surveys (for example Busemeyer et al. 2018), we argue that these attempts suffer from the limitation that survey research is still largely framed by the preconceptions of the researchers (see Chap. 1). This is why in this chapter we adopt a bottom-up strategy and seek to study people's opinions directly. By starting from below and assessing what citizens perceive as crucial challenges of the current and future labour market, and examining the way they link labour market issues to education, activation and other types of services and benefits, we seek to contribute to the literature by providing a more unfiltered view of citizens' perceptions and framings of these problems as well as of their preferred solutions.

The following section provides an overview of the different types of labour market strategies that have been developed over the years in European welfare states, situating social investment strategies within a larger range of labour market paradigms. This section also considers existing research on citizens' attitudes in this area and provides a brief description of recent labour market pathways in the countries chosen for our analysis because they typify different labour markets: the United Kingdom (liberal), Slovenia (post-socialist), Denmark (social democratic flexicurity) and Germany (modernised corporatist conservative). Section "Current Labour Market Policies in Europe: Pathways and Public Attitudes", sets out the findings from our research, and section "Labour Market Trends in the UK, Germany, Denmark, and Slovenia", presents our findings and analysis. We end with a discussion of the results.

ch
Current Labour Market Policies in Europe: Pathways and Public Attitudes

Labour Market Paradigms

Morel et al. (2012) distinguish three labour market paradigms: *Keynesian*, *neo-liberal* and *social investment*. The first understands unemployment and slow growth as caused by a demand deficit and argues for state stimulation of demand through infrastructure investment and social benefits. The principles of equality and full employment can be found at its core. Neo-liberal approaches conversely regard supply-side constraints (employment regulations, strong unions, benefits which reduce work incentives, taxation) as the problem and recommend privatisation and curbing inflation through monetary policy. They rest on principles of individual responsibility, activation and workfare. Social investment focuses attention on the skills and availability of workers and promotes (early) education, (lifelong) training and child and elderly care to release women workers. Its concerns are with individual capabilities and social inclusion.

Studies of Labour Market Attitudes using Large Samples

While these trends have been studied broadly by social policy scholars, we still lack substantial knowledge of their legitimacy among European citizens. In the context of welfare attitudes research (for example the European Social Survey [ESS] and the International Social Survey Programme [ISSP]), public perceptions of labour market policies are mostly measured through items on governments' responsibilities, spending priorities or redistribution preferences for unemployment benefits.

If we look at country-specific findings in the literature on welfare attitudes, it seems that there is a relationship between people's attitudes and the welfare regime they live in. As Andreß and Heien (2001, 352) conclude:

> people in liberal welfare regimes show comparatively low levels of support for the range of governmental action. While we find medium levels of support

in conservative regimes, support is much higher in welfare states categorized as being social democratic. Nevertheless, the highest level of support can be found in East Germany. Obviously, the communist ideal of social policy did not disappear with the end of the regime.

Although the relationship becomes more blurred if we dig deeper into the study of causes and effects in this regard (Arts and Gelissen 2001; Jæger 2006), country-specific differences are undeniable. In general, citizens in Denmark and Slovenia seem to see greater government responsibilities in fields such as unemployment protection, employment opportunities, and support for reconciling work and family life, while UK and to some extent also German citizens are less enthusiastic about public interventions. In accordance with what we know from the literature on 'worlds of welfare attitudes', we might interpret these patterns as being related to the liberal and individualistic system in the UK, to a socialist and state-centred legacy in Slovenia and to a social-democratic regime in Denmark. When it comes to citizens' attitudes towards job creation or protection, generally high support for public financing of projects to create new jobs can be observed in all countries, but again Slovenes are most supportive of public interventions (88.4 per cent, compared to 72.7 per cent in Denmark, 67.8 per cent in Germany and 75.1 in Great Britain; ISSP 2008). Turning towards people's preferences on unemployment protection, Germany stands out with a very high support for status-protecting unemployment benefits (57.7 per cent), while in the other countries—and particularly in Denmark—a flat-rate model is preferred: the option 'higher and lower earners should get the same amount of benefits' was chosen by 76.5 per cent in Denmark, 70.8 in the UK and 57.9 per cent of the Slovenes (ESS 2008).

Although this data from the ESS and ISSP already provides us with interesting insights into country-specific patterns of attitudes towards labour market policies, the items disregard more recent trends such as activation or social investment. However, we also find some support for social investment when examining people's preference data on spending priorities and government involvement in childcare provision. For instance, large majorities in all four countries support more education spending (ISSP 2008), and support for public childcare for working parents is very high

(Chung and Meuleman 2017). However, this information does not tell us much about broad acceptance of social investment strategies.

More recently, a few survey projects have sought to cure these data limitations. The 'Investing in Education in Europe' project addresses individual preferences towards education and includes a trade-off perspective (Busemeyer 2017; Busemeyer and Garritzmann 2017; Busemeyer et al. 2018). Highly educated, left-leaning and pro-state individuals are more likely to support increased education spending, even if it means higher taxes, whereas those with little education, a right-wing ideological orientation and a greater scepticism regarding the role of the state tend to be more opposed (Busemeyer and Garritzmann 2017). Furthermore, the welfare attitudes module in the European Social Survey 2016 includes a few items on activation policies and social investment (ESS 2016), and the data (not available at the time of writing) will provide fresh insights into the legitimacy of current trends in labour market policy.

While the large sample surveys provide us with representative comparative data, they necessarily draw on pre-defined analytical concepts and thus may fall short in capturing complex developments in the legitimacy of a changing work-welfare nexus and the arguments supporting such policies. As we outlined above, the changes in labour market policies in Europe had substantial impact on numerous dimensions of citizens' lives and social conditions, and we have little knowledge of how these changes are assessed and evaluated by the public. We argue that we need to study citizens' attitudes towards labour market policies from a bottom-up perspective to capture their framing of the issues and understand the impact of recent policy trends. Before we turn to our empirical analysis of the debates in the four countries we will provide some insights into recent labour market trends and developments.

Labour Market Trends in the UK, Germany, Denmark and Slovenia

The UK, Germany, Denmark and Slovenia have all experienced specific labour market and employment developments and have undergone substantive changes in their work-welfare nexus in the last few decades. In

Labour Market Challenges and the Role of Social Investment 249

most countries, we can see a fluctuation in unemployment rates at a relatively similar rate, with a sharp increase due to the financial crisis of 2008–2009 and then falling slowly over the following years. Examining the key indicator for labour market policies, we see that in 2015 Denmark is preeminent in activation, accounting for nearly 1.5 per cent of GDP (see Fig. 8.1). Germany and Slovenia on the other hand spend a tenth of this. In addition, these countries have cut spending in this area since 2010. We do not have data for the UK for 2015, but in 2010 it was one of the lowest spenders in Active Labour Market Policy (ALMP) in 2010 and has if anything reduced spending since.

When we turn towards passive labour market policy spending (income maintenance for the unemployed), we can see that again Denmark shows the highest spending rates among the four countries under study (see Fig. 8.2). However, as in almost all other European countries—including Germany, Slovenia and Denmark, while we again have no 2015 UK data, though benefit rates here were cut and numbers receiving them fell—passive spending decreased between 2010 and 2015.

From a broader perspective, the reduced spending can be read as expressions of a broader welfare state retrenchment and the ongoing re-commodification trend across Europe. However, different countries show different detailed patterns of change.

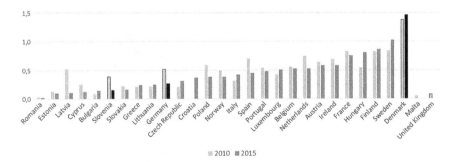

Fig. 8.1 Expenditure on active labour market services in 2010 and 2015 (% GDP). Source: Eurostat (LMP expenditure; categories 2–7)

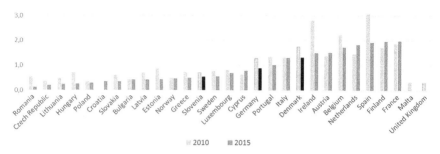

Fig. 8.2 Passive labour market expenditure in 2010 and 2015 (% GDP). Source: Eurostat (LMP expenditure; categories 8 and 9)

The United Kingdom

A typical liberal regime (Esping-Andersen 1990), the UK provides low employment protection for standard workers and thus a relatively flexible labour market (OECD 2004). The UK labour market is also characterised by low levels of income security based on a means-tested low flat-rate job seekers' allowance. In addition, there is considerable income disparity across socio-economic groups, and income inequality has risen more rapidly over the years compared to other countries (OECD 2011). As outlined in greater detail by Taylor-Gooby et al. (2017), in the context of the 'Third Way' approach of the early 2000s, the social investment approach became highly prominent, and policy spending was presented as 'targeted investment' (Giddens 2001; Lister 2004), that is, a cautious expansion of state provision/social policies and investment for the future. However, many of these policies have been curtailed by the Conservative and Coalition government from 2010 (Taylor-Gooby et al. 2017).

Germany

At the time when Esping-Andersen created his seminal welfare regime typology (Esping-Andersen 1990), Germany could be classified as a typical conservative welfare state, characterised by a Bismarckian, insurance-based social protection scheme, highly exclusive labour markets, low female employment and a crucial role for vocational training schemes.

However, since the late 1990s, the country has introduced far-reaching reforms, as depicted in greater detail by Heuer and Mau (2017). Besides cost reduction, the aim of this reorganisation was to establish a governance system providing targeted investment measures, especially to those who encounter difficulties (re)entering the labour market. The focus was mainly on the activation of long-term unemployed. Nevertheless, although (female) employment rates have significantly increased, the German labour market is still highly exclusive, and insiders (employees with jobs subject to social insurance contributions) are in a much better position than outsiders (with short-term contracts, mini-jobs or low-wage jobs).

Denmark

Denmark is a typical social-democratic welfare regime (Esping-Andersen 1990). The well-known flexicurity system—or 'golden triangle' (Madsen 2004)—was introduced in the 1990s to tackle issues of high and long-term unemployment and is typified by a flexible labour market, generous unemployment benefits and a high level of ALMP engagement. Nevertheless, in the context of economic recession, several changes occurred in Denmark. Most importantly, eligibility for unemployment benefits was tightened, but also access to training or education during the period of unemployment has been increased (Madsen 2013). Furthermore, benefits levels, eligibility and entitlement for immigrants were tightened in the context of debates on immigration that challenged the balance of Danish flexicurity and welfare.

Slovenia

Although Slovenia belongs to the post-socialist countries of Central and Eastern Europe, it did not adopt the strong market- and individualisation-oriented pathway of other countries in this region (Bohle and Greskovits 2007). Slovenia benefitted from strong economic growth in the aftermath of 1990. High living standards and a comparably generous social protection system made it an 'affluent enclave' (Fenger 2007, 13) in the region. However, even in the early years of transition, the country also showed high labour market segmentation between insiders with permanent employment and outsiders with short-term contracts or part-time jobs (Filipovič Hrast and Rakar 2017, 119). In 2008, the country was hit hard by the economic recession. This put strong pressure on the welfare system, and pension and labour market reforms were adopted, followed by welfare and family policy reforms. Consequently, Slovenia underwent a development from a highly universalist welfare state with a high level of decommodification towards a much more targeted, marketised and individualised system in the context of austerity policies.

Problem Perceptions and Key Topics in the Four Countries: The Democratic Forums

Labour market and employment issues were set as a topic for discussion by researchers on the second day of the Forums in all four countries (see Chap. 1). However, in three countries (UK, Germany and Slovenia) they were already chosen by the participants as a topic on the first day, while in Denmark they were only discussed on the second. In all cases the discussion of the topic started with brainstorming in which the moderators encouraged the participants to express freely their views on which aspects of the labour market and employment they believe will matter in the future. A more in-depth discussion on the different aspects followed in all breakout groups. Table 8.1 lists the different aspects mentioned during the breakout discussion (with the most relevant aspects highlighted in bold).

As Table 8.1 shows, the participants in the Democratic Forums raised topics which spanned several dimensions of labour market policy, including unemployment and unemployment benefits, fraud and benefit conditionality, working conditions and wages, education and vocational training, macroeconomic conditions and productivity, immigration, and reconciliation of work and family life. The broad range of topics is of course not surprising, since the everyday life of citizens is strongly shaped by the various dimensions related to their jobs and working life. However, if we take a closer look at the differences and similarities across the coun-

Table 8.1 Labour market topics raised by democratic forum participants in the UK, Denmark, Germany and Slovenia

Germany	UK
Secure job positions	(Youth) unemployment and work prospects
Work for everyone	
Wages, taxes, social insurance contributions and net income	**Education and training**
	Access to education (costs)
Minimum wage	**Investment in vocational skills**
Qualifications	Discouraging unemployment benefits
Education and training	
Investment in early education	Mandatory work in return for social benefits
Reconciliation of work and family life	
Shorter working hours	**Motivation, fraud, laziness**
Flexible working time	**Immigration**
Childcare availability	Economy and productivity
	Zero-hour contracts
	Childcare costs
Denmark	**Slovenia**
Incentive to work, activation, welfare conditionality	**Unemployment (particularly young and old)**
Work as contribution to society	Employing the disabled
Work ethics	Job guarantee
Unemployment benefits	Work motivation; work prospects
Public Employment Services (role and efficiency)	Unemployment brings laziness
	Work as social inclusion and individual happiness
Immigration	
Reconciliation of work and family life	**Tax contributions too high**
Working time	Net income
Minimum wage	Living standard
Work for everyone	**Minimum wage**
Flexicurity model	Pensions—financing problems
Collective agreements	Education and training
Technological developments and changing labour markets	**Investment in skills**
	Economy and jobs
Investment (in productivity)	
Education and training	

tries, we can see different emphases in the debates. For instance, unemployment was a crucial aspect in Slovenia and the UK, while it was less important in Denmark, and not an issue at all in Germany. Immigration was brought up in Denmark and the UK, but not in Slovenia and Germany, and precarious work and job conditions were particularly raised in Slovenia and Germany, while in the UK, zero-hour contracts, a very UK-specific issue, was one of the most discussed topics.

The only cross-cutting topics which were brought up in all four countries were 'work for all/job guarantee' and 'investment'. This is interesting, since these two topics clearly relate to the trends towards active welfare states and social investment as outlined above. A strong demand for work for all suggests that people have accepted the principle of high employment rates for all social groups, and the salience of investment claims indicates that the social investment concept has reached citizens' perceptions of 'good' labour market policies. However, if we take a closer look at the debates in the countries, it becomes clear that below the surface of the similarities regarding social investment and high employment, there are also fundamental differences: in Denmark, social investment was discussed in the context of investment in productivity, in Germany in the context of investment in early education, and in Slovenia and the UK in the context of investment in vocational skills. Furthermore, while in the UK and Denmark benefit fraud and benefit conditionality were highly salient, in Slovenia people emphasised the relevance of work motivation and work as social inclusion, and in Germany work for everyone was brought up in the context of job security.

Thus, similar topics and problem perceptions were raised in highly different contexts—a fact which indicates that a simple focus on the salience of themes falls short when it comes to a more complex assessment of citizen's perceptions of labour market policies. We provide more in-depth insights into the debates in the four countries in the following sections by revealing patterns of argument. Here we will particularly focus on the connections between problems and solutions, as we believe that this sheds light on participants' framing of the link between the different dimensions of work and welfare in their country.

Causes of Problems and Suggested Solutions

Denmark

Both the problem perceptions and the solutions suggested by participants in the Danish forum show a strong emphasis on productivity. The debates mainly focus on the questions of how growth and employment could be increased, and how the social protection scheme could be rendered more efficient. As unemployment was mostly perceived as a cause for insufficient productivity and growth, high employment was seen as the best solution. Here, both demand and supply-side measures such as job creation and work incentives were suggested. The Danish flexicurity model was mostly embraced as a highly useful way to ensure productivity and at the same time enhance social security. A respective policy proposal ('We believe that the Danish labour market model, also known as the Danish model, must be maintained, including the flexibility that allows for negotiation between the social partners') received 31 'yes'-votes and zero 'no'-votes. However, challenges such as immigration were mentioned by some participants as causes for a decreasing potential to keep the balance within the flexicurity scheme:

> when there are more and more coming into the country and there are low wages, there's an informal economy, there are eastern Europeans and a large number of immigrants.... In our previous model the trade unions were able to manage it by applying pressure. Now trade union affiliation overall is falling and more and more people are coming in. So it will probably become necessary to legislate on a Danish minimum wage. (DK-68)

In fact, introducing a minimum wage in Denmark was, as also mentioned in the quote, a frequently suggested solution to the problem of decreasing wages. However, while this measure received high support across all breakout groups (and a respective policy proposal was supported with 23 'yes'-votes), concerns were also raised (and the policy proposal received six 'no'-votes).

A further challenge for the Danish flexicurity scheme was identified with regard to the burdens individual employees experience within a flexible labour market. High individual stress, difficulties in reconciling work and family life, or increasing job insecurity were mentioned by participants as crucial problems. Potential solutions were suggested which emphasised the advantages of more flexible working time and lower working hours (particularly for parents).

Against the backdrop of the abovementioned focus on growth and productivity, investment in education but also in childcare was promoted as a crucial measure for addressing challenges such as demographic change or increasing productivity. A resource-oriented emphasis on social investment, not on equal opportunities, was at the core of the debates in all breakout groups, and statements like the following were made by several participants:

> There is no doubt that education is important ... we cannot avoid prioritising education. It would be the same as scrapping the welfare state. There was someone earlier who said that all these welfare services serve to increase productivity, because the reason we have our children in childcare is so that we can go to work. We need to have our parents cared for in order to be able to go to work. These things are rarely discussed and when they are, the idea is that childcare is there to benefit our children. (DK-69)

This resource-oriented focus was also particularly visible in the debates on immigration, where (frequently raised) welfare chauvinism was often rebuffed by arguments which emphasised the potential contributions immigrants could and should make to Danish society. Nevertheless, investment in education was not embraced as a means in itself, but understood as part of a well-designed labour market policy (which, the participants believe, is currently missing in Denmark). Here, a fundamental mismatch between demand and supply-side policies was identified as being responsible for the problem of 'educating for unemployment'. The educational system was criticised as not being able to educate for the market due to a strong focus on academic qualifications.

A similar critique was raised by some participants with regard to the vocational training schemes within the active labour market schemes. Although benefit conditionality and reinforced activation measures were supported by several participants across all breakout groups, training courses were considered as useless, and targeting of the measures was thought to be inefficient.

> I think it's daft that if you become unemployed you have to attend these completely pointless courses instead of being given the opportunity to retrain. Getting a daily allowance while you're in education. That would be much more motivating, instead of attending training courses that you're not interested in and that won't help you get a better or a new job. (DK-52)

As solutions to such problems some participants suggested making the activation scheme—including the job centres—more efficient by cutting parts of the administration and the training measures, but at the same time keeping the benefit conditionality and the respective monitoring alive. A relevant policy measure which requested 'Fewer resources on activation, job centres, activation programmes, work attitudes, etc.' received 16 'yes'-votes, and eight 'no'-votes.

In short, the debates in the Danish Democratic Forum broadly reflect the national welfare regime. Flexicurity was a crucial topic for the participants, and they were highly concerned about structural imbalances and decreasing productivity. Unemployment was understood as a crucial economic problem which puts strong pressure on welfare budgets and hampers productivity and growth. In this regard, investment in skills and early education was suggested as measures to be implemented by the state, and a stricter conditionality of benefits was requested. Nevertheless, the existing active labour market scheme was criticised as being ineffective and strongly bureaucratised.

United Kingdom

Discussions in the Democratic Forum in the UK were characterised by a strong notion of individualism. As we can already see from Table 8.1, aspects such as benefit fraud, a lack of motivation or mandatory work played a crucial role. Most respondents understood unemployment as due to a lack of skills or immigration or the unwillingness of businesses, especially multinational companies, to provide jobs to native Britons. One key solution to this problem was to invest more in skills development, especially for the unemployed but also those in employment. The state should provide further apprenticeships, but many participants believed individuals should also take responsibility. For example, income support should be made conditional on taking part in apprenticeships and training. Another option was to provide companies with tax incentives to provide apprenticeships. Furthermore, those on benefits, including free childcare, should contribute to society in some way. This can be summarised best in the statement made on the second day plenary session:

People who aren't working and they're receiving benefits, we discussed the fact that, and it's already been stated, that they should have to contribute in some way, be it charity, voluntary work or whatever. We said the current system effectively encourages people to stay out of employment. (UK-n.i.)

[O]ne of the priorities should be perhaps not investing in your own people for like 2040, so invest in people, you know, see where their needs are, education, employment. They want to be more skilled, experienced. Like, you know big companies out there tell them to give people opportunities to develop themselves. (UK-46)

Another solution was changing the education system, to create a more skill-based rather than academic-based system. Applied qualifications at General Certificate of Secondary Education[1] or even lower level for students that are less academically able were mentioned, thus providing education centred on skilled manual and service work rather than academic achievement. The participants believed that the current education system is largely irrelevant to the skills required by employers, and more linkages need to be made between the two systems, and also to job centres.

Many of the participants, especially in the ethnic minority oversampled break-out group (see Chap. 1), believed that young people who were unable to gain jobs should go into a mandatory national service.

Mandatory national service for all young, unemployed people under the age of 21. People who are in long-term unemployment that are not in education or in training. Our rationale was it improves individual's work ethos, discipline, provides a routine. It keeps unemployment low, it provides skills, provides things like references, so they become more employable, it increases their employability. Young people that are unemployed are going to benefit from it because they're getting more prospects for the future. It also opens up future careers in perhaps military, police, other types of services along those lines. (UK-67)

The role of employers was also mentioned: the government should provide tax relief to get employers to provide more apprenticeships and higher quality jobs. Also, there were some mentions of providing more incentives for small- (medium-) sized businesses, again through tax relief.

Some participants supported tax cuts to enable these businesses to hire more workers.

> So that's where our idea of, you know, having more government funding and tax incentives to companies to provide that apprenticeship so if you are working, more higher skilled workers. I mean one of the big issues with unemployment at the minute is, to get a job a lot of companies require experience, if you haven't got that experience then you can't get employed, can you? And you don't gain skills so yes. (UK-n.i.)

> To remain competitive, you have got to offer big organisations, foreign investors, some kind of tax invest … tax incentive to want to be based in the UK, which is going to create employment. (UK-66)

Zero-hour contracts were seen as a problem because they generate unstable incomes and prevent individuals from being able to contribute to society through tax. Participants believed that governments should abolish such contracts, ensuring a minimum number of hours in the contracts. Participants raised concerns about work incentives, the impact on workers' health and difficulty in maintaining rent payments, let alone a mortgage, as reasons for abolishing them. However, there were concerns regarding the implementation of other supportive measures for low socioeconomic status/disadvantaged workers, such as increasing the minimum wage, especially for smaller companies.

> Yes, but it's not on about Amazon and stuff like that, it's on about Joe Blogs the plumber who's got four or five staff who he's got to spend an extra thousand pound a month on wages. (UK-84)

In sum, the UK democratic forum displays a high level of individualism and adherence to a neo-liberal paradigm in views on labour market problems and unemployment. There are areas where participants believed that state involvement was necessary, for example in regulating unfair contracts and providing a minimum standard/wage. Other roles for the state included using tax breaks to provide incentives for companies and introducing a more stringent conditionality on benefits for both job seekers' allowance recipients but also childcare service recipients. The role of the state is seen generally as to enable individuals to take part in the labour market as much as possible, rather than to provide security or provide jobs. Employers should take responsibility in investing in people, with incentives provided by the state via tax breaks, but also through state regulations requiring hiring of UK natives (for more detail see Chaps. 2, 3, and 4). Social investment strategies were at the core of the participants' understanding of how to tackle issues in the future, with heavy reliance on apprenticeships and changes in the education system to fit the needs of businesses. There was a strong consensus on provision of free and extended childcare services to allow more women to enter the labour market and provide early education for the next generation (for more see Chap. 7).

Germany

In Germany, the discussions on employment and the labour market reflected by and large the current prosperous economic situation in the country and recent trends in society, including higher female employment and labour market deregulation. The participants in the forum rarely brought up the topic of unemployment, and it was particularly striking that even in the breakout group with an oversampling of unemployed persons, unemployment (more precisely: unemployment benefits) was only touched upon thrice in the two days. In general, participants in this breakout group agreed that the tax-funded minimum income (ALG II) was too low and the risk of ending up with ALG II or low pensions is too high due to precarious jobs and other structural mismatches. In the breakout group with an oversampling of self-employed people, only one participant demanded stricter activation in the sense of harsher benefit criteria and demanding measures. His position was not actively supported by other participants, and unemployment was not discussed further.

The participants in all three breakout groups were strongly concerned about low incomes, and hairdressers, nurses or bakers were held up as examples where wages did not cover living costs. While the discussions in general did not reflect much on the causes of low wages, some participants mentioned privatisation and a decreased influence of public actors and social partners on labour agreements:

> But particularly in jobs like yours or elder-nursing care, the state could see to it that the wages are increased. (DE-10)
>
> Exactly. (DE-2)
>
> How? How are they supposed to do that? They've given up their influence there, because many of these sectors like that as well as preschool and daycare, they have less influence, because they've all been privatized. The nursing homes too. (DE-11)

As a consequence of the high salience of the topic of precarious work, the—catchy but blurry—policy guideline 'work must be worthwhile' (suggested by the breakout group with many self-employed) found high support in the final voting. While the recently introduced minimum wage was supported by some, but considered as too low, other participants did not applaud it and suggested other measures, such as lower social insurance contributions, changes in taxation, or wage subsidies.

Most interestingly, precarious jobs were almost entirely considered as a demand-side problem, and only very rarely were supply-side measures suggested. We found no single statement that unemployed or precarious workers with low qualifications should receive vocational training, other active labour market services or social services to increase their individual competitiveness and improve their position in the labour market. This does not mean that participants in the German democratic forums did not see a need to invest in human capital, but they laid a strong emphasis on a more comprehensive investment approach and early education. In general, early education was a highly relevant topic in all three breakout groups, and it was mostly discussed under the heading of inequalities, as the following quote illustrates:

> It depends on what you're born into. If it's a wealthy family, then the children will have much better chances than those who have to fight for everything and who have little time to help support the children's learning themselves. (DE-27)

Besides low-paid jobs, job insecurity (particularly due to short-term contracts but also because of other deregulation measures) was perceived as a crucial problem, and here the state was considered responsible for finding a solution, for example by abolishing short-term contracts, as formulated as a policy guideline by the breakout group with an oversampling of migrants. However, labour market flexibility was also defended by individual participants in all groups. Nevertheless, public investment in job quality and employers' efforts to create better jobs were considered as major topics for the future. In this context, problems with work-life balance and a reconciliation of work and family life were also discussed.

> Elimination of limited-time work contracts and positions [should be a priority]. It's often the practice to hire people on three-month contracts or for a half year, and then you can never plan in your life. Some people are caught in this kind of track for 20 years, and people are afraid to have this limited situation. (DE-6)

Despite the high share of flexible working patterns in Germany compared to the rest of Europe (Chung 2017), several participants from each group report that they suffer from inflexible work schedules, find it hard to combine work and childcare, and do not have enough time for their family. While these topics were brought up in the context of family policies, they were also frequently mentioned in discussions of labour market issues, and causes were mostly seen in a high demand for flexibility at the workplace and the weak bargaining position of employees.

Suggestions for possible solutions included time banks, sabbaticals and childcare provided by employers and tailored to the needs of employees. The measures were mostly located at the employers' level, but they were expected to be backed up by statutory power (laws, sanctions, financial support to individuals or incentives to firms).

> I feel that the employers and employees should decide that [flexible working time] amongst themselves, because in the end the employer makes his company attractive by offering such opportunities, and employees like such things. The state can do things to make it easier or more attractive to take such steps, but they should keep out of it for the most part, because

those are contractual conditions that the employer and employee decide with one another. (DE-22)

In general, the discussions in the German Democratic Dorum indicate that the reforms of recent decades, which included deregulation of the labour market, brought along certain challenges for citizens, where were reflected in the debates in our Democratic Forum. Several participants complained about job insecurity and low wages, and people repeatedly used the 'old model' of the corporatist welfare state as a point of reference when discussing labour market topics. Indeed, stronger regulation of both employment conditions and wages was requested from the state, but also flanked by initiatives from employers, such as a flexibilisation of working time to allow for a better reconciliation of work and family life. Unemployment was very rarely discussed, and also active labour market policies and investment in skills were not a relevant topic for the German participants. At the same time, investment in early education was a major concern for almost all participants. Here, the state was seen as responsible to ensure more equal opportunities for education, since the schooling system was perceived as highly unequal.

Slovenia

As demonstrated in Table 8.1, the discussion on labour market aspects in the Slovenian Democratic Forums were mostly characterised by participants' concerns about the cost of living. Employment was considered to be a core aspect of the economy and the welfare state, and the state was often seen as responsible for ensuring high employment rates:

> The society's prosperity greatly depends on high employment rates; it is up to the state to establish such environment. (SI-75)

One of most crucial topics here was the problem of unemployment, in particular for the young and the old. While the labour market situation for core workers seems to be judged as relatively good, those who are at an age to start their career, or who are at the end of it, were considered as particularly vulnerable. In this context, well-targeted human capital investment played a crucial role as a suggestion for the problem of unemployment. Regarding older people, the debate was linked to the need for requalification, and regarding the younger ones, the debate on unemployment was linked by several participants to the need of better linking education and needs of the labour market, as quotes like the following illustrate:

> we don't know in which direction we'd like to go, they are opening places for students in university courses without knowing exactly what the needs of the economy are. (SI-84)

The strong emphasis in the debates on social investment targeted towards the needs of the labour market is also reflected in the policy recommendation 'improving the link between education and economy', which received the highest number of positive votes among all proposals in Slovenia (37).

Furthermore, in the discussion on unemployment, effects at the individual level such as decreasing motivation were mentioned, as well as concerns about unemployed people's unwillingness to work and abuse of unemployment benefits:

> and they'll also have more self-esteem. Now they are latched on their parents, mommies coddle them because they are unemployed, or we coddle them, whatever, and when reaching their forties, they—or we—are not capable to live independently, without parental support. And the unemployment brings laziness and…. (SI-77)
>
> …crime, drugs, everything. (SI-82)

In relation to this, the role and efficiency of Employment Service was discussed in all three groups to a significant extent, and participants were mostly dissatisfied with its work, as the following statement illustrates:

> and as far as employment agency is concerned: nobody has any information there. I asked them where I should ask, where I could find more information, where to turn, because I have certain limitations—they know

nothing. I think there should be training at the employment agency as well, instead of money being used for benefits, financial support.... (SI-52)

Here again, the relevance of the topic for the participants is reflected in the high number of 'yes'-votes (32) for a respective policy recommendation ('proactive role of employment services').

As mentioned above, living standards were a crucial concern of participants in all three breakout groups, and a (higher) minimum wage was widely discussed in this context as a way to increase equality and reduce poverty, but also as a measure to fight undeclared work:

And if the minimum wage is high enough, you'll go to work more, but it should provide at least something, because for the majority, if they don't have a place to live, you can't survive on minimum wage. (SI-88)

...undeclared work should be penalized by the system, if you receive benefits and then do a bit of undeclared work because you won't do it for a minimum wage that's certainly too low.... Are we aware of what undeclared work means? Undeclared work means that then the employers are taking advantage of this and of course, the minimum wages are lower accordingly. (SI-83)

Besides the minimum wage, taxation was discussed in the light of living standards. Furthermore, high taxes where not only seen as a problem particularly for low income groups, they were also mentioned as a barrier for employers to hire; and thus lower taxes were seen as a measure to fight unemployment:

It would be very useful if taxation of labour would be lowered. Our labour taxation is extremely high, among the highest, it costs too much to employ a person to the point it is simply not profitable. If taxation would be lower, businesses could hire two persons instead of one, and one unemployed person would get a job. (SI-60)

In this context, a topic that was prominent in all three breakout groups, namely shorter working hours, was linked to taxation and job creation. While several participants expressed their concerns about high workload and problems of reconciling work and family life, flexible and short working hours were also seen as a tool to increase both individual productivity and the number of available jobs:

> We also had the suggestion to reduce the working hours from 8 to 6. It would improve efficiency and give parents more time with their children, we'd all have more free time, we'd all have time to relax and the next day we'd come to work with more energy, rested, and they'd get more from us. That's connected in a way to the employer being able to afford shorter working hours for the same pay. But if the taxes were lower, it's all connected. Then they'd have three employees instead of one or two, they could afford a six-hour working day for the same pay and we'd all be happy. (SI-60)

In sum, the Slovenian democratic forum was particularly characterised by participants' concerns about unemployment, living standards and poverty (both out-of-work and in-work poverty). The participants in all three groups seemed to be highly aware of the state of the Slovenian economy and the pressure on the welfare systems, and they mostly agreed that job creation, economic stimulation and labour market flexibility were the right answers to the challenges they identified, and that the government had the responsibility to target its educational system towards the needs of the labour market in order to fight and prevent unemployment. At the same time, decent wages, lower taxes and job security were also understood as highly relevant in order to confront the increasing pressure on people at the margins of the labour market—a group which is seen as rapidly increasing.

Discussion and Conclusion

The previous sections provided a relatively detailed picture of the discussion of labour market issues in the four countries under examination. As already seen in the analysis of the way the participants perceived and understood the topics in the initial brainstorming plenary, participants across all countries identified problems related to unemployment, job insecurity and precarious work, work-life balance, productivity, a mismatch of demand and supply, or educational inequalities. Some of the topics played a crucial role in all countries, while others only appeared in one or two.

At first sight, the similarities and differences reflect those in the key challenges faced in each of these countries. As outlined above, Germany has considerably lower unemployment rates—thus, the low salience of unemployment as a problem in the German debates is not surprising. At the same time, the labour market flexibilisation reforms of the past decades led to an increase in low-paid and non-permanent jobs, which might explain the relevance of precarious work and job conditions in the discussions in Germany. The recently increased female labour market participation rates might well be reflected in the concerns about reconciliation of work and family life. Similar explanations could be found when linking the developments in the other countries to the topics raised by the participants: the strong work-first focus in the UK most probably relates to a highly stigmatic culture towards welfare beneficiaries as well as the historical legacy as a liberal regime where individual responsibilities come first; the prominence of the flexicurity model and the high ALMP expenditure in Denmark make it plausible that people bring up these aspects in debates, yet debates about immigration were prominent in other countries as well; and the increasing unemployment rates after some prosperous years in Slovenia seem to be reflected in the Slovenes' concerns about unemployment and living standards, and so on.

However, if we dig deeper into the patterns of argument behind the problems and solutions that people identified, we can see that a great part of these differences also lies in areas that are present in debates and public discourse in these countries as well. As outlined above, social investment was (besides a demand for 'work for all') the only topic which was raised in all four countries and promoted as a solution to existing problems. However, the framing of the problems and the argumentative patterns behind social investment were highly divergent. In all countries, the problem of a mismatch between education and labour demand is mentioned (this was strongest in Denmark: 'educating for unemployment').

However, in Denmark, the UK and Slovenia, the request for an alignment of the educational system to the market is stronger than in Germany, where job creation is mentioned in this context. Consequently, in the UK, Denmark and Slovenia, investment in labour market skills is a crucial measure, while not in Germany. However, here we can observe even more fine-grained differences: in Denmark, investment in vocational skills was regarded as a right of the individual to take part in the welfare state, and as a tool to boost the productivity of the economy, while in the UK, the provision of skills training was meant to achieve equality in access to allow individuals to take full responsibility for their own labour market outcomes. In Germany, where investment in skills and vocational training was not high on the agenda, social investment was nevertheless a crucial topic—but here educational inequalities and the role of early childhood investment, and investment to allow more women's employment, were discussed intensely. These and other argumentative patterns raised by the participants in the four countries are depicted in Table 8.2.

As we can see from Table 8.2, the different argumentative patterns raised by the participants of the Democratic Forums display a mixture of all three different labour market paradigms mentioned above (Keynesian, neo-liberal and social investment). Unemployment is linked to both a lack of skills and a mismatch in demand and supply, people support both benefit conditionality and labour market re-regulation, and social equality is embraced alongside individual responsibility. Overall, it was not possible to say that for any particular country the identification of problems and their solutions followed a specific paradigm. However, the distinction between some of the principles and support as to why these step should be taken emerged more clearly in some cases than in others. In the UK, a more individualised neo-liberalism was evident, in Denmark the ideas of solidarity and equality emerged, and in Germany and Slovenia the principles of the social-investment paradigm, such as equality of opportunities and quality jobs, were dominant.

Summing up, this paper provides a unique insight into the perceptions of citizens in four distinct welfare regimes against the backdrop of a changing work-welfare nexus in the last few decades. Our contribution to the existing literature is threefold. First, in so far as the literature on citizens'

Labour Market Challenges and the Role of Social Investment 269

attitudes towards labour market policies and outcomes has mainly neglected major transformations, we provide a first overview of people's perceptions of trends such as activation and social investment. Second, we found—in line with the discussions among policymakers and academics—that the social investment paradigm has become a salient issue across different welfare state regimes. However, as a third result we also found crucial differences in how people understood and contextualised the social investment paradigm, including framing in terms of productivity, equal opportunities and human capital investment. We observed complex argumentative patterns, since citizens had a multifaceted understanding of the causes of and the solutions to the current labour market challenges. This particularly demonstrates the potential of Democratic Forums to unravel the complex nature of citizens' perceptions, preferences and ideas.

Table 8.2 Problems, their causes and their solutions

Problems	Causes and patterns	Solutions	Countries
Lack of productivity	→ Lack of skills	→ Investment in skills	Slovenia, Denmark, UK
Unemployment	→ Mismatch of demand and supply	→ Align vocational training and market needs	Slovenia, Denmark, UK, Germany
	→ Welfare moochers	→ Benefit conditionality	UK, Denmark, Slovenia
Job insecurity and low wage	→ Immigration	→ Regulate immigration	Denmark, UK
Work life balance	→ LM deregulation	→ Minimum wage und LM regulation	Germany, Slovenia, Denmark
	→ Low wages (make dual earners necessary); job requirements	→ Working time policies	Germany, Denmark, Slovenia
Educational inequalities	→ High childcare costs → Unequal school system	→ Investment in (early) education	UK, Germany

Note

1. This is the standard academic qualification taken by almost all school students at age 16.

References

Andreß, H.-J., & Heien, T. (2001). Four worlds of welfare state attitudes? A comparison of Germany, Norway, and the United States. *European Sociological Review, 17*(4), 337–356.

Arts, W., & Gelissen, J. (2001). Welfare states, solidarity and justice principles: Does the type really matter? *Acta Sociologica, 44*(4), 283–299.

Aurich, P. (2011). Activation reforms and the middle class: Attitudes in a European comparison. *German Review of Social Policy/Sozialer Fortschritt, 60*, 295–302.

Bohle, D., & Greskovits, B. (2007). Neoliberalism, embedded neoliberalism and neocorporatism: Towards transnational capitalism in Central-Eastern Europe. *West European Politics, 30*(3), 443–466.

Bonoli, G. (2010). The political economy of active labour-market policy. *Politics & Society, 38*(4), 435–457.

Busemeyer, M. (2017). Public opinion and the politics of social investment. In A. Hemerijck (Ed.), *The uses of social investment*. Oxford: Oxford University Press.

Busemeyer, M., & Garritzmann, J. (2017). Public opinion on policy and budgetary trade-offs in European welfare states: Evidence from a new comparative survey. *Journal of European Public Policy, 24*(6), 871–889.

Busemeyer, M., Garritzmann, J., Neimanns, E., & Neizi, R. (2018). Investing in education in Europe: Evidence from a new survey of public opinion. *Journal of European Social Policy, 28*(1), 34–54.

Chung, H. (2017). National-level family policies and the access to schedule control in a European comparative perspective: crowding out or in, and for whom? *Journal of Comparative Policy Analysis*, https://doi.org/10.1080/13876988.2017.1353745.

Chung, H., & Mau, S. (2014). Subjective insecurity and the role of institutions. *Journal of European Social Policy, 24*(4), 303–318.

Chung, H., & Meuleman, B. (2017). European parents' attitudes towards public childcare provision: The role of current provisions, interests and ideologies. *European Societies, 19*(1), 49–68.

Esping-Andersen, G. (1990). *The three worlds of welfare capitalism.* Princeton, NJ: Princeton University Press.
European Social Survey Round 4 Data. (2008). Data file edition 4.4. NSD - Norwegian Centre for Research Data, Norway – Data Archive and distributor of ESS data for ESS ERIC.
European Social Survey Round 8 Data. (2016). Data file edition 1.0. NSD - Norwegian Centre for Research Data, Norway – Data Archive and distributor of ESS data for ESS ERIC.
Fenger, M. (2007). Welfare regimes in Central and Eastern Europe: Incorporating post-communist countries in a welfare regime typology. *Contemporary Issues and Ideas in Social Sciences, 3*(2), 1–30.
Ferrera, M. (2005). *The boundaries of welfare: European integration and the new spatial politics of social protection.* Oxford: Oxford University Press.
Filipovič Hrast, M., & Rakar, T. (2017). The future of the Slovenian welfare state and challenges to solidarity. In P. Taylor-Gooby, B. Leruth, & H. Chung (Eds.), *After austerity. Welfare state transformation in Europe after the great recession.* Oxford: Oxford University Press.
Giddens, A. (2001). *The global third way debate.* Bristol: Polity Press.
Heidenreich, M. (2016). *Exploring inequality in Europe: Diverging income and employment opportunities in the crisis.* Cheltenham: Edward Elgar Publishing.
Heuer, J. O., & Mau, S. (2017). Stretching the limits of solidarity: The German case. In P. Taylor-Gooby, B. Leruth, & H. Chung (Eds.), *After austerity. Welfare state transformation in Europe after the great recession.* Oxford: Oxford University Press.
ISSP Research Group. (2008). International social survey programme: Role of government IV – ISSP 2006. GESIS Data Archive, Cologne.
Jæger, M. M. (2006). Welfare regimes and attitudes towards redistribution: The regime hypothesis revisited. *European Sociological Review, 22*(2), 157–170.
Lister, R. (2004). The third way's social investment state. In J. Lewis & R. Surender (Eds.), *Welfare state change. Towards a third way?* Oxford: Oxford University Press.
Madsen, P. K. (2004). The Danish model of 'flexicurity'. *Transfer, 10*(2), 187–207.
Madsen, P. K. (2013). Shelter from the storm? Danish flexicurity and the crisis. *IZA Journal of European Labor Studies, 2*(1), 6.
Morel, N., Palier, B., & Palme, J. (Eds.). (2012). *Towards a social investment welfare state.* Bristol: Policy Press.
OECD. (2004). Employment protection regulation and labour market performance. In *OECD employment outlook 2004.* Paris: OECD.

OECD. (2011). *Divided we stand: Why inequality keeps rising.* Paris: OECD.
Offe, C. (1984). *Contradictions of the welfare state.* London: Hutchinson & Co.
Pierson, P. (2001). *The new politics of the welfare state.* Oxford: Oxford University Press.
Svalund, J., Saloniemi, A., & Vulkan, P. (2016). Attitudes towards job protection legislation: Comparing insiders and outsiders in Finland, Norway and Sweden. *European Journal of Industrial Relations, 22*(4), 371–390.
Taylor-Gooby, P. (2004). *New risks, new welfare: The transformation of the European welfare state.* Oxford: Oxford University Press.
Taylor-Gooby, P., Leruth, B., & Chung, H. (2017). Where next for the UK welfare state? In P. Taylor-Gooby, B. Leruth, & H. Chung (Eds.), *After austerity: Welfare state transformation in Europe after the great recession.* Oxford: Oxford University Press.

9

Democratic Forums and Welfare State Attitudes

Peter Taylor-Gooby and Benjamin Leruth

This book contributes to the understanding of welfare state attitudes from three standpoints: methodological, empirical and political. Firstly, the Democratic Forum approach that we use gives ordinary members of the public much more control over the way the research is conducted than do the methods more commonly employed in attitude studies. As we argued in Chap. 1, the questionnaires and precoding categories used in structured surveys contain implicit assumptions about the key issues and how they are to be approached. Focus group schedules are designed to include some topics and exclude others. Democratic forums such as ours allow researchers access to popular discourse—the range of ideas present in interaction, the ones that are most widely shared and which predominate after extensive debate.

P. Taylor-Gooby (✉)
School of Social Policy, Sociology and Social Research,
University of Kent, Canterbury, UK
e-mail: p.f.taylor-gooby@kent.ac.uk

B. Leruth
Institute for Governance and Policy Analysis, University of Canberra,
Canberra, ACT, Australia

© The Author(s) 2018
P. Taylor-Gooby, B. Leruth (eds.), *Attitudes, Aspirations and Welfare*,
https://doi.org/10.1007/978-3-319-75783-4_9

They have limitations, most importantly in the impossibility of achieving a serviceable representative sample with the relatively small number of participants. The object of the forums is to trace debate and characterise the positions on which people can agree, rather than identify the views of different groups. Their chief virtue lies in the openness of the discussion, structured primarily by the participants.

Secondly democratic forums contribute to knowledge. Vernacular priorities receive due emphasis, the aspects of the issue that ordinary people see as important are stressed against those that are not, and linkages are drawn between ideas regardless of whether expert theory specifies them or not. We refer to this understanding of a particular topic in the context of how it relates to other themes as 'framing' and use the material from the forum discussions to explore such understanding in context. The forum data helps improve explanations of why people prefer the solutions they favour to the problems they identify.

Thirdly, this contribution is particularly relevant at a time when traditional welfare states are at a crossroads. Most mainstream political parties are in decline across Europe, especially on the left, and a new radical populism is gaining ground, especially on the right. We urgently need a better understanding of people's attitudes and aspirations and of why they prioritise particular issues, such as immigration, inequality and trust in government, and understand them in the way that they do. Political discontent, disillusion and disenfranchisement are symptoms of a deterioration in general support for the political system (see for example Dahlberg et al. 2014; Jennings et al. 2017; Norris 2011). Democratic forums generate new knowledge about popular ideas in a context of rapid political change and can thus contribute to the search for new policy directions that most people will find acceptable.

In this chapter we demonstrate the value of the democratic forum method by examining our main findings in the context of the picture presented by mainstream research. We pay particular attention to the framings of ideas that dominate in the discussion and go on to link them to the policies people want and those they reject.

Our Findings: Four Framings of State Welfare

In most areas our findings reinforce those of the welfare state attitude literature. Their chief contribution is to enable researchers to move beyond the picture presented in that literature to consider the overall framings that shape people's attitudes. In this chapter we examine four interlinked topics: inequality, fairness and social investment, intergenerational issues and social care, healthcare solidarity and responses to immigration. All are major issues in contemporary debate as the earlier chapters in this volume show, and all represent areas in which welfare states face major challenges (Taylor-Gooby et al. 2017). In each area we report briefly on the key findings of the mainstream and present our own work. We show how the forum findings parallel those of structured surveys and also how they help in developing explanations for similarities and differences in attitudes across the different European countries and in identifying effective and acceptable ways of addressing the problems that ordinary people recognise.

Up-to-date survey findings are conveniently summarised in the work of the leading cross-national study of welfare state attitudes, the European Social Survey (ESS) for 2016 (ESS 2017). The available data does not include Denmark. However, material from earlier surveys (the International Social Survey Project and ESS 2008) indicates Denmark follows a broadly social democratic pattern of attitudes with rather greater concern about the impact of future challenges than in Norway (see the material cited in Chap. 1).

The survey data shows that in most European countries most people endorse social provision to meet the needs commonly experienced during the life course, but with national variations, and that these can be summed up in terms of the influential regime typology. The main contrasts in Western Europe lie between three approaches: a social democratic commitment to universalism and equal citizenship across Scandinavian countries, corporatist orientation towards a more status- and work-related system of contribution and allocation typifying the heartland of the Continent, and a more liberal regime, leaning towards the market, individualism and privatisation, and found in the UK and Ireland. Post-Soviet Europe brings together an egalitarian heritage with acceptance of the market (Esping-Andersen 1999; Scruggs 2007; Kolarič et al. 2011). The regimes entail different approaches to fairness, to do with equal citizenship, work status, payment or work-effort and addressing needs. This fits with the main findings of attitude researchers who use structured surveys (Andreß and Heien 2001; Arts and Gelissen 2001; Blekesaune and Quadagno 2003; Likki and Staerklé 2015; Roosma et al. 2013; Svallfors 2012; van Oorschot et al. 2017; see also Chap. 1 of this volume).

ESS data show how regime differences are reflected in population attitudes for the countries we examine in detail in this book. For example, net agreement that 'the standard of living for unemployed people should be the government's responsibility' stands at 80 per cent in universalist Norway and 56 per cent in Slovenia, but at 36 per cent in Germany with its concern about linking reward to contribution and only 31 per cent in the more neo-liberal UK. Three-fifths of the UK population believe 'social services and benefits make people lazy' against half in Slovenia and one-eighth in Norway and Germany. The proportion agreeing with the minimalist conception that social benefits should be restricted solely to those 'with the lowest incomes' is roughly equal to that favouring a more substantial welfare state in the UK, but only about two-thirds as large in Germany and Slovenia and less than one-half the size in Norway. Scandinavian Europe tends to be more generous and universalist, the corporatist heartland more concerned with status and contribution, the post-Socialist countries with meeting needs in the context of limited resources and the liberal UK with reinforcing the work ethic.

We consider more detailed attitude patterns as we examine the forum discussions in the four topic areas.

Inequality, Fairness and Social Investment

Chapters 2, 4, and 8 deal with inequality and with the two discourses surrounding it: neo-liberalism with its associated individualist approach to welfare issues, and social investment in childcare and training, which is seen by its proponents to offer a way forward in a more market-centred world (Morel et al. 2012). Of the five countries studied the UK is the most unequal in income and in wealth. Germany follows, and then Denmark. Norway and Slovenia are the least unequal. ESS shows that national attitudes endorse this pattern. Net agreement with the statement that 'For a society to be fair, differences in people's standard of living should be small' stands at 64 per cent in low-income Slovenia, 57 per cent in Norway and Germany and only 41 per cent in the UK. However, in the majority of the countries, inequalities designed to reinforce incentives are tolerated, with more or less enthusiasm. Slovenian respondents emphatically reject the statement that 'large differences in income are acceptable to reward talents and efforts', with a net negative score (those in favour minus those against) of 27 per cent. Norway has a positive balance of 11 per cent and Germany of 22 per cent, while in the liberal UK those in favour outnumber those against by 28 per cent. These differences reflect the regime traditions: strong concerns about those at the bottom in Slovenia, inclusiveness at a high standard in Norway, some commitment to equality tempered by work-centred corporatism in Germany and a neo-liberal individualism in the UK.

Broadly speaking, national patterns of attitudes as revealed by the forums follow this framework, but the accounts of why people hold the views they do differ sharply, and here the forum work contributes to our understanding. In the UK many participants are accepting of existing inequalities (which they tend to underestimate) and reject state programmes of redistribution through progressive taxes or higher benefits. This is partly due to a general mistrust of the state, but partly because the primary conflict in society is seen (in the words of one participant) as not between 'rich and poor', but 'between working and non-working'. The liberal individualist ideology of the work ethic dominates over the welfare state logic of redistribution. In Germany, by contrast, there is also considerable scepticism about egalitarianism, following the corporatist emphasis on status differences as the basis for state interventions. However, when specific policy areas, such as education, taxation, benefits or pension entitlements, are discussed, most people are highly critical of inequalities and regard them as unfair. This appears to result from the fact that the inequalities they observe are completely incompatible with the corporatist ideal that links reward to social status and contribution. However, there is little appetite for major redistributive reform. In practice most people largely accept the inequalities implicit in recent labour market policies (to promote flexibility) and pension reforms (to encourage private saving) and are moving grudgingly towards greater individualism. It is the net acceptance of incentives that exerts an influence on their views.

In Denmark, often seen as typifying social democratic state-centred egalitarianism, the welfare state is valued highly. However, there is a surprising degree of criticism of state redistribution. People pay little attention to inequalities and their negative effects, but express some disquiet about the level of taxation. The impression is of a people surfeited with state welfare. In Norway by contrast the forum members (with a few exceptions) energetically reject the trend to greater inequality they see beginning to emerge in their society. The social democratic ideology of redistribution predominates, and a number of forum members state their willingness to accept tax increases or reductions in their own future pensions to benefit poorer citizens. There is also some limited concern about the workshy and about how important it is that everyone recognises their obligation to contribute. The upshot is an egalitarianism that rests clearly on collectivism.

In Slovenia inequality, as measured by quintile share, is roughly equal to that in Norway (3.6 as against 3.7: Eurostat 2017), but responses to it are very different. There is strong concern about low wages and benefits and about inequality, and an equally strong demand for aggressive redistributive and anti-corruption measures: sharp increases in the minimum wage and in pensions and other benefits, higher taxation of the better off and a drive against all those who seek to gain from their gatekeeper positions with welfare state services. This may be understood either in terms of the simple fact that incomes in Slovenia are at a very low level by European standards, so that any inequality bears heavily on the worst off, or the possibility that the recent transition to market society highlights exploitation and the opportunities for the better off to pursue their own interests.

Chapter 2 ('Neo-liberalism and individualism') and Chap. 8 ('Labour market challenges and the role of social investment') allow us to take the analysis a stage further and consider policy implications. These chapters deal with questions that are closely linked with debates about inequality, the former because neo-liberalism shifts inequality from centre stage to the sidelines and radically undermines the position of the interventionist redistributive state, and the latter because social investment is seen in many European policy debates as a way to take welfare state policies forward in a more market-centred and individualist world. These issues merited discussion in separate chapters because of their prominence in current debate and the way they highlight the value of democratic forum methodology by enabling researchers to trace the way participants frame the issues in each area.

The main finding of both chapters is the similarity between the overall policy directions endorsed across all five countries, despite the very real differences in general ideology and current circumstances. In all five the principal way forward is seen as social investment: state intervention to guarantee all citizens good access to the services and benefits they need to contribute to and succeed in the world of work. This broadly reflects ESS 2016 findings. Over half those interviewed in that survey want money diverted from passive unemployment benefits to education and training for unemployed people (53 per cent in Slovenia, 61 per cent in Germany, 80 per cent in the UK and 85 per cent in Norway). Poverty in Slovenia may explain the substantial support for maintaining benefit payments, but the fact that Norway and the UK reveal similar attitudes and that support in Germany is less emphatic is of interest. Social investment was discussed in different ways and with different emphases, but it formed a common policy core. To understand how and why very different welfare states generated at first sight similar desired policy programmes we need to explore framings: the way people perceive the problems and issues and the relationships between them.

Chapter 2 shows that the view that the Great Recession united the pro-market trends in modern society to create a decisive shift towards neo-liberalism is misleading. In four out of the five countries examined participants look to the state (perhaps with some misgivings or reservations) to guarantee their future welfare. The exception is the UK and here the issue is a lack of trust in the capacity of government to do what is needed rather than any ideological commitment to the market. Some indication of this is provided in the level of satisfaction that people reported in ESS 2016 in answer to a question about 'the way democracy works in your county'. The real contrast lies between 80 per cent satisfaction in Norway and less than 20 per cent in Slovenia with its concerns about corruption. Less than half are satisfied in the UK (a very low level for Western Europe), but over 60 per cent for Germany. As Chap. 2 shows, UK dissatisfaction appears to centre on the apparent incapacity of government, its failure to achieve what citizens want it to do, despite promises and tax. This leaves people with little alternative but to rely on their own efforts and to hope that government will at least support them.

If the neo-liberal approach is not seen as the way forward elsewhere in Europe, there is nonetheless concern about the capacity of governments to address some of the issues that people see as emerging in the future and considerable support for greater individualism in policy in the context of state provision: hence social investment. The key point is that the reasoning that lies behind the commitment to social investment differs between welfare states.

In Germany most forum members recognise the greater precarity affecting many groups in the labour market, the inequality in education opportunities and long-run demographic issues that affect future welfare state funding. Early years education is seen as crucial and this is as much a rationale for childcare as are the interests of parents or the desire to mobilise more women for paid work. Social investment also fits with the regretful acceptance of policy directions towards greater privatisation and labour market flexibility. Opportunity policies that fit under the social investment umbrella can be understood as achieving a fairer linking of outcomes to contribution, thus restoring some of the virtues of corporatism, but only in the context of disappointment at the potential loss of the established social insurance entitlements.

Danish participants are often critical of the existing active labour market policies as ineffective, but at the same time want a renewed emphasis on interventions, with much higher investment in skills and early years education alongside stricter conditionality in benefits. The social democratic welfare state model is greatly valued, but there is considerable disquiet about productivity and future growth prospects. Consequently, the objective of reinforcing social investment policies is primarily economic and not centred on the individual. The Norwegian participants see their country as already strong in social investment and want this to continue, both for economic reasons and in the interests of citizens. In Slovenia the stress is on unemployment and incomes. The benefit of investment is seen as directly individual in cash terms. Finally, in the UK there is undoubtedly a strong emphasis on individual responsibility in accord with the work ethic, but it is up to the state to provide the setting in which people can, as it was often put in discussion, 'better themselves' or 'stand on their own two feet'. One striking issue is the way state provision of childcare is endorsed as elsewhere, but with the proviso that those parents receiving it must be in work and if they are on benefits at least be allocated voluntary work so that they are not subsidised to relax at home.

Social investment is valued everywhere, but for different reasons: as compensating for inequalities in education and enhancing women's opportunities so that outcomes match status more closely in Germany; as enhancing the continuing and future viability of a social democratic welfare state in Denmark; as part of successful social democracy in Norway, to address pressing income inequalities in Slovenia; and for enhancing equal opportunities for those who make an effort and reinforcing the work ethic in the UK. Fairness remains defined in terms appropriate to the regime type: work-status based in Germany; to do with social democratic egalitarianism in Denmark and, more strongly, in Norway; as allowing needs to be met in Slovenia; and in strict opportunity terms in the UK. The value of the forum material is that it brings out the structure of the arguments used by ordinary people more clearly and enables researchers to examine the framing of ideas that lie behind similar policy conclusions in welfare states from different regime categories.

Intergenerational Issues and Social Care

When we turn to the chapters dealing with the long-term issues identified by welfare state commentators as confronting current patterns of service with the severest challenges—the intergenerational inequities associated with population ageing which impose severe pressures on the funding of pensions and health services (Chap. 5), and the problem of how care responsibilities are to be managed in societies where women are mainly engaged in paid work, and demographic shifts that both increase demand and reduce the number of potential carers (Chap. 6)—we find considerable similarities in national attitudes. The attitude survey literature demonstrates that pensions and healthcare are immensely popular in all the countries, even in the neo-liberal UK. This is equally true of older and younger participants. At least 85 per cent of ESS 2016 respondents agree that 'the standard of living of older people should be the government's responsibility'. The 2008 ESS showed that comparable proportions support healthcare. Support for state responsibility for childcare stands at a similar level (rather lower at 75 per cent in the UK). The forum discussions showed similar high levels of support, with a clear recognition of the pressures on provision. In both Denmark and Norway and particularly (and unsurprisingly) in the UK this led to acceptance of a stronger role for private pensions and for the private sector in healthcare. German participants also reluctantly accepted a role for private pensions in addition to basic and status-related state provision, as noted earlier. In Slovenia the demands are for better state provision, and there are sharp criticisms of the inadequacy of current pensions, with no support for the private sector.

The particular contribution of the forums is to show how, in the four continental countries, and most notably in Norway and Denmark, where forum members regard current provision as more than adequate, there is a willingness among older people to sacrifice some of the services from which they benefit to improve provision for younger people. This is not evident from the blanket endorsement of state provision for older groups in the structured survey literature, but emerges strongly in the forum discussions. There is also strong support for greater state involvement in childcare following from the enthusiasm for social investment noted above.

The UK stands out in its weak intergenerational solidarity because most people see pensions and healthcare as already unsatisfactory: the main current in the debate claims that the existing structure of provision is simply unsustainable and will not exist in 25 years' time. There is a rejection of higher taxation to improve services, in line with the market assumption that people have strong rights to what they have earned and the belief that the state is wasteful and unable to direct what money it levies to the priorities of ordinary people. The assumption that the welfare state is in a possible terminal decline fits with the demands for social investment as a viable way forward.

When the discussion focuses directly on social care, rather than the needs of older people for healthcare and pensions, the widespread recognition of the pressures on the care system leads to the assumption that solutions will be more individualist, requiring stronger commitment from family members. Again this is noted at opposite ends of the current spectrum of provision, both in the Scandinavian countries and the UK. The willingness of younger family members to contemplate providing or financing care for elderly relatives at the same time as their own pension prospects diminish in many of the countries may seem surprising. The intergenerational contract is remarkably resilient: people are aware of the pressures and willing to help mitigate them—older groups by accepting a reduction in provision in countries where this is practicable, and younger groups by making whatever contribution they can. Tensions emerge most noticeably in the UK, where the expectation of weaker state provision is strongest, where willingness to pay more tax or to tax the rich harder is weakest and where younger generations offer private and family support with reluctance. Elsewhere the assumption is that the state will continue to provide the greater part of the necessary services, and in Slovenia the demands for the state to make radical improvements across the full range of provision are particularly vehement. These findings cut across the regime approach (except again for the UK), fit with the evidence of support for the elderly, help explain enthusiasm for social investment, and help underpin the idea that in most of Europe the welfare state in its various regime forms will continue despite the neo-liberal challenge.

Debates about childcare (Chap. 6) bridge the gap between the inequality/social investment theme and the intergenerational aspects of state welfare. Childcare can contribute to social investment in three main ways: from the child's perspective, by promoting access to early years education; from the parent's perspective, by allowing them to work and earn; and from the economic perspective, by releasing workers at a relatively young age. As in the case of inequality, the detailed reasoning displayed in the framing of similar issues across states reveals differences in the justification of people's of attitudes.

One aspect reflects regime logic: in Norway and Denmark the central theme in the childcare debate concerns gender equality, and the equal division of leave entitlement and take-up between parents. In Germany it is more to do with the valuing of women's unpaid work in parallel to the formal sector work recognised in corporatist welfare policy, especially as regards social insurance pension entitlement. In the UK the questions are to do with containing costs and using childcare to encourage women into paid work in a market-centred system, and in Slovenia the focus is on the absolute necessity of cheap childcare to enable families to earn enough to survive. For eldercare the debate moves more towards the social virtues of family care in the richer countries and the excessive costs of provision in Slovenia and the UK.

Childcare attitudes fit with the framings of social investment encountered earlier: to do with impact broadly across society in Norway and Denmark, in relation to work-based entitlement in Germany, reflecting the individualist work ethic in the UK, and the expectations of a decent level of provision from the state in Slovenia. The emotional bonds of intergenerational solidarity figure in discussion about the role of the family in care, and the level of provision that people currently experience in the better-resourced welfare states and expect to continue clearly colours the debate.

Intergenerational issues are a complex area, and care aspects have not received as much attention as the big spending established areas of provision in the attitude literature. The forum work shows two things: the intergenerational commitments in most countries that are essential for continued funding are strong, and the demands for state involvement in childcare, following on from the logic of social investment, emphatic. The analysis shows how the various priorities stipulated by the regime framework fit with popular ideas.

Healthcare Solidarity: Linking Intergenerational and Inequality Issues

In Chap. 7 we examine ideas about inequality in the specific field of healthcare in more detail. Healthcare is interesting because it is consistently one of the most strongly supported areas of welfare state provision, an area in which there is relentless and growing financial pressure from demographic shifts, rising wages and improvements in technology, and where at first sight there is considerable similarity between the countries in the level of public enthusiasm, as ESS 2016 shows. All these factors make it a suitable area in which to examine ideas about solidarity. As we noted earlier each of these factors emerges in the forum discussions. However, in addition to the overall endorsement of healthcare and the strong commitment to a more or less universal service we find different framings of equality in this field that once again enrich our understanding of how ordinary people think about regimes.

The different framings we term 'universal' (social democratic, Norway and Denmark), 'contributory' (corporatist, Germany), 'egalitarian' (post-soviet, Slovenia) and 'exclusive' (neo-liberal individualist, UK) solidarity. The key differences lie not in the outcome of support for entitlement to good healthcare across the community, but in how it is understood and justified. The structured survey literature pays less attention to rationales than to the direction and strength of attitudes.

In Norway and Denmark the basic assumption is of a universal entitlement to healthcare, and this includes all citizens. There is some resentment of perceived overuse of the service by foreigners and also privileged access by high-status people, but these problems are not seen as reasons to exclude these groups, but rather as indications of a need for improvements in management to equalise waiting times. In Germany the basis of equality is contributory. Solidarity requires that all should contribute and that no groups should be advantaged. There is concern about privileged access by the better off and the possible implications of a greater role for private provision, and a determination to ensure this is kept to a minimum. The question of access by foreigners and immigrants resolves into a debate about ensuring that these groups are also able to contribute, and thus to the importance of integrating immigrants into the labour market.

UK participants are warmly supportive of the NHS ('a thing of beauty' as one put it) despite their misgivings about its sustainability in a harsher, more individualist world. There is a particularly strong sense of the importance of defending the system against the demands of outsiders, especially immigrants, to ensure that collective provision can continue for insiders in a context where the pressures on the service are seen as extreme and unwillingness to pay higher taxes absolute, hence an exclusiveness that sets strict limits to solidarity. Finally, there is strong support among the participants in Slovenia for universal healthcare. This leads to discontent about what has been lost through the move to the capitalist market model and unease at the entry of the profit motive into the system (Slovenia has the lowest proportion of public finance and the highest of private health insurance spending among the countries). In the forums many participants protested bitterly against corruption: particular individuals in gatekeeper roles are able to extort bribes in return for access to a public service. The strongly-felt egalitarian solidarity is linked with demands for more government spending and curbs on the private sector and reflects the underlying overall disquiet about the changes in Slovenian society.

The framings of healthcare solidarity reflect regime type. The forum approach helps explain similarities in attitude outcomes in very different social and institutional contexts and shows how the different understandings of the issues in those contexts leads to a common solidaristic framing of healthcare with national variations. It also shows how different policies might reinforce and retain solidarity. In Norway and Denmark the key concern is to maintain a universal service so that if cutbacks are necessary in view of the demographic pressures discussed in the previous section, they will be shared equally. In Germany the debate is about safeguarding the system of entitlement via contribution. In the UK the key concern is to maintain a defensive solidarity against external demands, and in Slovenia it is simply to increase finance and control corruption.

Immigration and Inclusion

Recent high levels of immigration and the explosive growth of populist anti-immigrant politics ensure that migration and the associated issues of inclusion, exclusion and integration are major themes in the social welfare debate across Norway, Denmark, Germany and the UK (see Chaps. 1 and 3). In Slovenia the issues are different and concern the converse problem of retaining highly-skilled workers attracted to jobs in richer parts of Europe, leading back to the arguments discussed earlier for social investment and better opportunities in work. However, among the countries where immigration is high on the agenda, the focus of the debate varies between exclusion and integration. Attitude surveys show real differences between countries.

Concern over immigration is strongest in the UK, although immigration rates compared to population are lower than in Scandinavia and Germany, as the OECD data discussed in Chap. 1 show. Sixty per cent of respondents to ESS 2016 think immigrants must 'work and pay taxes for at least a year' to become entitled to benefits, while the corresponding figure is 50 per cent in Germany, 40 per cent in Norway, despite its universalist traditions, and 35 per cent in low-immigration Slovenia.

In the Scandinavian countries immigrants are seen primarily as a potential economic benefit provided that they are successfully integrated into society. Most participants are aware of demographic pressures and that immigration offers a way of addressing them. There are real concerns about the way racism has entered the debate. In Germany the question is how to sustain the national culture in the face of high immigration, a problem to be addressed through measures to integrate immigrants and ensure that they are able to work and contribute within the corporatist structure.

The dominant strand in UK discussion is very different. Although a small number of forum members pointed out that immigrant workers form a substantial part of the workforce and are vital in key areas such as the NHS, immigrants are seen primarily as an economic and social burden, demanding strong regulatory and exclusionary policies. For mainland Europe the discussions follow a regime logic, valuing universalism in the Scandinavian countries and work integration in Germany. The exclusionary chauvinism of the UK forum contradicts the liberal assumption of a free market in labour. It brings home the way UK welfare state discourse is shaped by a defensiveness cutting across the liberalism identified in regime theory. This is reflected in the way both the work-shy poor and the state's counter-productive efforts, attacking bottom up and top down, are seen to damage the interests of most citizens.

Welfare Framings Overall: Social Integration and Economic Success

The evidence from the democratic forums underpins the regime approach and shows how it can be taken further by examining popular framings of the issues. It also provides an indication of the new policy direction that people will find acceptable. In this chapter we have explored how attitude framings can be explored in relation to inequality, intergenerational issues, solidarity and immigration.

In relation to inequality we showed how people's ideas about inequality and the role of the welfare state in addressing it differed between countries that typified the various regimes, but at the same time pointed to similar ways forward in policy. While social investment is seen as a key element in the general success of Norway's welfare state and one that needs to be maintained, in Denmark the debate is rather more focused on revitalising an approach that is felt to have grown less effective in guaranteeing good opportunities. In Germany social investment is seen as helping people contribute and attain an appropriate work status. In the UK it is about sharpening incentives and strengthening the work ethic. In Slovenia the objective is to provide better outcomes for those at the bottom while retaining more skilled workers in the country.

The participants in our democratic forums endorse the main services for older people (pensions and healthcare) and at the same time support good quality childcare alongside other services for younger age groups. The forum material reinforces the point that the intergenerational contract retains its force in most countries, and that older people in particular are willing (especially in the richer welfare states) to surrender some of their benefits to help their children's generation. The rationale for supporting childcare varies. The logic of social investment plays a part, but here also regime differences are evident. In Germany for example the capacity of a childcare programme to integrate women into paid work, or to recognise their unwaged work for social insurance entitlements, is emphasised. In the UK, liberalism requires that care subsidies must be targeted to those actually in paid work. In Slovenia, the concern is primarily to increase the family income.

The discussions of the solidarity surrounding the most popular service, healthcare, and the divisions over the extent to which immigration provides, on the one hand, the potential asset of labour or, on the other hand, the burden of welfare state dependency illuminate further issues. Attitude surveys show considerable consensus between countries in the first area and considerable divergence in the second. The forums show how these attitudes are related to ideas about social integration.

In relation to healthcare, the high levels of enthusiasm for universal or quasi-universal services derive from different background assumptions. In the Scandinavian countries, solidarity is universalist, derived from a model of integration through common citizenship. In Germany integration is contributory and the debate is about ensuring that individuals are in a position to participate appropriately and in fact do so. In the UK it is exclusionary, confining solidarity to insiders in a way that cuts across the liberal logic of integration through an open and free market. In Slovenia it is egalitarian, drawing on the socialist heritage.

For immigration, the discussion in Denmark, Norway and Germany centres on issues of integration, more in social terms in the first two countries and through work in the third. This leads participants to address the question of how this is to be achieved through language and cultural education, and access to resources and training. In the UK a defensiveness similar to that for healthcare emerges: immigrants are seen primarily as a burden, and the solution is stricter regulation or exclusion. Integration is confined to the insiders, the established population. It is as if the UK's healthcare system in the first case and rights of residency in the second are seen as the private property of citizens, to be carefully guarded.

These points suggest differences in the way people think about the economy and the state. A view of the economy and thus of society as open and dynamic underlies the Scandinavian and corporatist approach. This is associated with a view of the state as supportive and competent. The key problem is to ensure that dynamism continues and is sustained effectively and that the pursuit of economic objectives does not damage social integration. The perspective on immigration as providing a potential asset fits with this. The objective of policy is to ensure that the asset is used without disruption and this involves integration into the country's social and economic model. Similarly, the state provides obviously needed services such as healthcare within the framework of integration.

The UK approach differs. Despite its liberalism, the commitment to open markets is hedged with protectionism and exclusiveness. Partly this is a matter of people's lack of confidence in the capacity of government as a successful regulator and enabler—rather it wastes resources and featherbeds undeserving groups. Partly it is the strong presumptions about property rights that define access to jobs and resources as zero-sum, so that any benefit must involve a corresponding loss. Immigrants will take from the established population, not contribute; valued services such as healthcare must be protected from outsiders and integration centres on the protection of those already on the inside. The idea that intervention might help generate more for all is lacking.

The analysis of the framing that surrounds solidarity and immigration also suggests that, in many countries, policies to address the issue will include integration into social values as well as an emphasis on contribution to the economy through work. Again, this fits with the shift in policy emphasis towards younger groups and to opportunity that runs across ideas about inequality, the intergenerational shift of policy emphasis and the concern with childcare, apprenticeships and education encountered in the forums.

Implications for Policymaking: The Way Forward for European Welfare States?

Our findings improve understanding of ordinary people's aspirations and priorities for the future of the welfare state. We find cross-national differences in ideas about inequality, fairness and redistribution, but shared support for the big-spending services such as healthcare and pensions and willingness to sustain the intergenerational contract. There are real variations in the bases of such solidarity, common concerns about immigration, although only the UK endorses exclusion, and agreement on the value of social investment, again for different reasons in different national settings. Can we think in terms of convergence towards a sustainable social policy across Europe, at least in the intergenerational areas and in social investment which would make up the greater part of a future state welfare system?

One possibility is that the EU might bring welfare policies together over the next quarter century. It lacks competence in most welfare state areas although it does have considerable powers in relation to inter-EU immigration, derived from member states' commitment to free movement of people under the Treaty of Maastricht.

The EU is currently facing a multifaceted crisis, driven by financial, economic, social, political, migratory and security elements (Leruth 2017). Whether welfare state programmes might help it or damage it in its response is unclear. Despite limited competence, the EU has sought to promote social investment as part of its Lisbon (2000) and (mostly) Lisbon II (2005) strategies, and its Europe 2020 programme (European Commission 2010), further developed in 2013 (European Commission 2013). As we pointed out in Chap. 1, national policies have been more successful in meeting the targets on education and training and on the proportion of women in paid jobs set by this programme than in addressing those for poverty, job quality or overall employment. There is considerable variation between the Southern and Eastern members, and Ireland and the rest, and few signs of convergence. The European Commission's health programme is concerned chiefly with the promotion and coordination of public health initiatives (European Commission 2014) and, apart from one recommendation in 2012 on the use of tobacco in confined public spaces, has low public visibility.

Our participants, even in the fully committed EU member states (Denmark, Germany and Slovenia), made little reference to the EU in relation to social investment and none in relation to health. The Commission could do more to communicate its activities, but it seems unlikely to play a strong role in public opinion without greater competence and, most importantly, without greater effectiveness in these areas.

In relation to migration within the Union, the EU has strong powers, but its objectives are challenged by substantial minority parties in most member countries. Our findings indicate that in most cases the balance of the debate, so far as public attitudes go, is to recognise the value of immigrants as workers and to press for urgent efforts to achieve more successful integration, but also to recognise that this will not be achieved without tension. Only in the UK has immigration, the major driving force behind the Brexit vote, led to a rejection of EU principles. The pre-Brexit negotiations included the offer of an 'emergency brake' to permit particular members to deny EU migrants in-work benefits and social housing. Whether such measures will be implemented more broadly or will help defuse the conflicts over immigration is unclear.

In sum, while our findings show some variation in terms of attitudes towards immigration, inequality and redistribution, they also show signs of convergence in sustaining the intergenerational contract at the heart of the welfare state and in developing social investment programmes. The foundations of these attitudes vary depending on the welfare regime, with the strongest divisions between corporatist and social democratic regimes and with the liberal UK an outlier. Immigration is the real concern. However, there is a real possibility that a distinctively European direction in social welfare will endure into the future, driven from the national level, with little indication that the EU will bulk large in it. More research is needed to understand these issues in other European countries and particularly in Southern Europe where the Great Recession hit hardest.

Concluding Summary

This review of the findings from our research demonstrates that democratic forums can contribute to improved methodology in attitude research, to generating new knowledge about how people think about major social issues and to policy debate. It supports seven points:

1. Democratic forums offer a new way to explore popular understanding of welfare. Extended discussion of the issues with limited moderation generates results that parallel the main findings from structured surveys, but go beyond them to provide an account of how ordinary people understand the issues and why they come to the conclusions they do in very different economic, social and institutional contexts. Despite limitations, forums are valuable assets in research on public policy attitudes.
2. The regime approach provides a useful typology of European welfare states. The democratic forum material helps understand why the different national patterns of attitudes fit loosely into the general regime categories.
3. The UK differs from other European welfare states in its extreme emphasis on individual responsibility and the work ethic (influencing the perception that the most important social division lies between working and non-working groups, highlighting paid work as the main justification for childcare and valuing social investment solely because

it promotes fairer opportunities in work), its exclusionary and defensive approach, as if existing services were the private property of those who enjoy them, and in its presumption that the state is incapable of sustaining the major services as pressures grow more intense.
4. People in other countries tend to understand their social world in more collective terms. Individual and family interests are to be advanced by contribution and allocation, and the economy is a dynamic and collaborative enterprise requiring management and regulation to achieve the most good, and government is capable of delivering this. State welfare is part of this and not an optional luxury.
5. Immigration emerges as a major issue in most countries, but not one that leads to an overt exclusionary approach, except in the UK. There are indications that the issues are more to do with social and cultural integration in most countries and that policies to promote this are seen as essential. Immigration is a potential area of conflict between old and new Europe as anti-immigrant parties enter parliament in a number of countries at the same time as other countries export workers north and west. The forum discussions point to an integrative approach to manage the issue.
6. The intergenerational contract remains remarkably resilient in most countries, and older people in particular are willing to support provision for younger age groups and (especially in richer countries) make sacrifices in their own entitlements to pay for it.
7. Social investment is seen as the way forward across European welfare states, but for different reasons in different countries. This reflects the policy emphasis of *Europe 2020*. It fits with a general shift of emphasis in public policy attitudes away from older groups and towards the needs of younger groups and the belief that the primary role of welfare is to help people meet the challenges of a new more globalized and competitive world.

In short, democratic forums build on structured survey research to enrich our understanding of welfare state attitudes in Europe. They show that in most countries the intergenerational contract is secure, but the emphasis is shifting in social policy debate from old to young and from consumption to social contribution and investment. Public debate in different countries can endorse similar opportunity-centred policies for different reasons, appropriate to national context. The European commitment to state welfare is being tested by population ageing, recession, rapid labour market change and conflicts over immigration. Our work shows that in most countries ordinary people see the welfare state as continuing into the future and as capable of developing new services to meet the new challenges.

References

Andreß, H.-J., & Heien, T. (2001). Four worlds of welfare state attitudes? A comparison of Germany, Norway, and the United States. *European Sociological Review, 17*(4), 337–356.

Arts, W., & Gelissen, J. (2001). Welfare states, solidarity and justice principles: Does the type really matter? *Acta Sociologica, 44*(4), 283–299.

Blekesaune, M., & Quadagno, J. (2003). Public attitudes toward welfare state policies a comparative analysis of 24 nations. *European Sociological Review, 19*(5), 415–427.

Dahlberg, S., Linde, J., & Holmberg, S. (2014). Democratic discontent in old and new democracies: Assessing the importance of democratic input and governmental output. *Political Studies, 63*(1), 18–37.

European Commission. (2010). *Towards a strategy for smart, sustainable and inclusive growth*. COM (2010) 2020. Retrieved November 27, 2017, from http://ec.europa.eu/eu2020/pdf/COMPLET%20EN%20BARROSO%20%20%20007%20-%20Europe%202020%20-%20EN%20version.pdf.

European Commission. (2013). *Towards social investment for growth and cohesion-including implementing the European Social Fund 2014–2020*. COM (2013) 83 final. Brussels: European Commission.

European Commission. (2014). Third Public Health Initiative. Retrieved November 27, 2017, from https://ec.europa.eu/health/sites/health/files/programme/docs/factsheet_healthprogramme2014_2020_en.pdf.

Esping-Andersen, G. (1999). *Social foundations of post-industrial welfare states*. Oxford: Oxford University Press.

European Social Survey (ESS). (2017). ESS Round 8. Retrieved November 21, 2017, from http://www.europeansocialsurvey.org/.

Eurostat. (2017). Inequality of income distribution. Retrieved November 17, 2017, from http://ec.europa.eu/eurostat/tgm/table.do?tab=table&init=1&language=en&pcode=tsdsc260&plugin=1.

Jennings, W., Clarke, N., Moss, J., & Stoker, G. (2017). The decline in diffuse support for national politics: The long view on political discontent in Britain'. *Political Quarterly, 81*(3), 748–758.

Kolarič, Z., Kopač, A., & Rakar, T. (2011). Welfare states in transition: The development of the welfare system in Slovenia. In S. Dehnert & M. Stambolieva (Eds.), *Welfare states in transition: 20 years after the Yugoslav welfare model* (pp. 288–309). Sofia: Friedrich Ebert Foundation.

Leruth, B. (2017). The Europeanisation of the welfare state: The case for a differentiated European social model. In P. Taylor-Gooby, B. Leruth, & H. Chung (Eds.), *After austerity: Welfare state transformation in Europe after the great recession*. Oxford: Oxford University Press.

Likki, T., & Staerklé, C. (2015). Welfare support in Europe: Interplay of dependency culture beliefs and meritocratic contexts. *International Journal of Public Opinion Research, 27*(1), 138–153.

Morel, N., Palier, B., & Palme, J. (2012). *Towards a social investment welfare state? Ideas, policies and challenges*. Bristol: Policy Press.

Norris, P. (2011). *Democratic deficit: Critical citizens revisited*. Oxford: Oxford University Press.

Roosma, F., Gelissen, J., & van Oorschot, W. (2013). The multidimensionality of welfare state attitudes: A European cross-national study. *Social Indicators Research, 113*(1), 235–255.

Scruggs, L. (2007). Welfare state generosity across space and time. In J. Clasen & N. A. Siegel (Eds.), *Investigating welfare state change. The 'dependent variable' problem' in comparative analysis* (pp. 133–165). Cheltenham: Elgar.

Svallfors, S. (2012). *Contested welfare states: Welfare attitudes in Europe and beyond*. Stanford, CA: Stanford University Press.

Taylor-Gooby, P., Leruth, B., & Chung, H. (Eds.). (2017). *After austerity: The new politics of welfare in Europe*. Oxford: Oxford University Press.

van Oorschot, W., Roosma, F., Meuleman, B., & Reeskens, T. (Eds.). (2017). *The social legitimacy of targeted welfare*. Cheltenham: Edward Elgar.

Appendix: Details of the Participants in the Democratic Forums

© The Author(s) 2018
P. Taylor-Gooby, B. Leruth (eds.), *Attitudes, Aspirations and Welfare*,
https://doi.org/10.1007/978-3-319-75783-4

Note: There are minor variations in the data gathered in each country, according to national research practice.

Germany

Participant number	Vote for party in next election	Gender	Age	Highest level of education	Work status	Household's total net income, all sources	Ethnic minority
P01	SPD	Female	45–54	Tertiary	Unemployed, looking for job	<1400 € (1 + 2 decile)	No
P02	CDU	Female	35–44	Lower secondary	Unemployed, looking for job	1400–2100 € (3 + 4 decile)	No
P03	SPD + Grüne	Female	Under 24	Upper secondary	In full-time education	<1400 € (1 + 2 decile)	Yes
P04	Piraten	Female	45–54	Tertiary	Working full-time	2800–4000 € (7 + 8 decile)	No
P05	Grüne	Female	45–54	Tertiary	Working full-time	2100–2800 € (5 + 6 decile)	Yes
P06	SPD	Female	35–44	Upper secondary	Working part-time	2800–4000 € (7 + 8 decile)	Yes
P07	Linke + Grüne	Female	45–54	Tertiary	Working full-time	2100–2800 € (5 + 6 decile)	No
P08	Linke	Female	Under 24	Upper secondary	Working part-time	1400–2100 € (3 + 4 decile)	Yes
P09	SPD	Female	25–34	Tertiary	Unemployed, looking for job	1400–2100 € (3 + 4 decile)	No
P10	SPD	Female	55–64	Lower secondary	Retired	1400–2100 € (3 + 4 decile)	No
P11	CDU	Female	65+	Tertiary	Retired	2100–2800 € (5 + 6 decile)	No
P12	CDU	Female	25–34	Upper secondary	Stay at home to look after family	2100–2800 € (5 + 6 decile)	No
P13	CDU	Female	25–34	Lower secondary	Working part-time	<1400 € (1 + 2 decile)	Yes
P14	CDU	Female	25–34	Lower secondary	Working full-time	4000–5000 € (9 decile)	No
P15	CDU	Female	45–54	Lower secondary	Stay at home to look after family	2100–2800 € (5 + 6 decile)	No
P16	CDU	Female	Under 24	Upper secondary	In full-time education	2100–2800 € (5 + 6 decile)	No
P17	SPD	Female	65+	Tertiary	Retired	2800–4000 € (7 + 8 decile)	No

P18	AfD	Male	45–54	Lower secondary	Permanently sick or disabled	<1400 € (1 + 2 decile)	No
P19	Linke	Male	25–34	Lower secondary	Working part-time	1400–2100 € (3 + 4 decile)	Yes
P20	SPD	Male	25–34	Tertiary	Working full-time	2100–2800 € (5 + 6 decile)	No
P21	CDU	Male	35–44	Upper secondary	Working full-time	2800–4000 € (7 + 8 decile)	Yes
P22	FDP	Male	Under 24	Upper secondary	Working full-time	2100–2800 € (5 + 6 decile)	Yes
P23	SPD	Male	65+	Lower secondary	Retired	2100–2800 € (5 + 6 decile)	No
P24	SPD	Male	55–64	Tertiary	Working full-time	4000–5000 € (9 decile)	No
P26	CDU	Male	25–34	Lower secondary	Working full-time	4000–5000 € (9 decile)	No
P27	FDP	Male	65+	Tertiary	Retired	>5000 € (10 decile)	No
P28	CDU	Male	65+	Lower secondary	Retired	2100–2800 € (5 + 6 decile)	No
P29	CDU	Male	35–44	Tertiary	Working full-time	>5000 € (10 decile)	No
P30	SPD	Male	25–34	Lower secondary	Working full-time	4000–5000 € (9 decile)	No
P31	SPD	Male	45–54	Lower secondary	Working part-time	>5000 € (10 decile)	No
P32	CDU	Male	65+	Tertiary	Retired	2800–4000 € (7 + 8 decile)	No
P33	Piraten	Male	45–54	Lower secondary	Working full-time	<1400 € (1 + 2 decile)	No
P34	Grüne	Male	45–54	Tertiary	Working full-time	2800–4000 € (7 + 8 decile)	No
P35	CDU	Female	Under 24	Upper secondary	Working part-time	>5000 € (10 decile)	No

Denmark

Reference	Political orientation	Gender	Age	Highest level of education	Work status	Household net-income (in DKK)	Ethnic minority
DK-50	Alternativet—The Alternative (Green Party)	Female	65+	Skilled worker	Retired	100,000–200,000	No
DK-52	Declined to respond	Female	25–34	Tertiary	Employed	No info	Yes
DK-53	Radikale Venstre (the Danish Social-Liberal Party)	Male	25–34	Tertiary	Employed	300,000–400,000	No
DK-54	Alternativet—The Alternative (Green Party)	Female	under 24	Upper secondary	Student	0–100,000	No
DK-55	Socialdemokraterne—The Social Democrats	Male	45–54	Tertiary	Employed	500,000–600,000	No
DK-56	Socialistisk Folkeparti—Socialist People's Party	Female	25–34	Upper secondary	Student	0–100,000	No
DK-57	Dansk Folkeparti—Danish People's Party	Male	25–34	Tertiary	Employed	400,000–500,000	No
DK-58	Radikale Venstre (the Danish Social-Liberal Party)	Female	35–44	n.i.	Employed	300,000–400,000	No
DK-59	Socialdemokraterne—The Social Democrats	Female	65+	Tertiary	Retired	No info	No
DK-60	Venstre—Left, Liberal Party of Denmark	Male	35–44	Tertiary	Employed	300,000–400,000	No
DK-61	Venstre—Left, Liberal Party of Denmark	Female	35–44	Tertiary	Employed	800,000–900,000	No
DK-62	Socialistisk Folkeparti—Socialist People's Party	Male	25–34	Tertiary	Employed	400,000–500,000	No
DK-64	No party, don't know	Female	under 24	Upper secondary	Student	0–100,000	No
DK-65	Enhedslisten—Red-Green Alliance	Female	under 24	Upper secondary	Student	0–100,000	No
DK-66	Socialistisk Folkeparti—Socialist People's Party	Female	25–34	Tertiary	Employed	200,000–300,000	No

ID	Party	Sex	Age	Education	Employment	Income	Foreign background
DK-67	Dansk Folkeparti—Danish People's Party	Male	55–64	Tertiary	Retired	300,000–400,000	No
DK-68	Socialistisk Folkeparti—Socialist People's Party	Male	65+	Tertiary	Retired	100,000–200,000	No
DK-69	Declined to respond	Male	55–64	Tertiary	Employed	800,000–900,000	No
DK-70	Liberal Alliance	Female	55–64	n.i.	Employed	300,000–400,000	No
DK-71	Socialistisk Folkeparti—Socialist People's Party	Male	55–64	Tertiary	Employed	400,000–500,000	No, father from Germany
DK-72	Dansk Folkeparti—Danish People's Party	Female	45–54	Tertiary	Unemployed	100,000–200,000	No
DK-73	Enhedslisten—Red-Green Alliance	Male	under 24	n.i.	Self-employed	200,000–300,000	Yes
DK-74	Did not vote	Male	25–34	Tertiary	Employed	500,000–600,000	No, father from Sweden
DK-75	Socialistisk Folkeparti—Socialist People's Party	Female	25–34	Tertiary	Employed	300,000–400,000	No
DK-76	Enhedslisten—Red-Green Alliance	Female	55–64	Tertiary	Self-employed	No info	No
DK-77	Alternativet—The Alternative (Green Party)	Female	45–54	Tertiary	Self-employed	400,000–500,000	No
DK-78	Dansk Folkeparti—Danish People's Party	Female	55–64	n.i.	Unemployed	No info	No
DK-79	Venstre—Left, Liberal Party of Denmark	Male	65+	Tertiary	Retired	200,000–300,000	No
DK-80	Venstre—Left, Liberal Party of Denmark	Female	55–64	Tertiary	Early pensioner	200,000–300,000	No
DK-81	Venstre—Left, Liberal Party of Denmark	Male	65+	Tertiary	Employed	600,000–700,000	No
DK-82	Venstre—Left, Liberal Party of Denmark	Female	45–54	Tertiary	Self-employed	600,000–700,000	No
DK-83	Liberal Alliance	Male	55–64	Tertiary	Employed	No info	No
DK-84	Liberal Alliance	Male	65+	Tertiary	Retired	0–100,000	No
DK-85	Alternativet—The Alternative (Green Party)	Female	25–34	Upper secondary	Student	0–100,000	No
DK-87	Did not vote	Female	under 24	Upper secondary	Student	100,000–200,000	Yes

Appendix: Details of the Participants in the Democratic Forums

Norway

Reference	Vote for party in next election	Gender	Age	Highest level of education	Work status	Household's total net income, all sources	Ethnic minority
No-01	Labour	Female	Under 24	Tertiary	In full-time education	n.i.	No
No-02	Labour	Female	25–34	Tertiary	In full-time education	M—4th decile	No
No-03	Conservative Party	Female	25–34	Tertiary	Working full-time	n.i.	n.i.
No-04	Red Party	Female	25–34	Tertiary	Working full-time	F—5th decile	No
No-05	Labour	Female	35–44	Upper secondary	Working full-time	C—3rd decile	Yes
No-06	Labour	Female	35–44	Tertiary	Working part-time	C—3rd decile	Yes
No-07	Conservative Party	Male	Under 24	Tertiary	Working part-time	R—2nd decile	No
No-08	Christian Democrats	Male	25–34	Tertiary	In full-time	M—4th decile	No
No-09	Conservative Party	Male	25–34	Tertiary	Working full-time	H—10th decile	No
No-10	Liberal Party	Male	25–34	Tertiary	In full-time education	S—6th decile	No
No-11	Conservative Party	Male	25–34	Tertiary	Working full-time	P—8th decile	No
No-12	Labour	Female	25–34	Tertiary	Working part-time	R—2nd decile	Yes
No-13	Socialist Left	Female	25–34	Tertiary	In full-time	M—4th decile	No
No-14	Conservative Party	Female	45–54	Tertiary	Working full-time	P—8th decile	No
No-15	Centre Party	Female	35–44	Tertiary	Permanently sick or disabled	R—2nd decile	No
No-16	Labour	Female	45–54	Tertiary	Working part-time	P—8th decile	No
No-17	Liberal Party	Male	Under 24	Upper secondary	In full-time education	J—1st decile	Yes
No-18	Labour	Male	25–34	Upper secondary	Working full-time	R—2nd decile	Yes
No-19	Conservative Party	Female	35–44	Tertiary	Stay at home to look after house/family	S—6th decile	Yes

Appendix: Details of the Participants in the Democratic Forums

No-20	Labour	Female	45–54	Tertiary	Working full-time	H—10th decile	No
No-21	Conservative Party	Male	45–54	Tertiary	Working full-time	H—10th decile	No
No-22	Conservative Party	Male	55–64	Tertiary	Working full-time	D—9th decile	No
No-23	Labour	Male	Under 24	Tertiary	Working full-time	P—8th decile	Yes
No-24	Conservative Party	Male	25–34	Tertiary	In full-time education	R—2nd decile	No
No-25	Progress Party	Male	35–44	Tertiary	Working part-time	S—6th decile	No
No-26	Conservative Party	Female	45–54	Tertiary	Permanently sick or disabled	F—5th decile	No
No-27	Red Party	Female	35–44	Tertiary	Unemployed, looking for job	C—3rd decile	No
No-28	Labour	Female	45–54	Tertiary	Working full-time	H—10th decile	No
No-29	Labour	Female	45–54	Tertiary	Working full-time	M—4th decile	No
No-30	Labour	Female	65+	Tertiary	Retired	D—9th decile	No
No-31	Socialist Left	Female	65+	Tertiary	Retired	S—6th decile	No
No-32	Labour	Male	55–64	Primary	Permanently sick or disabled	R—2nd decile	No
No-33	Labour	Male	65+	Tertiary	Retired	K—7th decile	No
No-34	Conservative Party	Male	65+	Tertiary	Retired	P—8th decile	No

Appendix: Details of the Participants in the Democratic Forums

Slovenia

Reference	Political orientation	Gender	Age	Highest level of education	Work status	Number of children under 16 in household	Household's total net income, all sources	Ethnic minority
SI-50	Middle	Male	35–44	Tertiary	Working full-time	2	P—8th decile	No
SI-51	Middle	Male	25–34	Secondary	Unemployed	0	S—6th decile	No
SI-52	I don't care about politics	Male	35–44	Secondary	Unemployed	3 or more	R—2nd decile	No
SI-53	Right	Female	55–64	Secondary	Unemployed	n.i.	n.i.	No
SI-54	Right	Female	45–54	Secondary	Retired	0	S—6th decile	No
SI-55	Left	Male	35–44	Secondary	Working full-time	1	P—8th decile	No
SI-56	Middle	Male	65+	Secondary	Retired	2	D—9th decile	No
SI-57	Middle	Female	35–44	Tertiary	Working full-time	0	M—4th decile	No
SI-58	Left	Female	45–54	Secondary	Working full-time	0	K—7th decile	No
SI-59	Middle	Female	25–34	Tertiary	Unemployed	0	R—2nd decile	No
SI-60	Left	Female	35–44	Tertiary	Working part-time	0	n.i.	No
SI-61	Middle	Female	45–54	Secondary	Working full-time	2	C—3rd decile	No
SI-62	Middle	Male	35–44	Tertiary	Working full-time	2	D—9th decile	No
SI-63	Don't know	Female	35–44	Secondary	Working full-time	2	K—7th decile	No
SI-64	Middle	Male	65+	Secondary	Retired	0	K—7th decile	Yes
SI-65	Right	Male	25–34	Tertiary	Working full-time	2	K—7th decile	No
SI-66	Middle	Female	Under 24	Secondary	In full-time	0	P—8th decile	No
SI-67	Right	Male	65+	Tertiary	Retired	0	K—7th decile	No
SI-68	Left	Female	45–54	Tertiary	Working full-time	0	S—6th decile	No
SI-69	Middle	Male	35–44	Tertiary	Working full-time	2	K—7th decile	No
SI-70	Left	Female	25–34	Tertiary	Working full-time	0	D—9th decile	No
SI-71	Left	Female	35–44	Tertiary	Working full-time	0	H—10th decile	No
SI-72	Middle	Male	55–64	Secondary	Working full-time	0	C—3rd decile	No
SI-73	Don't know	Female	45–54	Tertiary	Working full-time	0	R—2nd decile	No

Appendix: Details of the Participants in the Democratic Forums

SI-74	Middle	Female	35–44	Tertiary	Working full-time	0		H—10th decile	No
SI-75	Left	Male	35–44	Tertiary	Working full-time	0		D—9th decile	No
SI-76	Middle	Male	35–44	Tertiary	Working full-time	0		D—9th decile	No
SI-77	Middle	Female	35–44	Tertiary	Working part-time	3 or more		P—8th decile	No
SI-78	Middle	Male	45–54	Secondary	Working full-time	3 or more		C—3rd decile	No
SI-80	Don't know	Male	65+	Secondary	Retired	0		C—3rd decile	No
SI-81	Right	Female	55–64	Secondary	Retired	0		F—5th decile	No
SI-82	Middle	Female	35–44	Secondary	Working full-time	2		P—8th decile	No
SI-83	Middle	Male	45–54	Tertiary	Working full-time	1		D—9th decile	No
SI-84	Left	Female	35–44	Tertiary	Working part-time	2		K—7th decile	No
SI-85	Right	Male	35–44	Tertiary	Working full-time	2		F—5th decile	No
SI-86	Left	Female	25–34	Tertiary	Working full-time	0		K—7th decile	No
SI-87	Middle	Male	45–54	Tertiary	Retired	0		J—1st decile	No
SI-88	Left	Female	45–54	Tertiary	Working full-time	2		P—8th decile	No

Appendix: Details of the Participants in the Democratic Forums

UK

Reference	Vote for party in next election	Gender	Age	Highest level of education	Work status	Household's total net income, all sources	Ethnic minority
UK-40	n.i.	Female	25–34	Tertiary	Working full-time	M—4th decile	Yes
UK-41	n.i.	Female	45–54	Upper secondary	Working part-time	S—6th decile	No
UK-42	Labour	Female	25–34	Lower secondary	Stay at home to look after house/family	R—2nd decile	Yes
UK-43	Labour	Male	Under 24	Upper secondary	In full-time education	K—7th decile	No
UK-44	Conservative	Female	35–44	Upper secondary	Working part-time	D—9th decile	No
UK-45	Don't know	Female	65+	Upper secondary	Retired	M—4th decile	No
UK-46	Don't know	Male	35–44	Upper secondary	Working full-time	M—4th decile	No
UK-47	Don't know	Female	65+	Upper secondary	Retired	J—1st decile	No
UK-48	Labour	Male	45–54	Upper secondary	Permanently sick or disabled	C—3rd decile	Yes
UK-49	Labour	Female	45–54	Upper secondary	Working part-time	J—1st decile	Yes
UK-51	UKIP	Female	Under 24	Lower secondary	Stay at home to look after house/family	S—6th decile	No
UK-60	Don't know	Male	25–34	Upper secondary	Working full-time	J—1st decile	Yes
UK-61	Lib Dems	Male	25–34	Upper secondary	Working full-time	M—4th decile	Yes
UK-62	Labour	Male	25–34	Tertiary	Working full-time	D—9th decile	Yes
UK-63	Conservative	Female	Under 24	Upper secondary	In full-time education	Unassigned	No
UK-64	Lib Dems	Male	25–34	Tertiary	Working full-time	P—8th decile	No
UK-65	Don't know	Female	11	Tertiary	Working full-time	P—8th decile	Yes
UK-66	Labour	Male	45–54	Tertiary	Working full-time	H—10th decile	Yes
UK-67	Labour	Male	25–34	Tertiary	Working full-time	P—8th decile	No
UK-68	Labour	Female	35–44	Upper secondary	Working part-time	F—5th decile	Yes
UK-69	Labour	Male	25–34	Tertiary	Working full-time	D—9th decile	No
UK-70	Lib Dems	Male	55–64	Upper secondary	Working full-time	D—9th decile	Yes

Appendix: Details of the Participants in the Democratic Forums

UK-71	Don't know	Female	25–34	Tertiary	Working full-time	P—8th decile	Yes
UK-80	Conservative	Female	45–54	Upper secondary	Working part-time	R—2nd decile	No
UK-81	Don't know	Female	Under 24	Tertiary	Working full-time	D—9th decile	No
UK-82	Conservative	Female	35–44	Upper secondary	Working full-time	H—10th decile	No
UK-83	Don't know	Female	45–54	Tertiary	Working part-time	S—6th decile	No
UK-84	Conservative	Male	45–54	Upper secondary	Working full-time	P—8th decile	No
UK-85	Conservative	Male	65+	Lower secondary	Retired	J—1st decile	No
UK-86	UKIP	Male	25–34	Upper secondary	Working full-time	D—9th decile	No
UK-87	Conservative	Female	65+	Tertiary	Retired	S—6th decile	No
UK-88	Don't know	Male	25–34	Upper secondary	Working full-time	H—10th decile	Yes
UK-89	Labour	Male	45–54	Tertiary	Working full-time	K—7th decile	No
UK-90	Labour	Female	25–34	Upper secondary	Working full-time	F—5th decile	Yes

Note: *ISCED 2* lower secondary education; *ISCED 3, 4* upper secondary education

Author Index

A

Albrekt Larsen, C., 34
Alesina, A., 8, 64
Arts, W., 6, 96, 215, 247, 276
Atkinson, B., 94

B

Béland, D., 218
Blekesaune, M., 7, 190, 276
Bonoli, G., 6, 33, 244
Busemeyer, M., 9, 34, 245, 248

C

Cantillon, B., 31
Chung, H., 8, 34, 189–191,197, 201, 208, 244, 247, 262

D

Daly, M., 184–186, 209
De la Porte, C., 4
Dwyer, P., 191

E

Erikson, R.S., 94
Esping-Andersen, G., 95, 140, 185, 186, 243, 250, 251, 276

F

Ferrera, M., 6, 33, 244
Fong, C., 7, 95
Frederiksen, M., 68

Gelissen, J., 6, 96, 215, 247, 276
Goerres, A., 13, 190
Goul Andersen, J., 8, 33

Hemerijk, A., 3
Heuer, J.-O., 118, 251
Hrast, M.F., 98, 252
Hvinden, B., 137

Immergut, E.M., 139, 220

Jæger, M.M., 7, 96, 247

Kangas, O., 190
Kenworthy, L., 96
Kohli, M., 137, 139, 140
Kootstra, A., 276
Korpi, W., 187, 188
Kumlin, S., 95

Leruth, B., 4, 291
Lister, R., 144, 250

Mau, S., 7, 8, 34, 64, 68, 95, 96, 118, 215, 219, 244, 251

Offe, C., 243

Pierseon, P., 2, 32, 243, 244
Piketty, T., 93
Prinzen, K., 13

Quadagno, J., 7, 190, 276

Rakar, T., 252
Roosma, F., 6, 33
Rothstein, B., 111, 116

Schøyen, M.A., 137
Scruggs, L., 276
Seeleib-Kaiser, M., 185, 189, 208
Stiglitz, J., 31
Svallfors, S., 6, 8, 33, 95, 96, 137, 138, 190, 276

Taylor-Gooby, P., 2, 3, 6–8, 33, 35, 68, 189, 203, 227, 244, 250

Van Oorschot, W., 8, 9, 68, 96, 190, 191, 215, 219, 224, 245, 276

Zimmerman, K., 243

Subject Index[1]

A

Active labour market, 5, 256, 257, 261
Ambivalence, 14, 97, 108
Apprenticeship, 18–19, 36, 45, 46, 51, 52, 54, 81, 82, 130, 257–260, 290
Attitudes, 2, 5–10, 12, 14–16, 19, 33, 34, 36, 46, 55–56, 69–74, 85–87, 93–119, 121, 125, 138, 159–161, 163, 175, 190, 195, 196, 204, 216, 219, 224, 235, 236, 244, 246–248, 273–294
Austerity, 2–6, 9, 16, 22, 35, 138, 189, 252

B

Benefits, 6–8, 14, 18–21, 31, 37–39, 42–44, 46, 47, 51, 52, 54, 57, 69, 70, 72, 75, 78, 80, 81, 83, 84, 86, 98, 102, 105, 111–113, 116, 117, 120, 121, 125, 127, 128, 130–132, 139, 149, 150, 152, 157, 164, 166, 168, 172, 173, 178, 188, 190, 195, 196, 199–202, 208, 219, 249, 252, 254, 256–258, 260, 268, 276–280, 282, 287, 288, 290, 291

C

Chauvinism, 3, 4, 6, 9, 64, 65, 256, 287
Childcare, 3, 8, 19, 20, 22, 32, 33, 35, 37, 49, 54, 77, 139, 146,

---

[1] Note: Page numbers followed by 'n' refer to notes.

© The Author(s) 2018
P. Taylor-Gooby, B. Leruth (eds.), *Attitudes, Aspirations and Welfare*,
https://doi.org/10.1007/978-3-319-75783-4

Childcare (*cont.*)
  184–189, 191, 195–202, 208,
  210, 247, 255–257, 260, 262,
  280–284, 288, 290, 292
Citizen, 13, 49, 53, 68, 93–118,
  144–145, 189, 191, 195, 252,
  263, 269, 278, 279
Climate change, 3, 82
Coalition, 9
Collectivism, 30, 36, 37, 278
Community, 12, 29, 40, 44, 57, 79,
  101, 119, 131, 219, 220, 224,
  228, 233, 285
Conditionality, 19, 191, 219, 220,
  222, 223, 252, 254, 256, 257,
  260, 268, 280
Consensus, 13, 65, 79, 85–87, 145,
  158, 196, 288
Corporatism, 277, 280
Corruption, 18, 21, 47, 49, 50, 54,
  57, 105, 110, 117, 216, 236,
  279, 286
Crisis, 6, 16, 32, 75, 78, 206, 230,
  249, 291
Cross-country, 97, 141

Defamilialism, 184–186, 204, 208, 209
Democratic Forum (DF), 2, 6,
  10–17, 21, 29, 35, 36, 57, 63,
  65, 70–74, 77, 78, 83, 85,
  87–89, 94, 97, 100, 101,
  103–106, 108–111, 116–118,
  138, 144, 145, 152, 158, 184,
  195–207, 216, 218, 223–237,
  239, 252–254, 257, 259, 261,
  263, 266, 268, 269, 273–294

Denmark, 4, 14, 18, 19, 21, 35,
  36, 40–44, 48, 54, 57, 64,
  70, 72, 73, 79–83, 86–89,
  94, 97–99, 101–106, 116,
  117, 119, 121, 143,
  145–150, 158, 162, 163,
  189, 190, 217, 245,
  247–257, 267, 268, 275,
  276, 278, 281–286, 288,
  289, 291, 300–301
Dependency, 37, 52, 142, 148,
  244, 288
Deservingness, 8, 9, 74, 75, 78, 80,
  82, 83, 88, 190, 195, 205,
  215, 216, 219–221, 223–226,
  228, 231, 233
Differentiated disintegration, 4
Disability, 140
Dual earner, 162, 187, 210
Dualisation, 2

Education, 3, 15, 16, 18, 19, 22, 32,
  33, 37, 41, 45, 46, 49–51, 54,
  75, 76, 78, 86, 102, 104, 106,
  107, 109, 112, 118, 119, 121,
  122, 124, 126, 129, 140, 144,
  146, 150, 152, 162–164, 167,
  171, 186, 201, 210, 226, 230,
  244–248, 251, 252, 254–258,
  260, 261, 263, 264, 267, 277,
  279–281, 283, 289–291
Elder care, 16, 32, 37, 164, 284
Employer, 44, 49, 86, 87, 132, 157,
  178, 185, 197–201, 207, 208,
  258, 260, 262, 263, 265, 266
Ethnic diversity, 64

Subject Index

Eurobarometer, 190
European Central Bank (ECB), 3, 31
European Commission (EC), 10, 32, 291
European Social Survey (ESS), 15, 68, 70–73, 99, 100, 189, 220, 246–248, 275, 276, 279, 282, 285, 287
European Union (EU), 3, 4, 8, 31, 32, 48, 63, 65, 86, 88, 141, 180n1, 225, 226, 237, 290–292
Europe 2020, 3, 32, 291, 293
Eurostat, 3, 202, 250, 278
Exclusion, 8, 102, 141, 153, 234, 244, 286, 289, 290

F

Familialisation, 144, 146, 151, 158, 184, 185, 187–189, 203, 206, 209
Family, 35, 51, 70, 81, 122, 127, 138–140, 144–147, 150, 154, 156, 168, 178, 179, 184–186, 188–191, 195, 202–204, 206–210, 244, 247, 252, 253, 255, 261–263, 266, 267, 283, 284, 288, 293
Finance sector, 119
Flexicurity, 35, 245, 251, 255, 257, 267
Focus group, 273
Framings, 12–14, 16, 18, 21, 22, 30, 46, 50, 52, 54, 57, 67, 80, 85, 87, 94, 101, 111, 113, 118, 138, 184, 218, 237, 240, 245, 248, 254, 267, 269, 274–290

G

Gender, 15, 16, 36, 44, 47, 48, 70, 83, 102, 119, 122, 163, 196, 199–201, 207, 210, 283
Generation, 125, 137–180, 205, 230, 260, 288
German Democratic Republic (GDR), 44, 247
Germany, 4, 7, 14, 18–20, 32, 35, 36, 39, 44–46, 54, 57, 70, 72–74, 77–79, 84, 86–89, 94, 97–99, 101, 104, 106–109, 121, 123, 137, 140, 142–144, 151–153, 162, 170, 188–191, 195–199, 202–204, 206, 208–210, 216, 220–223, 228–232, 237, 238, 240, 245, 247–254, 260–263, 267, 268, 276, 277, 279–281, 283–289, 291, 298–299
Globalization, 1, 2, 5, 20, 22, 36, 102, 243

H

Hard-working, 74, 76, 111–113, 116, 166, 224
Healthcare, 6, 21, 35, 75, 84, 119, 144, 171, 175, 217, 221, 225, 236–238, 282, 283, 288, 290
Housing, 4, 21, 75–77, 86, 106, 190, 226, 291

I

Identity, 63, 66, 74, 84, 88, 219, 224–226, 231, 232
Ideology, 7, 16, 20, 35, 102, 277, 279

Subject Index

Immigrant, 8, 9, 12, 14, 19, 21, 53, 63, 69, 70, 72, 73, 75, 76, 78–85, 88, 89, 167, 202, 221, 225, 226, 232, 233, 251, 255, 256, 285, 287, 289–291
Immigration, 1, 3–5, 8, 12, 15, 19, 22, 34, 53, 63, 68, 70, 74–77, 79–81, 85–87, 103, 122, 202, 226, 227, 233, 251–253, 255–257, 267, 274, 275, 286–294
Incentives, 3, 37, 39, 43, 49, 80, 81, 84, 102–104, 110, 119, 120, 157, 164, 171, 246, 255, 257–260, 262, 277, 278, 288
Inclusion, 15, 19, 186, 224, 246, 254, 286, 287
Individualism, 8, 19, 21, 29–57, 204, 227, 257, 259, 275, 277, 278, 280
Inequality, 1–3, 7, 15, 16, 19, 30, 31, 33, 36, 38, 39, 43, 47, 48, 57, 93–123, 125–129, 234, 250, 261, 267, 274–281, 283–286, 288, 290, 291
Inflation, 31, 246
Insecurity, 118, 143, 166, 244, 255, 267
Insurance, 46, 76, 103, 107, 120, 123, 164, 169, 170, 188, 235, 239, 240, 280, 284, 288
Integration, 19, 78, 80–84, 87, 233, 286–290, 293
Inter-generational, 16, 19, 103, 137–141, 143–149, 151, 153–159, 162, 163, 165, 167, 168, 170, 172, 174, 175, 177, 178, 180n1, 188, 195, 206, 210, 275, 281–286, 288, 290, 292, 293

International aid, 11
International Monetary Fund (IMF), 4, 5, 32
International Social Survey Project (ISSP), 191, 220, 221, 246, 247, 275

Jobs, 4, 19, 33, 36, 38–40, 44, 48, 50–52, 63, 70, 74, 78, 81–83, 87, 97, 104, 108, 119–122, 130, 131, 143, 147, 152, 153, 155–157, 163, 167, 171–175, 177–179, 200, 201, 207, 236, 245, 247, 250–263, 265–268, 286, 289, 291

Labour market, 1, 2, 5, 9, 15, 16, 19, 31, 33, 44, 50, 54, 57, 66, 74, 78, 82, 86, 87, 102, 103, 106, 107, 110, 112, 115, 118, 121, 139, 140, 142, 144, 149–151, 153, 154, 156, 157, 162, 163, 167, 175, 183, 184, 195, 196, 201, 207, 210, 243–269, 277, 278, 280, 285, 294
Legitimacy, 11, 117, 218, 239, 240, 244, 246, 248
Liberalism, 30, 278, 288, 289
Local government

Majoritarian, 3, 6, 37, 40, 47, 48, 51, 52, 57, 63, 68, 84, 85, 109, 127, 147, 221, 226, 247, 265, 277
Manufacturing sector, 122, 127

Subject Index

Market, 2, 8, 14, 30–34, 39, 47, 81, 96, 98, 102, 184–186, 188, 189, 195, 204, 208, 217, 236, 256, 268, 275, 277–279, 282, 286, 287, 289
Means-test, 52, 111, 116, 145, 166, 220, 250
Media, 13, 14, 76, 112, 222, 240
Middle class, 9, 93, 109–111, 117, 118, 125, 127, 128
Minimum wage, 20, 47, 50, 57, 98, 105, 110, 113, 117, 120, 127, 128, 132, 174, 255, 259, 261, 265, 278
Mobility, 7, 32, 33, 104
Multinational company (MNC), 20, 257

N

Nationalism, 4, 63–68, 70, 72, 74, 75, 77–85, 87–89
Neo-Keynesianism, 4
Neo-liberalism, 5, 8, 9, 16, 29, 55–56, 246, 259, 268, 276–280, 282, 283, 285
Norway, 14, 17, 19, 21, 35–40, 54, 55, 57, 64, 67, 70, 72, 73, 81–83, 87–89, 140–142, 148–151, 158, 162, 165, 167, 186, 189–191, 195, 196, 198, 199, 202–204, 206–210, 216, 220–223, 231–234, 236, 238–240, 275–279, 281–286, 288, 289, 302–303

O

Opportunity, 5, 7, 8, 10, 16, 19, 29, 32, 33, 36, 40, 45, 50, 51, 53, 54, 63, 75, 104, 109, 120, 122, 124, 144, 147, 148, 152, 153, 155–157, 165, 167, 170, 195–197, 207, 228, 247, 256, 258, 262, 263, 268, 269, 278, 280, 281, 286, 288, 290, 293

P

Pensions, 2, 33, 67, 96, 137, 156, 173, 200, 229, 244, 277
Political challenges, 2
Population ageing, 1–5, 15, 16, 18, 20, 22, 137, 140, 144, 148, 152–155, 157, 158, 164, 171, 172, 183, 189, 281, 294
Populism, 2–6, 8, 9, 274
Post-socialism, 21
Poverty, 3, 16, 19, 32, 48, 98, 101, 103, 108, 110, 112, 117, 126, 128, 131, 141, 143, 151, 153, 155, 158, 159, 169, 173, 180n1, 244, 265, 266, 279, 291
Privatisation, 20, 33, 227, 232, 236, 244, 246, 261, 275, 280
Productivity, 3, 5, 101, 102, 106, 146, 150, 163, 252, 254–257, 266–269, 280
Public opinion, 6, 97–100, 239

Q

Qualitative, 7, 21, 74, 87, 97, 118
Quantitative, 5, 16, 18–21, 68, 74, 218
Questionnaire, 13, 15, 21, 70, 97, 273

Subject Index

R

Rationing, 239, 240
Recession, 1, 4, 5, 149, 176, 189, 251, 252, 279, 292, 294
Reciprocity, 7, 9, 67, 82, 195, 205, 219, 224, 225, 232, 237
Redistribution, 5–7, 9, 19, 20, 30, 33–35, 38, 43, 48, 51, 66, 94–96, 98, 106, 108–111, 116–118, 121, 123, 246, 277, 278, 290, 291
Refugees, 77–80, 82–84, 86–88, 230, 231, 233, 239
Regime, 7, 14, 16, 19, 21, 35, 53, 93–118, 184, 186–189, 191, 204, 209, 246, 247, 250, 251, 257, 267, 268, 275–277, 281, 283–288, 292
Reluctant collectivism, 53
Responsibility, 6, 8, 9, 16, 18–20, 29, 33, 34, 36–38, 41, 44–46, 50, 51, 53, 77
Retirement, 42, 45, 52, 107, 123, 142, 146, 148, 149, 151–153, 156, 158, 162–172, 176, 179, 205, 229, 231
Rich, 45, 47, 49, 50, 74, 110–112, 116, 120, 121, 124–126, 128, 129, 175, 283

S

School, 79, 108, 110, 123, 124, 126, 129, 167, 177
Service sector, 32
Skill, 32, 48, 51, 83–85, 122, 208, 258, 280, 288
Slovenia, 14, 18–20, 35, 36, 39, 47–50, 54, 55, 70, 72, 73, 83–84, 87, 89, 94, 97–99, 101, 109–111, 116–118, 125, 127, 140–144, 153–155, 158, 162, 173, 175, 186, 188–191, 195–199, 202–204, 206, 208–210, 216–218, 220–223, 234–236, 238–240, 245, 247–254, 263–268, 276–289, 291, 304–305
Social care, 2, 35, 36, 275, 281–284
Social class, 7, 116
Social democracy, 31, 95, 186, 216, 245, 247, 251, 275, 278, 280, 281, 285, 292
Social division, 292
Social housing, 21, 226, 291
Social investment, 3, 6, 8, 9, 16, 18, 22, 33, 34, 36, 50, 52, 53, 144, 145, 150, 160, 180, 201, 207, 243–269, 275–284, 286, 288, 290–293
Social risks, 19, 96, 215, 244
Social security, 49, 108, 151, 166, 169, 244, 255
Social services, 138, 261, 276
Social survey, 85
Sociotropic, 66–69, 74, 76, 78, 80–83, 88, 89
Solidarity, 8, 18, 19, 29, 30, 40, 41, 44, 49, 50, 57, 66, 67, 82, 88, 137–141, 143–149, 151, 153–159, 161–163, 165, 167–170, 172, 174, 175, 177, 178, 180n1, 191, 195, 206, 209, 210, 215, 216, 218–221, 223–240, 275, 282, 284–286, 288–290
Status, 18, 57, 75, 76, 80, 82, 96, 118, 128, 220, 277
Structural threats, 2

Subject Index 317

Sustainability, 16, 18, 20–22, 30, 36, 41, 43, 44, 50, 53, 76, 137–141, 143–149, 151, 153–159, 162, 163, 165, 167, 168, 170, 172, 174, 175, 177, 178, 180n1, 183, 203, 204, 206, 207, 209, 215, 216, 218–221, 223–237, 239, 240, 285

T

Tax, 7, 20, 21, 30, 35, 36, 38–41, 43, 45, 46, 48–53, 72, 76, 78, 82, 84–86, 94, 98, 103, 106, 108, 110, 112, 113, 117, 119–121, 123, 124, 127–129, 132, 139, 147, 148, 154, 157, 163, 175, 178, 198, 201, 208, 216, 222, 224, 227, 232, 239, 248, 257–259, 265, 266, 277, 278, 280, 283, 285, 287
Training, 3, 5, 9, 18, 22, 32–34, 36, 40, 54, 78, 87, 169, 201, 244, 246, 250–252, 256–258, 261, 265, 268, 279, 289, 291
Transport, 127
Trust, 14, 19, 20, 30, 38, 40, 41, 77, 101, 110, 166, 234, 235, 274, 279

U

Unemployment, 7, 12, 14, 31, 34, 35, 40, 46, 51, 52, 66, 68, 69, 76, 80, 81, 123, 131, 132, 140, 148, 150, 162, 167, 172, 173, 179, 201, 202, 225, 244–247, 249, 251–253, 255–261, 263–268, 276, 279, 280

Union, 20, 31, 185
United Kingdom (UK), 3, 4, 32, 50–53, 64, 74–77, 94, 97, 101, 111–113, 116, 128, 142–144, 155–158, 216, 224–227, 245, 247–252, 257–260, 275
Universal Credit, 12
Universalism, 17, 216, 234–236, 275, 287

V

Voter, 96, 116

W

Wealth, 93–118, 121, 123, 124, 236, 239, 276
Welfare magnetism, 72, 80, 81
Welfare state, 1–22, 55–56, 93–118, 137–141, 143–149, 151, 153–159, 162, 163, 165, 167, 168, 170, 172, 174, 175, 177, 178, 180n1, 215, 217–219, 223, 228, 243, 273–294
Work ethic, 12, 18, 31, 34, 35, 44, 46, 51, 67, 127, 276, 277, 281, 284, 288, 292
Working age, 6–9, 18, 76, 137, 138, 140–142, 144, 148, 153
Work-life balance, 195, 197, 206–208, 262, 267, 269
Workshy, 21, 34, 278, 287

Z

Zero-hour contract, 20, 112, 253, 259

CPSIA information can be obtained
at www.ICGtesting.com
Printed in the USA
LVHW02*0238050718
582681LV00013B/170/P